Religion in Life & Society

GCSE RELIGIOUS STUDIES FOR EDEXCEL 'A'

Michael Keene

Folens
Publishers

Acknowledgements

The author and publisher would like to thank the following for the use of copyright material:

Alex Keene/The Walking Camera on pp. 2, 5, 10, 11, 16, 19, 20, 21, 31, 33, 36, 39, 45 (x2), 51, 66, 67, 74, 75, 77, 78, 79, 82 (x2), 86, 87, 89, 91, 93, 96, 115, 135, 161, 165; Associated Press/Hasan Sarbakhshian, Stringer on p. 73, Associated Press/Themba Hadebe on p. 85, Associated Press/Amit Bhargava on p. 137, Associated Press/Stringer on p. 157; BBC Picture Archives on p. 97; World Religions Photo Library on pp. 3, 7, 27, 47, 53, 59, 63, 65, 139; Corbis/Hanan Isachar on p. 13, Corbis/Annie Griffiths Belt on p. 49, Corbis/Philip Gouldon p. 95, Corbis/Craig Lovell on p. 123, Corbis/Peter Turnley on p. 127, Corbis/Mark Jenkinson on p. 142, Corbis/Bettmann on p. 145; Digital Stock on pp. 18, 101, 117; Image State on p. 130; Jewish Care/Justin Grainge Photography on p. 17; John Birdsall Social Issues Photolibrary on pp. 43, 155; Network/Lookat/Robert Huber on p. 147; PA Photos on pp. 103, 133; Photofusion/Clarissa Leahy on p. 23, Photofusion/Jane Alexander on p. 71, Photofusion/Sam Tanner on p. 107, Photofusion/Crispin Hughes on p. 109; Rex Features/Richard Young on p. 55, Rex Features/Erik Pendzich on p. 57, Rex Features/Isopress Senepart on p. 159; Reuters/Stringer GG/2002 on p. 9, Reuters/Goran Tomasevic on p. 129, Reuters/Yves Herman on p. 143; Robert Harding/NJ Edison on p. 22, Robert Harding/N Penny on p. 25, Robert Harding/G Corrigan on p. 37, Robert Harding on pp. 41, 140; Science Photo Library/Ed Young on p. 119, Science Photo Library/Hank Morgan on p. 153, Science Photo Library/Victor de Schwanberg on p. 163, Science Photo Library on p. 167, Science Photo Library/Mark Garlick on p. 169; Topham/Press Association on p. 69, PressNet/Topham on p. 105, Topham Picturepoint on pp. 113, 121, 131, 134, 141, 149

Cover Images: Dr Yorgos Nikas/Science Photo Library, Robert Harding, Digital Stock

United Kingdom: Folens Publishers, Apex Business Centre, Boscombe Road, Dunstable LU5 4RL.

Email: folens@folens.com

Ireland: Folens Publishers, Greenhills Road, Tallaght, Dublin 24.

Email: info@folens.ie

Poland: JUKA, ul. Renesansowa 38, Warsaw 01-905.

Editor: Melody Ismail

Design: FMS Design Consultants Limited

First published 2002 by Folens Limited.

British Library Cataloguing in Publication Data. A catalogue record for this publication is available from the British Library.

ISBN 1 84303 295 3

Contents

CHAPTER 4: SOCIAL HARMONY

CHAPTER 5: WEALTH AND POVERTY, AND THE MEDIA

Part Two: Religion and Society

CHAPTER 6: RELIGION AND SOCIAL RESPONSIBILITY

CHAPTER 7: RELIGION AND THE ENVIRONMENT

CHAPTER 8: CONFLICT AND CRIME

CHAPTER 9: MEDICAL ISSUES AND SCIENCE

Introduction

You have chosen to study specification A of the Edexcel examination in Religious Studies. This textbook has been prepared to give you the best possible chance of doing well in this examination. Whilst planning this textbook we have taken great care to make it suitable for those taking both the long and short course options. We hope that you will find it both an interesting introduction to some very important topics and a book that is easy to use.

As you use this book you will notice, in particular, the following key features.

- The material is presented in the same order, and uses the same language, as the Edexcel syllabus itself. This is a real advantage. It means that if you carefully work your way through this book you will cover everything that the exam board requires of you. To help you further the material is presented in easy-to-digest, bite-sized chunks that are broken down by frequent sub-headings.

- An introduction leads you into each topic gradually. It then goes on to outline the main issues and questions that you are going to be looking at.

- A 'key question' at the beginning of the text introduces you to the most important issue in each spread. This is a good place to start. It helps you to focus your mind as you read what follows. It also cuts straight to the chase and lets you know what really matters.

- You will find significant words or phrases, when they are first introduced, listed under 'Important words'. You should try to learn as many of these as you can. Try to use them appropriately in your exam answers to give greater depth.

IMPORTANT WORDS

Conversion;	a sharp turn-around, a change of religious commitment
Miracle;	an event or act which breaks a law of nature
Numinous;	that which relates to God, an experience that arouses deep spiritual feelings
Prayer;	to commune with God, to express deep spiritual feelings to God

- Other words that you will come across in the text are explained in the 'Glossary' at the end of the book. When you come across a word that you have not met before be sure to look it up in the glossary. It will only take you a minute and will help you understand the text more easily. It is a good idea to keep your own dictionary of technical words that you can add to as you go along.

- You will find the teachings of the different religions on the various topics colour-coded to help you to find your way around.

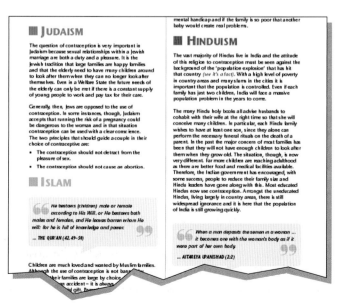

Introduction continued ...

- There are many quotations taken from the holy books, and other sources, dotted throughout the book. These are very important. They matter to the followers of the different religions but they also help you to understand why people believe what they do. Learn as many of them as you can. Try to use them in your examination answers.

- Throughout the book you will find various 'Exam tips'. Put the advice that you are given into practice and you will find your work improves noticeably. There is a skill involved in taking exams and these tips will help improve your exam techniques.

> ✓ **Exam tip**
> In the case of euthanasia and other social topics, candidates must know all sides of the argument. You should look in the newspapers for current examples. New and different circumstances are always arising. Use relevant and up-to-date information in your answers.

- Many spreads include a 'Think about' exercise. These encourage you to think about something that you have read. It is very easy to move through a course quickly without taking time out to think about some of the things that you have learned. Remember – in this course you are expected to learn about religion and also to learn from it. The 'Think about' questions are there to help you to apply the teachings of the world religions to very specific social, moral and personal issues. To do this you must regularly stop and think.

> **Think about ...**
>
> Look at the survey findings above. For which conditions did more than 50 per cent of those interviewed think that voluntary euthanasia should be allowed? Write down **TWO** comments to show how you feel about these findings.
> Do you think that they give a true indication of how the majority of people feel about euthanasia? Give **TWO** reasons for your answer.

- The 'Tasks' have been carefully chosen to help you to concentrate on the most important areas that you have studied. If you pay them attention they will direct you to those areas that you need to concentrate on.

> **Tasks**
> 1. Explain what you understand by the term 'mass media'.
> 2. Write about **THREE** parts of the mass media.
> 3. The quotation on this spread hints at a major problem of the mass media. What is that problem?

- There is a 'Summary' at the end of each spread. This gives you the key points of that spread. These summaries will help you to remember what you have learned before you move on to the next issue. When the exam draws near they can also be used as part of your revision programme.

SUMMARY

1 The term mass media refers to all forms of written and transmitted communication. These became very sophisticated by the end of the twentieth century.

2 The digital revolution has made information readily available to most people – but the poorest are likely to miss out.

- There are also carefully selected photographs that go with each spread. These are large enough for you to be able to learn a great deal from the detail. Do not rush past them without stopping to look and learn.

- Each section in the book ends with worked GCSE questions. This 'Exam help' is included to show you what should be contained within a full exam answer. The first question reflects the separate stages within the usual GCSE questions in the exam. The shorter questions that follow are intended to give an idea of the points you need to consider in an answer.

- At the end of the book there is also a comprehensive glossary of terms you should be aware of, and extra quotations across all religions and topics which supplement those you will find in the rest of textbook.

CHAPTER 1: BELIEVING IN GOD

1:1 Religious upbringing

How do people try to introduce their children to religious faith?

There are many different paths that people take to arrive at their religious faith. Some children are brought up in a religious atmosphere and do not feel the need to question that faith. Others are brought up similarly, but lose their faith as they grow older – some return to the faith later. Others do not have a belief in God until a dramatic spiritual experience turns them into a religious believer. This is often called a 'conversion' experience. Some people do not follow any religion or believe in the existence of a God – they are atheists. Agnostics are people who are uncertain as to whether or not God exists as they believe nothing is known, or can be known, about His existence.

Some religions, such as Christianity and Islam, actively go out to make converts whilst others, like Judaism, do not. There are also millions of people who go through the whole of their lives without seriously considering whether to believe in God or not. Every religious person, though, hopes that their children will believe as they do. The different religions have their own ways of trying to make sure this happens.

■ CHRISTIANITY

About 40 per cent of all children in the UK are baptised in an Anglican or Roman Catholic Church when they are a few months old. Some are dedicated to God in a Baptist church instead and then, years later, they will be given the opportunity to affirm their faith in God publicly, when they are either confirmed or go through the service of believer's baptism. In between these events, children are often taught to pray and read the Bible regularly. Christian children are taught more about their faith by attending Sunday school. They may also be taken to church regularly to meet other Christians. Children begin to understand that the Church is like a large family with members helping and caring for each other. This is the 'family' to which they belong.

■ JUDAISM

Boys are circumcised on the eighth day of their life and this is a continual physical reminder to them of their Jewishness. As soon as possible after their thirteenth

▲ Being allowed to read the Jewish scriptures in public is a sign of being accepted as an adult.

birthday, Jewish boys celebrate their barmitzvah as they take on the religious responsibilities of a Jewish adult. In some synagogues, there is a similar ceremony for girls, the batmitzvah, which takes place after their twelfth birthday. Both ceremonies provide Jewish young people with the opportunity to express their commitment to their faith publicly.

Each sabbath day begins with the family coming together and sharing a special meal and this 'togetherness' is also expressed at the many Jewish festivals, most of which centre on the home, rather than the synagogue. At an early age Jewish boys are taught to read and understand Hebrew as well as the meaning of the special articles which are so much a part of the Jewish way of life – including the tefillin and tallit.

■ ISLAM

Straight after birth a Muslim father whispers the adhan, the Muslim call to prayer, into the ear of his child. This means that the first word the baby hears on earth is the name of Allah. Muslim boys are circumcised either in infancy or any age up to puberty. A Muslim child is encouraged from an early age to join in the prayers that are offered five times a day. A child's religious education begins when they are taken along to the madrasah, the school attached to the mosque. Here the important religious traditions of Islam are taught, including the wudu and prayer rituals. A child is also taught how to read Arabic, the language in which the holy book, the Qur'an, is written.

▲ Mother instructing her children on the Qur'an.

HINDUISM

When a Hindu baby is born, the priest studies a horoscope to find out where the planets were at the moment of birth. From this he can work out which letter the child's name should begin with. He also highlights certain dates that are going to be important in the child's life. Several samskaras (special rituals) will be performed throughout the child's life to help them on their journey. The time when the baby takes its first solid food and has its head shaved are very important. When a boy is older, he will receive his sacred thread. Wearing this for the remainder of his life he will be reminded that he has particular duties to God, his parents and the gurus – his spiritual teachers.

IMPORTANT WORDS

Agnostic;	a person who does not believe there is enough proof to decide whether there is a God or not
Allah;	the name of the supreme being worshipped by Muslims
Atheist;	a person who does not believe that there is a God
Believer's baptism;	service in Baptist church by which people witness to their faith in Christ

✓ Exam tip
There are many important words in this book you may not be familiar with. It is important that you learn the meaning of these words. If you do this and use them correctly it will give your exam answers extra value. There are 'important words' boxes throughout, with fuller explanations in the glossary.

Tasks

1. Describe **THREE** things that are likely to be true of the upbringing of most Christian children.

2. What are the barmitzvah and batmitzvah?

3. How do Muslim parents try to make sure that their children will grow up to be practising Muslims?

4. What are the samskaras and which is the most important of them?

5. 'If you want your children to share your religious faith you should start helping them to do so from the moment they are born.' Do you agree? Give reasons for your opinion. In your answer you should refer to Christianity.

SUMMARY

1 Baptism and confirmation or believer's baptism are important events in the lives of many young Christians. So, too, are reading the Bible and learning to pray.

2 Circumcision and barmitzvah are important events for Jewish boys. Celebrating the sabbath day and different festivals are also important.

3 The first word a Muslim child hears is the name of God. Later the child learns to read the Qur'an. Learning to pray properly is an important part of a Muslim upbringing.

4 The most important event in the life of a Hindu boy is receiving the sacred thread – a reminder of his duties to God, his parents and his guru.

1:2 Religious experience

What part can spiritual experiences play in leading people to believe in God?

Spiritual experience, experiencing God, is a very important part of belonging to a religion, but not everyone who has a spiritual experience belongs to a religion. These experiences can come to people in different, and sometimes unexpected, ways. Most spiritual experiences come in four different forms.

The experience of worship

Meeting together with other people in a place of worship – whether it is in a church, a synagogue, a mosque or a temple – gives many people a spiritual experience. Some of the buildings in which people meet for worship are stunning. People may find themselves being spiritually moved by the singing, the prayers, the readings from the holy book, the sermon or the architecture of the building – all of which are key parts of most acts of worship. One important purpose of such worship is to create the kind of atmosphere in which a spiritual experience can take place. Many people find this happening to them week by week. The experiences of God that they have, though, may not be dramatic but quiet and peaceful. Spiritual experiences, like religious buildings, come in all shapes and sizes.

The experience of solitude

The experience of being alone with God in a place of worship, a natural place of beauty or a familiar location, like home, is one known to many religious believers. Silence, solitude and peacefulness are important parts of many genuine spiritual experiences. Quakers, for instance, are a Christian group whose acts of worship are mainly made up of silent times of waiting for the 'voice of God' to speak to them. Acts of meditation, which are so important to many people, are times when the human heart is silenced, the senses are stilled, to become receptive and ready to hear God. Although prayer may involve words it does not necessarily do so. Nuns and monks, in particular, have always found their deepest experiences of God in waiting and silence.

The 'conversion' experience

Religious literature is full of examples of people being 'converted' to a religious belief. Of the four religions covered in this book this is most likely to happen in Christianity and Islam – both are religions in which attempts are made to change people's minds from unbelief to belief. During the 1950s and 1960s, for instance, large Christian rallies and meetings were held and conducted by preachers, such as Billy Graham, at which people were invited to come forward and 'commit their lives to Christ'. The important thing about a conversion experience is that the initial experience of God is intended to lead to a continuing day-by-day experience of the Christian life. Muhammad, the Prophet of Allah, had many overwhelming experiences of Allah and these form the basis of his revelations, which are recorded in the Qur'an.

Many people have experiences of a more general nature that seem to have a religious element built into them. They might have an experience like this when they enter a magnificent building for the first time or unexpectedly stumble on a beautiful view. They are simply overwhelmed by what they see. Some people may understand this type of feeling as an experience of God. Others see it as an experience for which they can find no adequate words. Rudolph Otto (1869–1937) spoke of experiences of God as being experiences of the 'numinous' (other worldly). Such experiences, he said, were 'mysterium, tremendum et fascinans' (mysterious, overwhelming and fascinating).

Experiencing the miraculous

A miracle is an event that seems to break all known natural laws and has no natural explanation. Most religious people believe in miracles but few have ever experienced one, although many are recorded in the various holy books. Jesus, for example, was believed by those who met him to be capable of healing the sick and altering the laws of nature. We are told that he walked on water, stilled a storm, healed a demoniac and turned water into wine, amongst other miraculous acts. At the heart of Christianity is believed to be the greatest miracle of all – the rising of Jesus from the dead.

Not all miracles, though, are confined to the pages of holy books. There are many accounts in the Roman Catholic Church, for instance, of modern appearances of the Virgin Mary, the mother of Jesus. The most well known of these are associated with Lourdes, in France. In recent years the Christian Church appears to have rediscovered its ministry of healing. Healing services are held regularly in many churches. Many people, though, are doubtful about reports that people have been healed by God. Some find the thought that God can act in this way faith-strengthening, others find it unlikely in the scientific age in which we live.

▲ Many people experience God through prayer or reading the holy scriptures.

IMPORTANT WORDS

Conversion; a sharp turn-around, a change of religious commitment

Miracle; an event or act which breaks a law of nature

Numinous; that which relates to God, an experience that arouses deep spiritual feelings

Prayer; to commune with God, to express deep spiritual feelings to God

Tasks

1. What is the aim of religious worship?

2. What is meant by being 'converted' to a religious faith?

3. Describe an experience that you have had that with hindsight you might call 'religious' or 'spiritual'.

4. Describe **TWO** miracles associated with a religious leader.

5. 'Religious experiences prove that God exists.' Do you agree? Give reasons for your opinion showing that you have considered another point of view.

SUMMARY

1 Many people have spiritual experiences as part of an act of worship. Worship sets out to create the atmosphere in which such experiences can happen.

2 Silence can bring many people an experience of God. Quakers listen for the inner voice of God. Monks and nuns use silence and solitude to hear God speaking to them.

3 Some people have a conversion experience that changes the whole direction of their lives.

1:3 Everyday experience

What arguments have traditionally been put forward to persuade people to believe in God?

Few people are argued into believing in God. Faith is more important than argument as far as believing in God is concerned. Yet three arguments, that take as their starting point the external and internal worlds, have been put forward by distinguished thinkers and philosophers to lead people to think that belief in God might be rationally necessary. Look at the facts, they say, and then see whether you believe in God.

> *Fools say to themselves, 'There is no God.' They are all corrupt, and they have done terrible things … .*
>
> **… THE BIBLE (PSALMS 14.1)**

The argument from causation

This argument is associated with Thomas Aquinas (1225–74). He argued that everything in the world is an effect. It is the result of something else happening (the cause). Take an example: I have a black eye (the effect) and so we know that someone must have hit me or else I walked into a door (cause). Take another example: I am an effect, but what caused me – my mother and father having sexual intercourse. Nothing exists that does not have a prior cause. The universe is an effect but what, or who, caused it? This can only be the First Cause – God. Only the First Cause did not have a cause before it to bring it into existence.

Nothing happens by accident. There is an explanation for everything that exists in the universe. Science depends on this principle. It also believes that everything is, in the end, open to explanation. The only thing that cannot be explained in this way is God – the First Cause or ultimate mystery. This argument is called the 'cosmological argument' for the existence of God – the argument from causation.

The argument from design

This argument is associated with William Paley (1743–1805). He argued that if you look at the universe around you carefully you will be impressed by one thing above everything else – it has obviously been very carefully designed. You will see this whether you scan the heavens with a telescope or examine the smallest organism through a microscope. To illustrate this, Paley asked his readers to imagine stumbling across a watch lying on the ground in an uninhabited place. Open up the watch and look at its intricate machinery of wheels, cogs and balances. Do you think the watch was created by accident? You would be more inclined to think that it was made by a skilled watchmaker. Yet the universe is far more intricate than a watch. Could it exist by chance? Does it require a designer? The implications are obvious. Something as complicated as the universe demands a designer who put it together. This argument is called the 'teleological argument' for the existence of God – the argument from design.

The moral argument

Instead of looking outside to the world in which we live, as the other two arguments do, this argument looks within to what Immanuel Kant (1724–1804) called the 'categorical imperative'. Just think how many times each of us say that we 'ought' to do something. This is a kind of inner urge and is often what we call our conscience. Almost all the time we know the right thing to do although we do not always do it. Where does this categorical imperative come from? We can only know what is right and wrong from one source – God. This is the answer given by the religions of the world.

IMPORTANT WORDS

Causation;	the act of bringing something into being that previously did not exist
Design;	to plan and execute something, to create something that has a purpose

▼ You can see evidence for design wherever you look in the world.

▲ For some people the beauty of nature makes them aware of the presence of God.

The meaning of life

The religions of the world teach that life itself must have a meaning because this is what God gives to it. The Psalmist in the Bible speaks for many from different religions when he says that it is the fool who declares that God does not exist *(see quotation)*. Yet many people do not believe in God. The 'atheist' is someone who does not believe that God exists whilst the 'agnostic' says that the jury is still out – there is not enough evidence to say one way or another.

Tasks

1. Describe **TWO** ways in which believers might justify their faith in God.

2. Describe the cosmological argument for the existence of God.

3. Describe the teleological argument for the existence of God.

4. What do religious people believe about the purpose of life?

5. 'There are some very good reasons for not believing in God.' Do you agree? Give reasons for your opinion showing that you have considered another point of view.

 Think about ...

If a person does not believe in God (an atheist), do you think it would be difficult for them to live a moral life in which they cared for other people, as the Psalmist indicates in the quotation from the Bible?

SUMMARY

1 Three arguments have been put forward in favour of the existence of God. The first argues that every effect has a cause. The universe is an effect – so, who created it? The only possibility is God.

2 The second argument points out the presence of design and purpose in the whole of life (Paley's watch). The only possible designer of the universe is God.

3 The third argument looks at the conscience of human beings. Everyone knows that they often 'ought' to do things. Why do they feel like this? This 'categorical imperative' could only come from God.

1:4 Suffering and belief in God

Does the existence of evil and suffering in the world challenge religious faith?

Atrocities and suffering are amongst the most serious issues that any believer in God has to face. One of the main reasons given for the rejection of the idea of the existence of God by atheists and for the doubts expressed by agnostics is the evidence all around of human anguish. This seems to be so contradictory to the teachings of the world religions about God that stress that He is omnipotent (all-powerful), benevolent (all good and loving) and omniscient (all-knowing). Suffering is also linked to evil and the question of evil challenges the minds of believers and non-believers alike.

Every illness can make us glimpse death.

... CATECHISM OF THE CATHOLIC CHURCH, 1994

Examples of suffering

Although all forms of suffering concern many people, they present a problem for the believers of different faiths as God's actions may seem questionable. It is often asked 'how can there be a God?' after a natural disaster or similar. There are many examples.

- Natural disasters – floods, earthquakes, volcanoes and so on. These natural disasters kill thousands of people each year and the human race has little, if any, control over them. They usually strike at the poorest and most vulnerable people. This is called 'natural evil'.

- Adults and children dying each year from hunger and malnutrition – simply because they are unfortunate enough to have been born in the wrong place. Malnutrition is directly responsible for the deaths of 20 million people a year of whom 5 million are children under the age of 5.

- Children who are born with incurable illnesses or massive handicaps through no fault of their own or of their parents.

- Illnesses or accidents which rob loving families of parents or children.

It is not just the 'fact' of suffering which causes anguish but also the 'unfairness' of it all. Some people go through life with little suffering, at least until the end, whilst millions have never known an extended period free from suffering and pain. The inevitable questions are – 'Why does it happen this way?' 'Is there an overall purpose behind life – or not?' These are questions that the believer in God cannot evade. In the end it all boils down to a dilemma, which can be simply stated:

- **Either** God wants to remove suffering but He cannot – in which case He is not all-powerful.

- **Or** God can remove suffering but He does not – in which case He cannot be all-loving.

Naked came I out of my mother's womb, and naked shall I return there. The Lord has given, and the Lord has taken away; blessed be the name of the Lord.

... THE TANAKH (JOB 1.21)

Religion and suffering

No answer to the problem of suffering can ever be totally satisfactory. Three answers, though, are found in the religions covered in this book.

1. Suffering is the direct consequence of human sin. This might be true in many situations. A sufferer from lung cancer may have contracted the disease due to prolonged smoking. How, though, can the child who contracts HIV from her mother be blamed?

2. Suffering comes from an evil power, opposed to the goodness of God. This is an explanation favoured by Christianity, Judaism and Islam. Christians and Jews call this evil force Satan, whilst in Islam he is referred to as Iblis. Thoughtful people wonder, though, who created this evil force? If it was God, why did He do it? If it was not God, who did?

3. God alone knows the meaning of suffering. The most well-known book about suffering is found in the Jewish scriptures, the book of Job. Job was a righteous man whose faith in God was tested when Satan was allowed by God to rob Job of everything – his health, his family and his wealth. Job's final answer is that suffering is a mystery and to question God about it shows a complete lack of faith.

Clearly no single answer to the problem of suffering is wholly satisfactory. Yet how can anyone witness suffering on a vast and indiscriminate scale without questioning the existence of a loving, all-knowing and all-powerful God?

▲ Ecuadoreans rescue an elderly woman from flood waters in April 2002. Heavy rains set off landslides and flooding in Ecuador.

! Think about ...

Do you think that trying to understand suffering in the world is more of a challenge to those that believe in God? Or do you think that it is equally hard to explain if you are an atheist? How do you understand such suffering?

IMPORTANT WORDS

Benevolence;	the belief that God is all-caring, all-loving and good
Moral evil;	suffering that stems from actions for which a person could be held responsible
Natural evil;	suffering which results from natural disasters such as floods and earthquakes
Omnipotence;	the belief that God is all-powerful and that nothing is beyond His power
Omniscience;	the belief that God knows everything that has happened, is happening and will happen

Tasks

1.a. Describe **THREE** different kinds of suffering.

   b. How do you think that each of them presents a challenge to the person who believes in God?

2. What are **THREE** of the explanations for suffering put forward by the different world religions?

3. 'Suffering makes it impossible to believe in God.' Do you agree with this comment? Give reasons for your opinion showing that you have considered more than one point of view.

SUMMARY

1 There are many different kinds of suffering that offer particular challenges to people who believe in God. The unfairness of suffering is as much a challenge as its actual existence.

2 Religion is not able to offer a totally satisfactory answer to the problem. It is suggested that human beings are to blame, that suffering stems from a power of evil and that God alone knows the reason for suffering.

1:5 Christianity and suffering

What is the Christian approach to suffering?

Most Christians accept the scientific view of creation that the whole universe, including human beings, is part of an evolving process, which began in the distant reaches of time and still continues today. As far as human beings are concerned, suffering plays a very important part in this process of evolution since it helps people to grow and develop in many ways – including their spiritual growth.

The traditional Christian viewpoint is rooted in the story of creation in the book of Genesis which shows that God created a perfect world but that sin soon entered the picture. Suffering is the direct result of sin. Suffering is a part of God's punishment of humans for sin.

The suffering God

Many modern Christians have found a way of reconciling their belief in a loving God with the existence of suffering in the world. At the heart of the Christian faith is the story of Jesus, the Son of God, who lived a genuinely human life on earth and died on a cross. This encourages Christians to believe that God has not left them on their own to suffer – He shared their suffering in Jesus and suffers alongside them today. The cross, the symbol of that suffering, has become the central symbol of the Christian faith.

▼ Healing services are held in many churches.

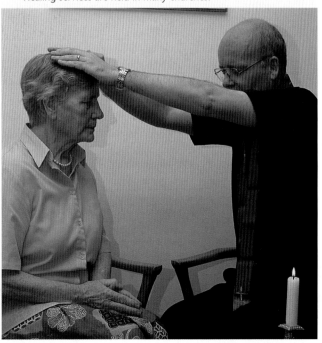

> The only thing that makes it possible to believe in God at all is the cross. We do not begin by explaining evil away, justifying God, excusing him for the mess he has made of creation … Jesus experienced even more acutely the abandonment and desolation that I knew … there, in that utter absence of God, was the presence of God.
>
> **... FRANCES YOUNG, MOTHER OF A SEVERELY DISABLED SON**

Suffering is the beginning – not the end

The cross is at the heart of the story of Jesus but it does not tell the whole tale. The story goes on to tell how he came back to life after 3 days and, 40 days on, went to be with his Father, God, in heaven. The resurrection of Jesus is the most important Christian belief. It has very important consequences for all Christian believers. They take it to show that they, too, will come back to life and spend eternity with God in heaven. Death will not end their relationship with God – that will continue for ever. Even if their life on earth has been characterised by pain and suffering that will pale into insignificance beside what they can look forward to beyond the grave. This is at the heart of the Christian understanding of suffering and provides Christians with the strength to accept everything that life brings them.

> [In heaven] there will be no more death, no more grief or crying or pain. The old things have disappeared.
>
> **... THE BIBLE (REVELATION 21.4)**

> Pain is God's megaphone to rouse a deaf world. We are like blocks of stone out of which the sculptor carves the forms of men. The blows of his chisel, which hurt us so much, are what make us perfect. We think our childish toys bring us all the happiness there is and our nursery is the whole big world. But something must drive us out of the nursery to the world of others. And that something is suffering.
>
> **... CS LEWIS**

▲ The crown of thorns and the cup of suffering are reminders of the suffering that ended the life of Jesus.

Meaning in suffering

Christians try to find some meaning in all the suffering. A full understanding may elude them but they can begin to find some meaning beyond it all. CS Lewis, the writer of the Narnia books, suggested that pain is part of God's preparatory work on every man and woman *(see quotation)*. Christians pray for those who are suffering, that God might be with them and heal them. Christians have always been in the forefront of those seeking to bring comfort and healing to those who suffer in hospitals and hospices. Anointing the sick with oil is one of the sacraments carried out by the Roman Catholic Church.

Tasks

1. Give **TWO** ways in which Christians have tried to explain why there is suffering in the world.

2. How do Christians believe that God suffers in the world today and what example is provided for Christians to follow?

3. Describe **TWO** ways in which Christians try to help people who are suffering.

4. 'A good God would not allow suffering in the world.' Do you agree with this comment? Give reasons for your opinion showing that you have considered more than one point of view.

 Think about ...

How do you think that having the cross as the central symbol of Christianity might help people to find meaning in their own experiences of suffering?

SUMMARY

1 Christians have different explanations for the existence of suffering. One is that it is essential to the continual evolution of the human race. Another is that it was God's punishment for the sin of Adam and Eve.

2 At the heart of the Christian faith is the suffering of Jesus on the cross. This shows that God Himself suffers through the sufferings of the human race.

3 Christians believe that they can see, by faith, beyond their suffering to the time, in heaven, when suffering and pain will no longer exist.

1:6 Judaism, Islam and Hinduism, and suffering

What light can Judaism, Islam and Hinduism throw on the question of suffering?

■ JUDAISM

> Not to have known suffering is not to be truly human.
>
> ... *JEWISH MIDRASH*

Jews ask the usual questions relating to suffering and God, but there is one extra important Jewish question: 'How could God allow 6 million Jews to die in the German concentration camps in the Second World War?' This event, known as the Holocaust, put a whole new perspective on suffering. Some Jews lost their faith as a result, blaming God for what happened to their fellow believers. Others have come to the conclusion that, at best, they are worshipping a God with limited power. God simply was unable to save His chosen people.

The Jewish scriptures contain many stories of people suffering. Underlying all these stories is the belief that such suffering is ultimately for the benefit of the person. Suffering is a fact of life. It comes from God and so there has to be a positive side to it. People who suffer have to draw on an inner strength that they never knew they had and this means that they emerge as better people as a result.

■ ISLAM

Muslims believe that nothing can happen to them that is outside the plan of God. Nothing happens unless Allah wills it. Suffering and pain are part of the divine plan. Suffering is a test set by God. When God created the world he appointed Adam to look after it as his vice-regent. Human beings were made superior to the angels because they were given the precious gift of free will. The angels were commanded to bow down to humans and respect their superiority but Iblis refused to do so. As a result Iblis was given the kingdom of hell as his dominion and told to test the faith of the people in Allah. Evil and suffering are the ways in which he does this.

> Be sure. We shall test you with something of fear and hunger, some loss in goods or lives or the fruit (of your toil), but give glad tidings to those who patiently persevere – Who say, when afflicted with calamity: 'To Allah we belong and to Him is our return.'
>
> ... *THE QUR'AN (2.155–156)*

IT'S A FACT

In the Qur'an Allah is given 99 different names. One of them is 'the Compassionate One'. Because of this, Muslims believe that they should show compassion to those who are suffering.

■ HINDUISM

Hinduism recognises two kinds of evil.

1. **Natural evil.** Samsara, the cycle of birth, death and rebirth, is a natural evil since the individual life-force or atman (soul) has to go through death and rebirth many times. Death comes as a result of committing different forms of natural evil.

2. **Moral evil.** Hindus believe that some people have a tendency to commit such moral evils as incest, theft, adultery, lying and murder. Moral evil is explained by the law of karma. All suffering comes from human actions. There is a fault in creation that results in suffering. If a person experiences suffering in this world it is because of bad karma in a previous life. A good life is the result of good karma. Suffering is not the fault of God or anyone else. Every human being is responsible for their own suffering – either in this life or in a previous one.

> Great souls who have become one with Me have reached the highest goal. They do not undergo re-birth, a condition which is impermanent and full of pain and suffering.
>
> ... *THE BHAGAVAD GITA (8.15)*

! Think about ...

Both Judaism and Islam believe in an evil power to help explain sin and suffering. What do you think are the strengths and weaknesses of this approach?

 Exam tip
Note the very different approach to suffering between Judaism and Islam and Hinduism. Hinduism does not feel its belief in God is challenged by suffering, whereas Judaism does. Make sure you understand the reason for this.

Tasks

1. Why is the problem of suffering particularly important for all Jews to consider?

2. How do Muslims deal with the problem of suffering and how is Allah involved in it?

3.a. Who is Iblis?

 b. What work does Iblis carry out?

4.a. What is natural evil in Hinduism?

 b. What is moral evil in Hinduism?

5. 'The only way to explain the presence of suffering is to put it down to the activity of an evil power.' Do you agree with this comment? Give reasons for your opinion showing that you have considered more than one point of view.

SUMMARY

1 The slaughter of 6 million Jews in the Holocaust is a key event in Jewish history. Many Jews lost their faith in God because of it. Suffering, though, is viewed as a fact of life by Jews.

2 Muslims believe that everything happens within the will of Allah. Suffering is a test of faith. Iblis tests the faith of believers in Allah.

3 In Hinduism, natural and moral evil are recognised – the first comes from the natural life-cycle and the second because certain people have a tendency to commit evil acts.

▼ Yad Vashem, Holocaust memorial site in Jerusalem depicts twisted bodies resembling a barbed-wire fence.

 **Exam help ...**

This opening chapter is mainly concerned with how people come to religious faith. The ceremonies for each religion that are carried out on young children are clearly important. Some people may have a later experience of God. People come to religious faith by a variety of routes. You should be aware of the different arguments for God's existence, although these are unlikely to lead to religious faith for many. Then there is the greatest obstacle to religious belief for many people – the existence of suffering. It is important to understand how Christianity, Judaism, Islam and Hinduism deal with this problem and the reasons for their different approaches.

1.a. What is an atheist?

   b. Outline the reasons a person might give for being an atheist.

   c. Explain how religious experience may lead to, or support, belief in God.

   d. 'Children should be allowed to make up their own minds about whether to believe in God.' Do you agree? Give reasons for your opinion, showing that you have considered another point of view. Your answer should refer to the teaching of at least ONE religion.

1.a. An atheist is someone who believes that God does not exist – *a* [without] *theos* [God].

   b. The reasons that an atheist might give include:

- The scientific explanations now available for the creation of the world and so-called mysterious events in the world. In the past people accepted the explanations put forward in the holy books – the creation of the world in Genesis, the miracles in the Old Testament and Gospels, for example.

- Miracles do not happen today – there is no evidence, for example, that there is a God who answers prayers. Even the seemingly miraculous can now be given a scientific explanation.

- The existence of evil and suffering. The many examples of meaningless suffering in the world. Faced with the many natural disasters that strike, how could anyone believe in a God who should be helping people?

- The lack of any real evidence that God exists. Traditional proofs for God's existence do not amount to much. The faith of religious people can easily be misplaced.

   c. You need to begin by defining what a religious experience is. A religious experience is one that affects a person's spirit or soul, the deepest part of their personality. People can have religious experiences when they are with others, during an act of worship or when they are on their own.

- Some children are taken to a place of worship regularly and surrounded by reminders of God's presence or of their faith. They may have religious experiences from an early age but it is not always possible to decide which comes first – the religious experience or belief in God.

- People may have no belief in God until they have a particular experience leading them to a religion – called a 'conversion' experience. They may have many later experiences and these will deepen their faith. It is unlikely that these later experiences, though, will be as dramatic as the first.

- Some people believe that they have experienced a miracle. There are many miracles in the Bible and other holy books.

- Some people may believe in God without having 'experienced' Him. Some experiences are more general and merely lead people to believe that there is another world, a spiritual world, beyond the present one.

   d. Children must be free to make up their own minds about believing in God. All religions agree that belief is a personal decision. No one can make another person's mind up for them. All religions teach that each person has free will. However, most religious parents will try to guide their children into following the same faith, they can do this by various means.

- Religions try to surround children with influences that will help them to believe. Religious parents want their children to share their own religious faith.

continued ...

continued ...

- The children will take part in religious ceremonies – circumcision, infant baptism, child dedication and so on. These are reinforced by later ceremonies, such as confirmation, believer's baptism and the sacred thread ceremony. Some young people, though, are turned off religion between the early and later ceremonies.

A belief in God cannot be forced on someone. It is a matter of free choice. Surrounding a child with religious influences may make belief in God more likely – or it may have the opposite effect. Non-religious adults were often put off following a religion in childhood by over-zealous parents. It is natural for parents to want their children to share their own religious faith and many children do continue to follow the chosen faith of their parents.

- Rather than hold God responsible for much of the suffering in the world, Christians have pointed out that suffering causes God Himself to suffer. God was present in the world in Jesus. Jesus suffered through no fault of his own. His suffering was totally undeserved. Christians believe that God still identifies with those who suffer today. Christians also believe in the idea of the 'vale of suffering'; suffering is a spiritual benefit to those who experience it.

3. **'Miracles do not happen today and so cannot support religious faith.' Do you agree? Give reasons for your opinion, showing that you have considered another point of view. Your answer should refer to the teaching of at least ONE religion.**

2. **What is the response of ONE religion to the problem of suffering?**

2. The chosen religion is Christianity. This religion provides several ways of approaching the problem of suffering.

- Christianity shares many beliefs with Judaism. Both Christians and Jews believe that there is a devil (Satan) who is responsible for the evil and suffering in the world. This can be seen in the story of Job in the Old Testament and the temptations of Jesus in the New Testament.

- The story of Job teaches that suffering cannot be understood. There is no reason why it happens. It just has to be accepted.

- Christians believe that people need to fight suffering. Jesus fought against it and healed those who were suffering. The Church has continued this principle through its ministry of healing and its medical work at home and overseas (Christian Aid and The Salvation Army are good examples).

- Some suffering, moral evil, is brought by people on themselves. An example of this is the person who suffers from blocked arteries after a lifetime of greed. This links with the Christian belief in human free will. People must be free to act, even if their actions cause them to suffer. God cannot be held responsible for this suffering.

continued ...

3. A miracle is an event that is 'out of the ordinary' and does not seem to have a natural explanation. God is thought to be able to perform miracles. Christians believe that Jesus also had this power. There are many reasons why people think that miracles do not happen today.

- Science can explain the world and all events within the world. The things that cannot be explained scientifically are put down to human ignorance. Given time, there is little that science will not be able to explain.

- There is no proof for the miraculous. Many 'miracles' from the past are now explained in another way. There is no concrete evidence that miracles took place. This is true of the miracles of Jesus, as it is of others. There is little reason to believe that the miraculous takes place. However, it is sometimes impossible to disprove what people call a miracle.

- In the past miracles have been used to support religious faith. It is a matter of faith whether people still continue to believe them. Did Jesus perform miracles? Has the Virgin Mary appeared to people at Lourdes and elsewhere? Are people being healed by God today? No scientific proof is possible to support these claims. There is no proof for the most important miracle in Christianity – the resurrection of Jesus from the dead. Millions of people, though, believe that it happened. Science cannot prove or disprove it. It is a matter of faith.

2:1 The sanctity of life

What do religious people mean when they speak of the 'sanctity of life' and why is it important?

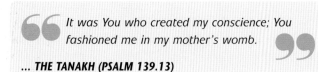

> It was You who created my conscience; You fashioned me in my mother's womb.
>
> ... **THE TANAKH (PSALM 139.13)**

Followers of each religion in this book believe in a God, the Supreme Spirit, who created all life in the beginning and continues His creative work in the world today. All life is believed to be a free gift from God. That life is sacred or holy is a basic religious belief that, in the case of Hinduism, extends beyond human life to include all forms of life. The basic religious understanding of this can be put simply: God creates all life in His own time; God ends all life in His own time. It is against the will of God to interfere with this process unless it is for a very good, life-giving, reason.

All religions teach that human beings are free to believe or not to believe in God. God has given all human beings free will and this is one of His most precious gifts. Without this gift human beings would be little more than puppets in God's hands. Possessing free will makes human beings different from every other form of life. The freedom to make free choices, though, brings with it enormous responsibilities, since the choice could be between life and death. These are choices that no sensible human being will take lightly, particularly in the areas of abortion and euthanasia.

Religion and the sanctity of life

At the root of all religious teaching lies the belief that life, especially human life, is sacred and holy. It follows that, if all life is a gift from God, then it must be cherished and valued.

■ CHRISTIANITY ■ JUDAISM

The Jewish scriptures and the Christian Bible teach that God is found at the very centre of life. He created life in the beginning and each new life is a gift from God. Christians believe that Jesus, the Son of God, showed how God Himself viewed human life when he became a human being. This event, the birth and life of Jesus, is known as the Incarnation (God becoming flesh).

Jews and Christians mostly agree that all life and death decisions, including those involving abortion and euthanasia, are ones that belong rightly to God alone and should not be taken by human beings. After all, they are asking whether an unborn baby has the right to life and whether a human being should have its life prematurely ended. These are decisions that the two religions believe have always rightly belonged to God and are not for human beings to make, except in particular circumstances.

■ ISLAM

The Qur'an is the holy book for all Muslims. It teaches that Allah alone breathes life into every new human being at conception. It also teaches that only Allah can decide when each person will die. Human beings cannot take this responsibility away from God since they do not have the authority to do so.

▼ This sculpture expresses the religious belief that all life is sacred and in the hands of God.

▲ Jewish elderly people enjoying themselves. All religions teach that everyone, young and old, matters to God.

▨ HINDUISM

Hindus believe that after death every soul is reborn into another body, this process is called reincarnation. Most Hindus believe that the soul is released from rebirth by people doing their duty – their dharma. If this is done for every rebirth of the soul then in the end they will reach moksha. Moksha is the release from the cycle of rebirth and is thought of as the soul coming together with God or a joining of the soul with Brahman. Some Hindus also believe that moksha can come through devotion or meditation, but it is the soul rather than the body, that is important.

> ❝ *Reverence for all life is the greatest commandment ... we take this so lightly, thoughtlessly plucking a flower, thoughtlessly stepping on a poor insect, thoughtlessly disregarding the suffering and lives of our fellow men and women.* ❞
>
> *... DR ALBERT SCHWEITZER (1875–1965),*
> *A CHRISTIAN MISSIONARY WORKING IN AFRICA*

IMPORTANT WORDS

Sanctity of life; the belief that there is something holy and sacred about human life, meaning that it must be treated with great care

Tasks

1. The word 'sacred' can mean many things – amongst them holy, revered and hallowed. Look up these words and any others suggested by the word 'sacred' in a dictionary then write a full definition of the word.

2.a. Read the quotation by Albert Schweitzer. Explain what you think the phrase 'reverence for all life' means.

  b. Give **TWO** examples of how we seem to revere life in the modern world and **TWO** ways in which we seem to treat it cheaply.

3. 'Human life is more sacred than any other kind of life.' Do you agree with this comment? Give reasons for your opinion and show that you have considered more than one point of view.

SUMMARY

1 The belief that life is sacred is at the heart of all world religions.

2 There is also a belief that life is a free gift from God. God has the right, which no one else has, to give and take life.

2:2 Christianity and the after-life

What do Christians believe about life after death?

> 66 *For God loved the world so much that he gave his only Son, so that everyone who believes in him may not die but have eternal life. For God did not send His Son into the world to be its judge, but to be its saviour.* 99
>
> **... THE BIBLE (JOHN 3.16–17)**

The teaching of Jesus

The Bible teaches that Jesus, the Son of God, was born as a human being, suffered, died and came back to life before returning to his home in heaven. As Jesus taught, this makes it possible for those who have faith in him to share in the joys of heaven after they die. Jesus spoke of his life and death as if he was like a seed that falls into the soil and dies *(see quotation below)*. It is only when it is sown and then dies that many other seeds – the early Christians and all later followers of Jesus – can be spiritually re-born. The gift of eternal life, offered to all those who believe in Jesus, could only have come out of his death on the cross and his resurrection from the dead.

> 66 *I am telling you the truth: a grain of wheat remains no more than a single grain unless it is dropped into the ground and dies. If it does die, then it produces many grains.* 99
>
> **... THE BIBLE (JOHN 12.24)**

▼ Christians believe that Jesus was crucified before, three days later, being brought back to life by God.

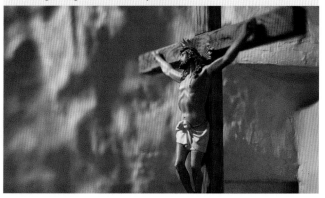

The first Christians

The message of Jesus was later preached by the early Christians. Paul wrote that if there is no resurrection from the dead then Christians are wasting their time. It is only because Christians believe that Jesus rose from the dead that they believe that they, too, will share in eternal life. Without the one there could not be the other.

> 66 *Any man's death diminishes me because I am involved in Mankinde; and therefore never send to hear for whom the bell tolls: it tolls for thee.* 99
>
> **... JOHN DONNE (1571–1631), POET AND CLERGYMAN**

A vision of heaven

The book of Revelation in the Bible claims to be a vision of heaven that was given by the Holy Spirit to one of the disciples of Jesus, St John. In heaven, it is claimed, Christians will be with God and He will wipe away every tear from their eyes – there will be no more death or mourning; no more crying or pain because everything associated with human life on earth will be replaced by a totally new way of life. This is the hope that all Christians share and the Bible leads them to expect.

There is, however, a sharp disagreement among Christians about what they expect to happen to them when they die. There are two broad views on what will happen.

1. **The Protestant view.** After death, Protestants believe that they either stay in the grave until Jesus returns to the earth and then they are judged; or that they go immediately to heaven or hell. Protestants all agree that each person must be judged and this is when their eternal destination is settled. Like Roman Catholics, Protestants believe in the 'immortality of the soul' – the soul never dies but lives on in some spiritual realm shared with God. They also believe in the 'resurrection of the body' – a body which will have the same spiritual characteristics that Jesus had when he returned from the dead.

2. **The Roman Catholic view.** Death is followed by some time spent in purgatory – a place between earth and heaven. This is a time of preparation for the soul before entering heaven. People left behind on earth can influence the amount of time the soul spends in purgatory by praying that God will have mercy on it and offering up special prayers.

▲ Headstones often express Christian beliefs about life after death.

Believing in eternal life

Although fewer Christians today strongly believe in life after death than in the past, it is still a very important part of the Christian faith. It makes sense of the fact that life on earth often appears to be very unfair. It also provides comfort for those people who are mourning the loss of someone close if they believe that they will 'see' the person again. It gives a sense of purpose to people in their everyday lives – they are more careful how they live in this life if they believe that God will hold them to account on the Day of Judgement.

IMPORTANT WORDS

Immortality of the soul;	Christians believe that the soul does not die but is eternal
Resurrection;	Christians believe that the spiritual part of the human being is given a new body, sharing in the life of Christ

✓ **Exam tip**
There are two basic religious attitudes to the after-life – resurrection and reincarnation. Resurrection is the basic teaching of Christianity, Judaism and Islam. Reincarnation is taught by Hinduism. In the exam you will be expected to know the differences between the two – and who believes what.

Tasks

1.a. Make a list of **FIVE** things that Christians associate with heaven.

b. Make a list of **FIVE** things that you associate with heaven.

c. Where do these two lists overlap and where are they different?

2. Write down **THREE** things that Roman Catholics believe about purgatory.

 Think about ...

What do you think happens to people after they die? Give reasons for your answer.

SUMMARY

1 Jesus taught that there is a life after death.

2 Christians believe that Jesus died so that their sins can be forgiven and they can receive eternal life from God.

3 Roman Catholics believe that the soul spends time in purgatory after death. Protestants believe that the soul goes to heaven or hell at death or on the return of Jesus to the earth.

2:3 Judaism, Islam and Hinduism, and the after-life

What do Jews, Muslims and Hindus believe about life after death?

Although they disagree over the form it takes, all religions teach that death is not the final word and that there is some form of survival beyond the grave.

▌ JUDAISM

> ❝ I believe with perfect faith that there will be a resurrection of the dead at the time when it will please the Creator, blessed be His name, and exalted be the remembrance of Him for ever and ever. ❞
>
> ... THE JEWISH 'THIRTEEN PRINCIPLES OF MOSES MAIMONIDES'

Although Jews believe that there is some form of life beyond death their holy books do not contain much on this issue. Judaism teaches that a person's soul survives death. It does this because the good work a person has performed cannot be extinguished nor can their memory be removed from the people who loved them. Beyond this Jews believe it is dangerous to speculate about the nature of life beyond the grave. Its details must remain a mystery – known only to God. The only thing that can be known for sure is that the good will be rewarded and the evil punished in the life to come. The rest is down to the will of God and will be made known to us in His good time and not before.

▌ ISLAM

> ❝ To Allah we belong and to Him is our return. ❞
>
> ... THE QUR'AN (2.156)

Muslims believe that when a person dies their soul is taken by the Angel of Death to a place of waiting in the grave until the Day of Judgement. On this Day, the universe will be destroyed and everyone will be brought before Allah, the Judge of all. Those who have lived by Allah's standards, shown in the Qur'an, will be rewarded by spending eternity in heaven. Those who have rejected the light of God that Muhammad brought, will be sent to hell.

Both heaven and hell are described very graphically in the Qur'an.

- Heaven is a beautiful garden with rivers that flow as milk and honey. Heaven is a paradise in which true believers are at one with Allah. Heaven is a place of unsurpassable beauty and plenty.

- Hell is a frightening place of great heat and torment where people are confronted with the stark truth about their evil deeds on earth. They will have the whole of eternity to regret that they did not listen to Allah's Prophet, Muhammad.

> ### ! Think about ...
>
> The Jewish name for a cemetery is 'Bet ha-Hayyim'. This mean the 'house of life'. Why do you think that this name is thought to be spiritually appropriate?

▼ Once a person has been dead for a short time Jews often erect permanent, or temporary, memorials in their honour.

▲ Hindus believe that after death the body has no further use and so can be burned.

HINDUISM

Hindus believe in reincarnation. The atman (soul) cannot die; it is destined to be eternally reborn. The state in which the atman is reborn is down to the law of karma, which covers all life. The law dictates that what a person does in this life will affect what happens to them in the next. The aim of this life is to be free from rebirth in the next, so the fate of everyone depends on their behaviour in this life. Karma is carried over from one life to the next. People will not necessarily be rewarded or punished in this life but it will happen at some time. That is the unbreakable Hindu law and the only certain fact of life.

> *From the unreal lead me to the real! From darkness lead me to the light! From death lead me to immortality!*
>
> ... ***BRIHADARANYAKA UPANISHAD (1:3.28)***

Tasks

1. Write down **THREE** pieces of information about:

   a. resurrection   **b. reincarnation**

   Make sure that your information highlights the differences between the two beliefs about life after death.

2. Explain the beliefs held by **ONE** religion, other than Christianity, about life after death.

3. There are two clear beliefs about life after death – resurrection and reincarnation. Which of these are you most inclined to believe – or do you find it impossible to believe in any form of survival after death? Produce clear reasons for your answer.

SUMMARY

1 Both Islam and Judaism teach that the body will be resurrected after death. Islam believes strongly in a time of judgement that leads to heaven or hell. Jewish beliefs about the after-life are less clear.

2 Hinduism teaches that the soul is reborn many times – reincarnation. It is eventually hoped that this cycle will be broken and that the soul will be reabsorbed into God. This may take many rebirths.

2:4 Abortion

What does the law say about abortion?

Abortion – the law

In 1967 the Abortion Act became law in England, Scotland and Wales. The new Act legalised an abortion if two doctors agree that:

- The life of the mother would be at risk if the pregnancy was allowed to continue.

- The mental or physical health of the mother could be damaged if the pregnancy was allowed to continue. (80 per cent of all abortions are carried out because of this clause.)

- The child could be physically or mentally disabled.

- The mental or physical health of other children in the family could be endangered if another baby is born.

Although the time limit for an abortion was not set it was agreed that the pregnancy would be terminated before 28 weeks of pregnancy. In 1990 it was decided that an abortion could only be legally performed before 24 weeks of pregnancy. This made little difference to the overall number of abortions performed. It is unlikely that an abortion would be carried out after 18 weeks of pregnancy unless there are compelling medical reasons for doing so.

▼ The law does not allow a father any say as to whether or not an abortion should be performed.

> *The child, by reason of his or her physical and mental immaturity, needs special safeguards and care, including appropriate legal protection, before as well as after birth.*
>
> **... THE UNITED NATIONS DECLARATION OF THE RIGHTS OF THE CHILD**

Abortion – the facts

- Before 1967 at least 200 000 abortions were carried out illegally each year in the UK. About 70 women died annually from their injuries. Thousands more were scarred for life or rendered infertile by a botched back-street abortion.

- During 1971 104 000 abortions were performed in the UK and by 1999 this figure had risen to 177 000. One in every 12 abortions is carried out on a woman who is more than 12 weeks pregnant. Few women have gone beyond 16 weeks.

- 10 per cent of all the abortions, about 17 000, are carried out on women who come to the UK from countries where abortion is illegal, such as Ireland.

When does life begin?

In any discussion of abortion the most important question is 'When does life begin?' There are three possible answers to this question.

1. Life begins at the moment when the sperm fertilises the egg. Groups opposed to abortion believe that life begins at the moment of conception although, at this stage, no organs have begun to develop.

2. Life begins at some point during pregnancy. Religions have traditionally taught that this happens when God implants a soul in the body. This is the moment when the person becomes a spiritual person.

3. Life either begins when the baby could survive independent of its mother (viability) or at the moment when it is born.

Abortion – the issues

The teaching of most religions is that abortion is morally and spiritually wrong – even if it is legal. The main arguments are as follows.

Arguments for abortion

- Every woman has the right to decide what should happen to her own body.

- It is not possible to say with any certainty when human life begins.

- There is no such thing as a totally safe contraceptive and so mistakes are bound to occur.

- If abortion were illegal then women would be forced to go back to very dangerous, back-street abortions.

- A child should not have to be born as an unwanted baby.

Arguments against abortion

- The unborn child is a human being from the moment of conception. Killing is a very serious moral evil.

- Abortion is too convenient as an easy way out of a difficult or inconvenient situation.

- A foetus has the same rights as every other human being – including the right to live. There is no difference between abortion and murder.

- People with serious physical or mental disabilities can live long, and very happy, lives. They can also be a great blessing to those around them.

IMPORTANT WORD

Abortion; the medical expulsion of an embryo or foetus from a woman's uterus

 Think about ...

Do you agree with the United Nations Declaration that society has a particular responsibility to look after its most vulnerable groups? Which groups fall into this category? What are the implications of this for abortion?

Tasks

1. **Carry out a class brainstorming session. Come up with as many answers to these questions as you can:**

   a. What is the meaning and purpose of life? Why are we here?

   b. When is abortion acceptable?

   c. When is abortion unacceptable?

   Bring together the answers of the class and see whether there is a general level of agreement or not.

▲ The decision over whether or not to have an abortion is one that the expectant mother has to make.

SUMMARY

1 Abortion has been legal since 1967 in parts of the UK. It was made legal to make it unnecessary for pregnant women to seek dangerous back-street abortions. Two doctors must agree to any abortion. It is most likely to be granted because the physical or mental health of the mother would be damaged.

2 No one agrees about exactly when life begins. This makes an assessment of abortion very difficult. Those who support it say that a woman has a right to decide what happens to her own body. Those who disagree maintain that a baby is a human being from the moment of conception – so abortion equals murder.

2:5 Christianity and abortion

What is the teaching of Christianity on abortion?

> The greatest destroyer of peace in the world today is abortion. If a mother can kill her own child, what is there to stop you and me killing each other? The only one who has the right to take life is the One who created it.
>
> **... MOTHER TERESA, ROMAN CATHOLIC NUN WORKING IN INDIA**

Two churches – two very different opinions

The various Christian Churches do not agree about abortion. For much of the twentieth century it was one of the most divisive issues separating Christian from Christian. The Quaker Movement, for example, accepts that there is a lack of consensus among Quakers and so no official statement has been made on the issue. Here are two examples putting forward very different points of view.

1. **The Roman Catholic Church.** This Church teaches that it is very wrong to take human life at any time. It is very strongly opposed to contraception, abortion and euthanasia. Mother Teresa's comment represents this viewpoint. The Roman Catholic Church will not support an abortion even if the woman has been raped or is known to be expecting a severely disabled child. Even in a situation in which both mother and baby are at risk, the teaching of the Church is that the life of the baby should take precedence. Abortion is murder, the Church argues, and murder is wrong in all situations. There is no conceivable situation in which it could be justified. This is called an 'absolutist' viewpoint. God's rules are 'absolute' and cannot be broken, whatever the situation.

2. **The Methodist Church.** This Church does not believe that abortion is always wrong. Each case is individual and must be judged on its merits. It argues that there are situations in which abortion can be morally justified or can be, at the very least, seriously considered. As the quotation shows, there are situations where a mother's life is in danger or where she knows that she is expecting a disabled child. This is called a 'situationist' viewpoint. Each case must be judged within its 'situation' and a responsible decision taken when all the relevant facts are considered.

The Bible and abortion

There is not much in the Bible to help a Christian to form an opinion about abortion. There are two comments, however, that may indicate a viewpoint on the issue. The Bible teaches that man is made 'in the image of God' (Genesis 1.26) and people are told in the Ten Commandments that murder is always wrong (Exodus 20.13). For many Christians abortion is murder and there are no exceptions. For other Christians, though, it depends on just when life begins and agreeing on that, as we have seen, is far from straightforward.

When Jeremiah was called by God to be a prophet he was told: "I chose you before I gave you life and before you were born I selected you to be a prophet to the nations." (Jeremiah 1.5) God knows everybody from the moment they are conceived. The Roman Catholic Church teaches that both contraception and abortion are contrary to the will of God – and so are wrong.

Most Churches agree that a woman who is struggling with this decision needs serious counselling and support – both before and after the decision has been made. At the same time she must be left free to make the decision for herself without any outside pressure. It is hers, and hers alone, to make.

> Circumstances which may often justify an abortion are direct threats to a mother's life or to the probable birth of a severely abnormal child. The woman's other children, bad housing and family poverty should also be considered.
>
> **... THE METHODIST SYNOD, 1976**

Christians in action

Abortion arouses very strong feelings. Christians have been in the forefront of those opposed to abortion and they have shown this in various ways.

1. Protesting by writing letters to newspapers or to their local MP. These protests were particularly popular in the 1960s and 1970s.

2. Joining 'pro-life' groups such as LIFE and SPUC (Society for the Protection of the Unborn Child). Most of the members of these organisations are Roman Catholics.

3. Taking abortion into consideration when they vote. Many British Christians find out the opinions of the candidates on this, and similar issues, before they vote. In the USA, where abortion is a very bitter issue, people sometimes only vote for a representative who promises to oppose abortion if elected. As there are millions of Roman Catholics in the USA this can be a very powerful weapon.

Tasks

1. How do Christians sometimes show that they are opposed to abortion?

2.a. Explain why Christian Churches can, and do, disagree about abortion.

  b. Do you think that such disagreement is surprising? Give **ONE** reason for your answer.

3. 'I do not see how any Christian could possibly support abortion.' Do you agree with this comment? Give reasons for your opinion showing that you have considered more than one point of view.

Think about ...

Why do you think that abortion raises such strong feelings? Do you think that there is a hidden danger in debates about abortion when it raises such strong feelings? If so, what is it?

SUMMARY

1 Abortion is a very serious issue for many Christians and one that brings about serious disagreements. The Roman Catholic and Methodist Churches hold different opinions on the issue.

2 Some Christians take every opportunity to show their opposition to abortion.

▼ Many Christians are opposed to abortion since it involves the destruction of a potential, or actual, life.

2:6 Judaism, Islam and Hinduism, and abortion

What is the teaching of Judaism, Islam and Hinduism on abortion?

All religions disapprove of abortion but the strength of this disapproval depends on several factors. Amongst the factors involved are the stage reached in the pregnancy; the condition of the pregnant woman; the rights of the unborn child; the interests of the father and the teaching of the scriptures.

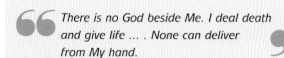

JUDAISM

> 66 There is no God beside Me. I deal death and give life ... . None can deliver from My hand. 99
>
> ... THE TORAH (DEUTERONOMY 32.39)

To Jews abortion is much more objectionable than contraception. It stands in the way of the will of God by destroying potential human life. At the same time Jewish thinking does not give the foetus, which is only a potential life, the same importance as the life of the pregnant woman. Abortion is acceptable if the pregnancy has become dangerous for the mother or is likely to become so or the mother would be gravely psychologically affected if the pregnancy were to continue. Some rabbis also permit an abortion if the unborn child is likely to be so physically or mentally damaged as to make a normal life impossible. The earlier an abortion is performed the more acceptable it is. The Talmud, an important Jewish holy book, teaches that the foetus does not become a human being until the forty-first day of pregnancy – the day on which the soul is planted by God in the body.

ISLAM

> 66 Kill not your children for fear of want. We shall provide sustenance for them as well as for you. Verily [truly] the killing of them is a great sin. 99
>
> ... THE QUR'AN (17.31)

The Qur'an teaches that abortion is a sin against Allah and so is forbidden. Many Muslims, however, believe that an abortion can go ahead if the life of the mother is in danger. This is because the mother is alive and has great family responsibilities, whereas the foetus has not yet developed a human personality. In this situation abortion is far from desirable but is the lesser of two evils.

Muslims regard all life as a gift from Allah. No one has life as a right: it is a loan. Like all loans it must be paid back to the person who lent it. Allah can call in this gift whenever He pleases. The Qur'an reminds women that, on the Day of Judgement, aborted infants will want to know from their mothers why they were killed.

HINDUISM

> 66 His being is the source of all being, the seed of all things that in this life have their life. He is God, hidden in all beings. He watches over the work of Creation, lives in all things, watches all things. 99
>
> ... THE UPANISHADS

Abortion is legal in India, where over 80 per cent of the population is Hindu, as long as it is carried out in a government clinic. It is supported by most Hindus both as a way of ending an unwanted pregnancy and also as a means of birth control. It is thought that as many as 5 million abortions take place in India each year.

However, Hinduism teaches that all life is sacred because all life is part of God. Human beings should not interfere with the natural processes. Since all new life comes from God, all new life is very special. Abortion results in bad karma. The amount of bad karma involved depends on the circumstances. It is very small when carried out to save the life of the mother. It is much greater when there is no compelling reason for the abortion.

> ✓ **Exam tip**
> When dealing with the attitudes of different religions to issues such as abortion, it is very important to know the individual teaching of each religion and also the main reason behind that teaching.

Tasks

1.a. Choose one of the religions in this spread. Write down **THREE** pieces of information about the attitude of your chosen religion towards abortion.

b. What appears to be the key reason of your chosen religion for opposing abortion?

2.a. What factors are taken into account by most religions when considering abortion?

b. Place these different factors in the order which you think they might have for the members of the different religions.

c. Which do you think are the most important, and the least important, when considering an abortion?

3. 'Abortion is no more than a form of murder.' Do you agreed with this comment? Give reasons for your opinion showing that you have also considered another point of view. In your answer you should refer to **ONE** particular religion.

 Think about ...

It is generally accepted by most religions that an abortion is justified if the life of the mother is at risk. Is this a conclusion that you agree with? Explain your answer.

SUMMARY

1 Judaism, Islam and Hinduism all allow an abortion if the life of the mother is at risk. This must be carried out at a very early stage of the pregnancy.

2 Although Hinduism is strongly against abortion the practice is widespread in the predominantly Hindu society of India.

▼ Parents in Bahrain receive advice from a doctor on their new born baby.

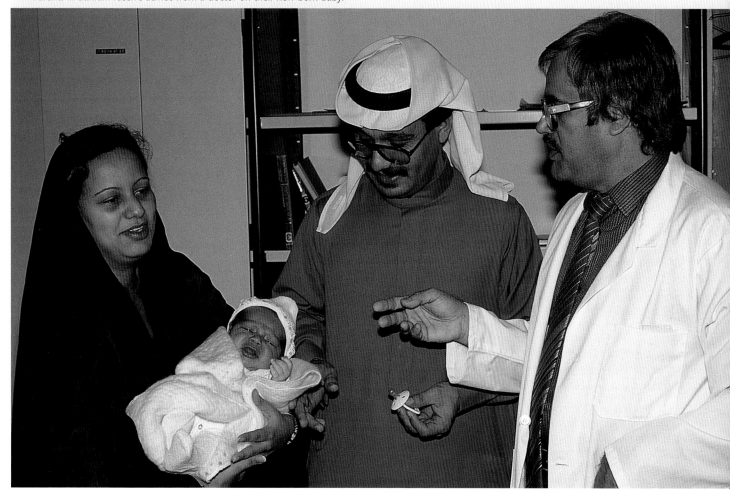

2:7 Euthanasia

What is euthanasia and what does the law say about it?

'Euthanasia' comes from two Greek words meaning a 'good death'. Today, though, the word is often taken to mean 'mercy killing'. There are two important things to remember about euthanasia.

1. Euthanasia involves the taking of someone's life.

2. It is done for the supposed benefit of the person being killed – often because their life has become intolerable because of the great pain they are suffering.

Types of euthanasia

Euthanasia is all about having the right to die at a time and in a manner of one's own choosing. The difference between euthanasia and suicide is that euthanasia involves another person – whether they provide the actual means of death or simply withhold treatment or medication. That person could be a doctor, a nurse, a relative or a friend. In the UK, whilst suicide is legal, it is illegal for anyone to help a person take their own life – 'assisted suicide'.

There are two forms of euthanasia.

1. **Passive euthanasia.** This is when a person is not helped to die, but their life is not prolonged in any way by using technology or drugs. For example, a person who is terminally ill may have their pain controlled but no further effort is made to prolong their life. The 'law of double-effect' also comes into play here in many cases. This is when steps are taken to help with a medical condition, although it is known that side effects of these steps will hasten death.

2. **Active euthanasia.** This is when active steps, usually by administering poison, are taken to bring about the end of a person's life.

Euthanasia can be voluntary (the person themselves taking the decision) or non-voluntary, where a decision is taken by a third person to allow a person to die because they are incapable of making that decision for themselves.

Euthanasia – the law

Active euthanasia is illegal in the UK. In the Netherlands, however, it is now legal for doctors to give injections to patients who have terminal illnesses to hasten their deaths – as long as they have freely given their consent. There is a 'cooling-off' period during which time a person can withdraw their consent. Two doctors must agree

that the person's condition is terminal. EXIT (the Voluntary Euthanasia Society), a society dedicated to making voluntary euthanasia legal in the UK, has existed since 1935.

Whilst opinion polls in the past have shown that most people do not believe that voluntary euthanasia should be legalised, recent evidence suggests that public opinion is changing. At the moment, though, the majority seem to believe that as long as a person is able to communicate with others and is not in unbearable pain they should not be helped to terminate their life. The Hospice Movement believes that it is possible to control pain so well now that no one needs to live in overwhelming distress. A 'hospice' was traditionally a resting place for travellers and pilgrims. Now it refers to a home for those who have reached the last part of their journey through life.

Euthanasia – the issues

Euthanasia is highly controversial, arousing very strong feelings in those who support the idea and those who oppose it. The main arguments are as follows.

Arguments for euthanasia

- People should have the right to do as they wish with their own lives – including choosing the moment of their death.

- If the future offers nothing but pain and a loss of dignity each person should be able to choose to die.

- Euthanasia removes the possibility of someone being a great burden to others, especially their own family.

- We curtail the lives of animals when they are terminally ill so why not do the same for humans?

Arguments against euthanasia

- It would undermine the confidence that patients have in doctors to save life.

- The principle that human life is sacred must be maintained at all costs.

- Hospices show that people can die with dignity and almost painlessly.

- All human beings, young and old, are precious to God.

- God gives life and God alone should decide when it will end.

▲ In 2002, Diane Pretty campaigned unsuccessfully for her husband to be allowed to help her die.

IMPORTANT WORDS

Assisted suicide; the act of helping someone to take their life

Euthanasia; the act of putting someone painlessly to death because they have an incurable illness

Non-voluntary euthanasia; euthanasia in situations where the person cannot make the decision for themselves – such as a person on a life-support machine

Voluntary euthanasia; situation in which a person can make the decision to end their life but is not physically capable of doing so without the help of someone else

Tasks

1.a. The word 'euthanasia' means a 'good death'. What do you understand by the phrase a 'good death'?

b. If you had the chance to choose a 'good' death what would that mean to you – and why?

2. Here are two comments about euthanasia. Decide which you agree with and give **TWO** reasons to support your view.

a. 'Everyone has the right to a peaceful death at a time of their own choosing.'

b. 'Life is sacred and no one has the right to take it.'

Show in your answer that you have considered one religious point of view.

 Think about ...

Tony Bland was in a 'persistent vegetative state' (PVS) after he was injured in the Hillsborough football disaster in 1989. His body continued to function internally, but there was no chance of him regaining consciousness. He had severe brain damage. After many months the court gave permission for the doctors to stop feeding him and giving him water. He soon died. Do you think the court was right?

SUMMARY

1 Euthanasia means taking one's own life with the help of someone else. This may be through the withholding of treatment or the administering of something that will cause death.

2 At the moment, active euthanasia is illegal in the UK. It is legal in the Netherlands.

3 There are strong religious and moral arguments for and against euthanasia.

2:8 Christianity and euthanasia

What do Christians believe about euthanasia?

Euthanasia, like abortion, is a very controversial subject among Christians. There is not a single view on whether people should be allowed to die at a time, and in circumstances, of their own choosing. However, most Christians would agree that:

- life is a free gift from God and has great value in itself
- every person should be able to live, and die, in true dignity.

> *The argument for euthanasia will be answered if better methods of caring for the dying are developed. Medical skill in terminal care must be improved, pre-death loneliness must be relieved, patients and family must be supported by the statutory services and by the community. The whole of the patient's needs, including the spiritual, must be met.*
>
> **... THE METHODIST CONFERENCE, 1974**

Although all of the Christian Churches that have expressed an official opinion are against euthanasia this is for slightly different reasons and with different degrees of certainty.

Nonconformist Churches and euthanasia

The Baptist and Methodist Churches both agree that abortion and euthanasia revolve around the same issue of who, in the end, has the right, to take human life. As the quote from the Methodist Conference shows, the argument for euthanasia is only persuasive if other important matters are not improved – such as the way we treat people in the last few weeks of their life. If the right support and help are available at this very difficult time then euthanasia is not necessary. Both Churches, though, accept that if a person is 'brain-dead' then relatives and doctors have no spiritual or moral duty to keep them alive artificially.

The Church of England and euthanasia

The Church of England makes two important points about euthanasia.

1. The sanctity of all life is a very important Christian belief and nothing must be allowed to interfere with this.

2. Doctors do not have to do everything to keep a person alive irrespective of the quality of their life. In particular, those who are 'brain-dead' do not need to remain on respirators.

A statement in 1992 emphasised that crucial life and death decisions must be made with the agreement of everyone involved. They should include the collaboration of more than one doctor. It is a Christian duty and the duty of the State to protect the most vulnerable people in society, especially those who may feel themselves to be unwanted or a burden to others. In addition, the Church believes that society should do everything in its power to make old people feel valued as members of the community.

The Roman Catholic Church and euthanasia

> *Euthanasia is a temptation, in effect, to take the life of a man under the false pretext of giving them a pleasant and quiet death ... this is a crime which cannot become legal by any means.*
>
> **... POPE PAUL VI, (1963—78)**

The Roman Catholic Church is the most outspoken Christian denomination on euthanasia. It bluntly states that euthanasia is wrong because all life comes from God and is sacred. Only God can take away a person's life. Human beings do not have that right. Any act that deliberately secures the death of someone else is murder. The Church does, though, accept that drugs given to relieve pain might, in the end, hasten death. This is called 'the law of double-effect' and is a common medical procedure. All Churches, including the Roman Catholic Church, accept that this is morally and spiritually acceptable.

The main Christian Churches are all officially against euthanasia in any form. This does not mean to say, however, that all individual Christians follow the teaching of the different Churches. There are undoubtedly millions of Christians who believe that the truth is not as clear-cut as the various Churches claim. Euthanasia is one of the issues on which the confusion of opinions within the Christian community reflects the uncertainty in society generally.

 Think about ...

The Church of England stresses that the elderly should be made to feel important members of society. What practical steps could the different Churches take to help to bring this about?

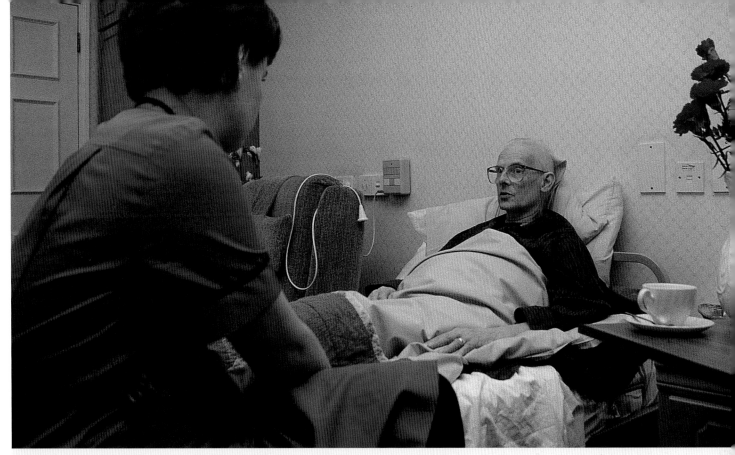

▲ Some people spend the last days of their life in a hospice.

Tasks

1.a. What is euthanasia?

  b. Give **TWO** reasons why most Christians are opposed to euthanasia.

2. Can you think of any situations in which someone, religious or otherwise, might find it very difficult to oppose euthanasia?

3.a. What is the 'law of double-effect'?

  b. Do you think that this is 'euthanasia by the back door'?

4.a. Summarise the teaching of Christianity on euthanasia.

  b. 'We have the right to choose the moment when we will die.' How do you think a Christian might respond to this statement? How would you respond?

  c. Do you think a believer can allow 'mercy killing' in any circumstances if their religion teaches them that it is wrong? Give **TWO** reasons for your answer.

> All those who work with dying people are anxious that terminal care everywhere should become so good that no one ever need ask for voluntary euthanasia.
>
> ... *DR CICELY SAUNDERS, FOUNDER OF THE MODERN HOSPICE MOVEMENT*

SUMMARY

1 Christians look on life as a gift from God and something to be cherished. Most Christian Churches are opposed to euthanasia.

2 The Nonconformist Churches and the Church of England stress that euthanasia would be morally and spiritually unacceptable. At the same time it is important that those who are terminally ill should receive suitable and loving care. All Churches stress the need for people to be able to die surrounded by love and with dignity.

3 The Roman Catholic Church is the strongest in its condemnation of euthanasia.

2:9 Judaism, Islam and Hinduism, and euthanasia

How do Jews, Muslims and Hindus feel about euthanasia?

Jews and Muslims agree that euthanasia is unacceptable and against the will of God. Within Hinduism, however, there is room for a difference of opinion.

 **JUDAISM**

> **IT'S A FACT**
>
> The Talmud, an important book of Jewish teaching, makes it clear that anyone who shoots a man as he falls off a cliff to his certain death is guilty of murder. It does not matter that the man's life may only have been shortened by a few seconds.

Judaism is totally opposed to euthanasia because life is the greatest of all God's good gifts. Whenever Jewish people raise their glasses and make a toast it is 'to life'. Judaism teaches that life is so important that a Jew may break any of the 613 laws to save a life except those that forbid murder, incest and idolatry.

> *It is forbidden to cause the dead to pass away quickly.*
>
> **... THE JEWISH LEGAL CODE**

Jewish teaching insists that:

- Nothing must be done to deliberately shorten a person's life. God alone decides when a person's life should end.

- Nothing should be done to prolong a person's pain. It might be acceptable to give drugs to ease a person's last hours even if they hasten their death (the law of double-effect). To prolong a person's life artificially is also to go against the will of God since it delays what should be coming into effect.

 ISLAM

The Prophet Muhammad reported on a man who was badly wounded in a battle. The wounds of the man were so bad that he cut his own wrists with a knife to hasten his death. Muhammad reported Allah as saying:

> *My slave hurried in the matter of his life therefore he is deprived of the Garden [paradise].*
>
> **... THE PROPHET MUHAMMAD, HADITH**

Muslims believe that the sufferings of this life are a test of a person's faith in Allah. Muslims must not give up on this life. They do not accept the idea that life may not be worth living. Life is always worth living – as long as Allah wills it. Both euthanasia and suicide are strongly discouraged because the length of a person's life can only be decided by Allah. A Muslim does not own his or her own life – it is on loan from God. The person who ends their life by sword, poison or any other means will be tormented by anguish on the Day of Judgement.

> *Nor can a soul die except by Allah's leave, the term being fixed as by writing.*
>
> **... THE QUR'AN (3.145)**

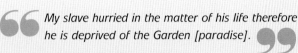 **HINDUISM**

> *Unborn, eternal, everlasting he [the soul] primeval: he is not slain when the body is slain. If a man knows him as indestructible, eternal, unborn, never to pass away, how and whom can he cause to be slain or slay?*
>
> **... THE BHAGAVAD GITA (2.20–21)**

An important Hindu belief is that of ahimsa (non-violence). This includes violence against oneself and that would seem to rule out euthanasia. The teaching of the Bhagavad Gita, a much loved Hindu holy book, however, seems to suggest something else. Many Hindus take this to permit euthanasia *(see quotation above)*. It is the soul that survives death and the soul cannot be harmed by anything that happens in this life. It is not harmful to speed up the soul's entry into the next life and a 'willed death', in which an old person refuses to eat and drink as they await death, might be right for certain Hindus.

Tasks

1. What do you think the old story from the Talmud *(see It's a fact)* has to say about the modern issue of euthanasia?

2. How would you explain the Muslim attitude towards euthanasia to a non-Muslim?

3. Explain what the Hindu idea of a 'willed death' has to do with euthanasia.

 Exam tip

There is a difference of opinion within Hinduism about euthanasia. Make sure that you know why most Hindus are against it, but also be aware of the teaching of the Bhagavad Gita, which seems to admit euthanasia and the idea of the 'willed death'.

! Think about ...

What do you think are the main arguments that an atheist might put forward for opposing euthanasia?

SUMMARY

❶ Both Islam and Judaism teach that the time of a person's death can be settled by God alone and it is wrong to hasten that time in any way.

❷ Islam teaches that human beings must accept willingly any suffering that Allah sends. All life belongs to God.

❸ Hinduism teaches that the body is unimportant and it is the soul that matters. This teaching allows many Hindus to accept a form of euthanasia. The belief in ahimsa, though, seems to rule out all forms of violence – including self-violence.

▼ Hinduism has always encouraged men, towards the end of their lives, to spend their time in spiritual activity.

 **Exam help ...**

In this section you must be aware of the importance of life after death in the teaching of the different religions. This forms the background to understanding the religious approach to abortion and euthanasia. You must understand the legal background to both topics. What does the law say about abortion and euthanasia? Why are all of the major religions opposed to both of them? Do human beings have the right to decide when a person's life should end? Does that right belong to God alone?

1.a. What is life after death?

b. Explain what Christianity teaches about life after death.

c. Explain why the followers of ONE religion, other than Christianity, believe in life after death.

d. 'People who are suffering should be allowed to take their own lives.' Do you agree? Give reasons for your opinion, showing that you have considered another point of view. Your answer should refer to the teaching of at least ONE religion.

1.a. By life after death people are referring to what happens to their body and soul after they die.

b. The Christian beliefs about life after death come from the Bible – especially the teachings of Jesus and Paul.

- The life, death and resurrection of Jesus make it possible for Christians to enjoy God's eternal life. Jesus spoke of a seed falling into the ground and dying to create life. Eternal life in heaven is offered to those who believe in Jesus.

- The teachings of the early Christians, especially Paul, tell Christian followers that there is life after death. Jesus rose from the dead to prove that there can be eternal life. Without the resurrection there is no life beyond the grave.

- There is a vision of heaven in the book of Revelation. Heaven is a place where there is no sadness, death or mourning. It is a totally new way of life where a spiritual body is promised to those in heaven.

continued ...

- There is a disagreement between Protestants and Catholics over the nature of the after-life. Both believe in the immortality of the soul. They also believe in the resurrection of the body. Protestants believe that heaven is experienced immediately after death; Catholics believe in purgatory – a place of cleansing after death.

- A belief in life after death gives meaning to the present life for Christians. It also provides much comfort when a loved one dies. Christians believe that they will be reunited in heaven.

c. The chosen religion is Islam. It is important to notice that this question asks 'why' and not 'what' the followers of Islam believe about life after death. Any answer that concentrates on the 'what' will be inadequate.

- All religions believe in some form of survival after death – whether resurrection as in Islam or reincarnation as in Hinduism.

- The main reason Muslims believe in a life after death is because of the teachings of their holy book – the Qur'an. The Qur'an is very clear on this subject. There is a life after death with judgement, punishment and reward. The Qur'an is believed by Muslims to be the word of Allah. Its whole teaching must be believed.

- Many sayings of the Prophet Muhammad are recorded in the Hadith. These, too, support the teaching of the Qur'an that there is a life beyond the grave.

- The teaching of the Qur'an is that life does not make sense unless there is an after-life. People are expected to live each day by the teachings of the holy book. After death they will be judged by Allah for the life they have lived. They will then spend eternity in heaven or hell. All of this only makes sense if there is an after-life.

d. This question is asking you to look at euthanasia. Euthanasia also means 'happy death' or 'easy death'. It is about a patient who is terminally ill and suffering being able legally to seek the help of somebody else to bring about their death. We will set the issues involved against the teachings of the Christian faith.

continued ...

Those who support voluntary euthanasia put forward many reasons.

- People have the right to do as they please with their own lives.
- A person should be able to choose to die with dignity.
- Euthanasia lessens the burden on friends and relatives.
- We release animals from unnecessary suffering, so why not humans?

Most Christian Churches oppose euthanasia. They put several reasons forward.

- Euthanasia would undermine the trust that patients have in doctors. The Hippocratic Oath obligates doctors to save life, not destroy it.
- Christians believe that all life is sacred. All human beings, whatever their condition, are precious to God. God gives life and only He can choose to end it. The principle that all human life is precious must always be maintained.
- Most hospices are based on Christian teaching. Hospices teach that pain can be managed by the careful use of drugs (palliative care). A person's life can still end in dignity. Hospices make euthanasia unnecessary.

It should be noted that many individual Christians do support euthanasia.

| 2. | **What reasons might people give for not believing in life after death?** |

2. It is not known how many people do not believe in life after death. It is not easy to see how such a belief can be held unless a person has a religious faith – unless one believes in spirits or ghosts. These reasons are often given for not believing in life after death.

- There is no proof. No one has returned from death – unless one includes Jesus and Lazarus. The 'near-death' experiences that people claim to have had are far too uncertain. These experiences may seem real for the person concerned, but other people do not always feel they are legitimate.
- There is medical and scientific evidence that 'brain-death' means the end. There is no evidence that a 'soul' lives in the body. The body disintegrates after death so the idea of resurrection after death does not make any sense.

continued ...

- There is widespread disagreement among the different religions about life after death. They only seem to agree about one thing – life is meaningless unless there is survival after death. Atheists disagree with this.
- Belief in an after-life is a matter of faith and not fact. Like everything else in religion, you either believe it or you don't.

| 3. | **Do all Christians agree about abortion?** |

3. Abortion is the destruction of the foetus in its mother's womb before it is fully grown. This is legal in most of the UK under certain conditions. Christians do not agree about abortion. They disagree over whether it is acceptable in certain situations.

- The Roman Catholic Church takes an 'absolutist' viewpoint – abortion is wrong in every situation. Abortion is seen as murder. If the life of the mother is under threat, the life of the baby must come first. If the mother has been raped she must still have the baby. If the baby is going to be severely handicapped it must still be born, as God values all life.
- The Protestant Churches take a 'situationist' approach – each case must be judged on its merits. If the mother's life is at risk or the baby may be born handicapped then an abortion can be justified. Sometimes an action can be justified if it is the lesser of two evils.
- Other Christian denominations, such as Quakers, do not take a stand either way on this issue.

3:1 Marriage and divorce

What are the facts about marriage, cohabitation and divorce in the UK?

> *What is the point of getting married to someone if you haven't lived with them first? How can you possibly know whether you want to spend the rest of your life with them?*
>
> **... YOUNG PERSON, AGED 17**

Marriage and cohabitation

Marriage and its popularity are in decline. A total of 267 961 marriages took place in England and Wales in 2000, compared with 393 500 in 1986. This continues the long-term downward trend generally seen since the peak in 1972, when 426 241 marriages took place.

On the other hand, cohabitation (two people living together but not married) has increased. Between 1979 and 1991 the percentage of women cohabitating had risen from 11 per cent to 23 per cent. By 2000 over 30 per cent of all women between the ages of 25 and 34 were cohabiting with their partner. In 1971 8 per cent of all births were outside marriage; by 2000 this had risen to 40 per cent. The popularity of marriage has decreased and the number of couples cohabitating has increased.

▼ Rings are exchanged at many weddings. Rings symbolise eternal love.

Possible reasons

Several reasons have been put forward to explain these figures.

- Many couples now see marriage as unnecessary to their happiness.
- Many couples see cohabitation as leading to marriage, as a kind of preparation.
- Some men and women want to have children but not to make a formal, legal and binding commitment to each other.
- Some couples do not want to spend money on a wedding ceremony and reception. The average cost of a wedding is over £12 000.

Divorce

Divorce increased dramatically, especially after 1971. This may indicate that marriage as an institution is in terminal decline and the number of divorces will continue to rise or it may be an indication that people are being more honest with each other – they are not simply staying together, 'for the sake of appearances'. During the twentieth century the increase in the divorce rate accelerated considerably due to two things.

1. **The Second World War.** There was a big increase in the number of divorces after the Second World War split up many relationships. Whilst men were away fighting, some women found new partners.
2. **Changes in the law.** Changes in legislation have made divorce easier to obtain if it is desired. However, there was also a steady increase in divorce in the 1960s prior to the divorce reform.

Divorce – the law

Since the middle of the nineteenth century there have been many changes in the law regarding divorce.

- Until 1857 an Act of Parliament was needed for a divorce. Divorces were rare.
- Until 1923 adultery was the main ground for a divorce. In 1937, insanity, desertion and cruelty were added as grounds for divorce.
- In 1948 the Legal Aid Act provided financial help for those who wanted a divorce.
- In 1971 the law allowed divorce for the 'irretrievable breakdown of marriage'. Couples could divorce after two years of marriage by mutual agreement or after five years if only one partner wanted a divorce.
- An Act of Parliament in 1984 reduced the time limit for a divorce from a minimum of three years of marriage to one year.

The effects of divorce

In 1971 74 000 people got divorced. In 1999 there were 144 000 divorces. In 2001 the divorce rate fell to its lowest since 1979. However, new marriages have a 1 in 2 chance of ending in divorce, this has consequences for society.

- There are now 1.2 million single parent families in the UK. 1 in every 3 children born since 1971 has found themself living in a family affected by separation or divorce. 75 per cent of all divorcing couples have children below the age of 16.

- 75 per cent of all divorce petitions are begun by women. In the 1950s a majority of those requesting a divorce were men. Increased financial independence means that a woman can now opt out of a marriage if she is unhappy.

- The stigma attached to divorce has virtually disappeared. Royal divorces in recent years demonstrate this. Couples now stay together less often 'for the sake of the children'.

IMPORTANT WORDS

Cohabitation;	arrangement between partners, with or without children, who are sharing a household without being married
Marriage;	a man and a woman who are legally recognised as husband and wife have passed through a religious or civil ceremony
Re-marriage;	when a person who has been divorced marries again

✓ **Exam tip**
Information about social topics, such as marriage and divorce, is readily available on various Internet sites. Collect this data to keep your statistical information up to date.

Tasks

1.a. What is cohabitation?

  b. What has happened to marriage and cohabitation in the UK in recent years?

  c. Give **THREE** reasons why more and more people are cohabiting.

2.a. What has happened to divorce in the UK in recent years?

  b. What is the major reason for the increase in the divorce rate during the twentieth century?

▲ Hindu wedding ceremony in India.

IT'S A FACT

Only 36 per cent of marriages that took place in England and Wales in 2000 involved religious ceremonies.

SUMMARY

1 Marriage has become less popular and cohabitation much more popular since the 1950s. For some couples cohabitation is an end in itself and for others the prelude to marriage.

2 Divorce has increased. This is largely because the Divorce Reform Act of 1971 made divorce easier to obtain. Many social problems, largely involving single parent families, have been caused as a result.

3:2 Christianity and marriage

How do Christians show the importance of marriage in their wedding service?

> *I, N, take you, N, to be my husband/wife to have and to hold from this day forward; for better, for worse, for richer, for poorer, in sickness and in health, to love and to cherish, till death us do part, according to God's holy law; and this is my solemn vow.*
>
> **... ANGLICAN WEDDING VOWS**

Marriages in the UK often take place in a church; some go through a ceremony in another place of worship and the remainder opt for a civil wedding ceremony. Those couples marrying in a church go through a Christian ceremony which, whilst it differs a little from denomination to denomination, always underlines the same beliefs about marriage.

The Christian wedding service

- Every Christian wedding service combines the religious and the legal aspects of marriage.

- An emphasis is laid on the fact that the marriage is taking place 'in the sight of God' and in front of relatives and friends. Whilst there must be a minimum of two witnesses to the ceremony the most important witness of all is God. It is this, more than anything else, that marks the difference between a religious and a civil ceremony.

- The marriage is intended to be a lifelong commitment between two people – as the Bible stresses. The couple promise that they will be faithful to each other 'until death us do part'.

- The vows that the couple make cover the whole range of human experiences through which they are likely to pass together – sickness and health, poverty and plenty. Through all of life's experiences the couple promise 'to love and cherish' one another until the end of their days.

- Rings are given, or exchanged, as a visible sign of the vows they have taken. The ring, a perfect unending circle, symbolises the love that will never end but will pass into eternity. Christians believe that marriage in the sight of God is unending. It is only with extreme reluctance that most Christian Churches accept divorce.

There are two important denominational variations to the wedding service.

1. A wedding service involving two Roman Catholics ends with the celebration of a Nuptial Mass at the altar in church. To Roman Catholics, marriage is a sacrament (a special vehicle of God's blessing) but it is unlike the six other sacraments, which are given to worshippers by a priest. The marriage sacrament is given by the man to the woman and vice versa and this makes them special.

2. In the Orthodox Church the service is called 'crowning' during which crowns are placed on the heads of the bride and groom. The two of them receive the power of the Holy Spirit to love each other. The crowns represent both joy and self-sacrifice – for a successful marriage the couple will need both in the years ahead.

Divorce

Jesus often reminded his followers about the purpose of marriage and the kind of relationship that God intended it to be. On more than one occasion Jesus seemed to rule out divorce altogether. He told the people that anyone who leaves their wife and marries someone else, commits adultery – women could not divorce their husbands in first century Palestine. Churches today, though, have mixed feelings about divorce.

- The Church of England recognises that divorce has become socially acceptable, although it will not usually remarry divorced people. It encourages divorced people to remarry in a civil ceremony and then go to church for God's blessing.

- The Roman Catholic Church believes that the marriage vow cannot be broken. An annulment can be granted, but this is not a straightforward process.

- Nonconformist Churches allow divorced people to remarry in church, although individual ministers are free to refuse to carry out the ceremony if it is against their conscience. Most nonconformists feel that if a person has made a mistake they should be allowed another chance.

> *A man who divorces his wife and marries another woman commits adultery against his wife. In the same way, a woman who divorces her husband and marries another man commits adultery.*
>
> **... THE BIBLE (MARK 10.11–12)**

Adultery;	sexual relations between a married person and another person who is not their marriage partner
Faithfulness;	remaining loyal to a partner and never having a sexual relationship with anyone else
Pre-marital sex;	sexual intercourse before a couple is married
Promiscuity;	having sexual relations with several partners; this is often called 'casual sex'; in the Bible it is called 'fornication'

Tasks

1. Describe what Jesus said about divorce.

2. Write down **THREE** important things about the Christian marriage service.

3.a. What is a civil wedding ceremony?

  b. Describe **TWO** differences between a Christian and a civil wedding ceremony.

4. Explain whether or not you are in favour of divorce and give your reasons. Refer to the Christian faith in your answer.

SUMMARY

1 The Christian wedding service combines legal and religious aspects. Such a marriage is taking place in the sight of God. It is intended to be permanent. The vows that the couple take stress their faithfulness to each other through every possible experience of life.

2 The Roman Catholic service ends with a Nuptial Mass. During the Orthodox service the couple wear crowns – to show the joy and self-sacrifice needed for a successful marriage.

3 The wedding service and the Bible both stress that marriage is for ever. Some churches will remarry divorced people, but most will not. The Roman Catholic Church grants an annulment in some circumstances but not a divorce.

▲ Christianity teaches that a marriage takes place with the blessing of God.

3:3 Judaism, Islam and Hinduism, and marriage

How do Jews, Muslims and Hindus show the importance of marriage in their wedding services?

■ JUDAISM

> *Hence a man leaves his father and mother and clings to his wife, so that they become one flesh.*
>
> **... THE TORAH (GENESIS 2.24)**

Marriage. Marriage and family life are at the heart of the Jewish faith. The marriage service may take place in the synagogue or elsewhere as long as the bride and groom stand under a chuppah – the wedding canopy. This represents the new home that they are going to set up together. The most important part of the service is the signing of the marriage contract, the ketubah, in which the groom promises that he will look after and care for his wife. The ceremony that follows is very brief. At its heart lies the promise made by the man as he gives his partner her ring: 'Behold, you are sanctified [made holy] to me by means of this ring, according to the rituals of Moses and Israel.'

During the ceremony the groom smashes a wine glass under his feet. There are different reasons given for this: some say it is a reminder that the most precious things in life, like marriage, are very fragile and easily broken. If they are to survive they need to be cherished.

Divorce. Although Jews believe that marriage should be for life they accept that it sometimes disintegrates. Orthodox Jews believe that for a woman to remarry she must obtain permission from her ex-husband to obtain a get (divorce certificate). Reform Jews do not follow this rule. All Jews agree that a divorce cannot take place within three months in case the wife is pregnant.

■ ISLAM

Marriage. In the simple Muslim wedding ceremony the declaration is made that the couple are marrying of their own free will. A marriage contract is signed which stipulates the mahr (dowry) that the groom is giving his bride. The bride need not be present when the contract is made.

In some Muslim weddings there are vows in which a couple promise to dedicate their marriage to Allah because stable marriage is at the heart of Muslim society. Some Muslim marriages are still arranged, but no couple can be married against their will. Under normal circumstances a Muslim man may only have one wife but the Qur'an does allow polygamy for men under certain strict conditions.

Divorce. Marriage between a Muslim couple is a legal rather than a religious contract and so can be ended. Divorce is lawful and allowed in Islam though is discouraged. A man cannot be granted a divorce if his wife is pregnant so a three-month 'cooling-off' time is stipulated – as in Judaism. During this time an attempt must be made to bring the couple together. The wife can free herself completely from the marriage by returning her mahr.

> *If a wife fears cruelty or desertion on her husband's part, there is no blame on them if they arrange an amicable settlement between themselves; and such arrangement is best.*
>
> **... THE QUR'AN (4.128)**

■ HINDUISM

Marriage. Hindu marriages are traditionally arranged, though in the UK many find their own partners. Marriage is a responsibility on every Hindu since it involves the bringing together, and uniting, of two families not just two people. The birth horoscopes of the man and woman are consulted before the time and place of the wedding are fixed. By tradition the wedding takes place in the home of the bride, although this is less common than it used to be. The priest lights a holy fire, in honour of the God Agni, whilst the bride is given away by her parents. They join the hands of the couple together with a scarf. The priest leads the singing of mantras, holy chants, whilst the groom repeats words that ask that their union might be blessed with children. The end of the bride's sari is then joined to her new husband's scarf as a symbol that they are now joined together for life in marriage.

The couple then take seven steps around the sacred fire. Each of these steps is symbolically important *(see It's a fact)*. The groom's right hand is placed on the bride's right shoulder. The guests and the priest then bless the couple asking that they will have a long and happy marriage blessed with children and grandchildren.

▲ Jewish groom signs a ketubah at his wedding.

Divorce. The teaching of Hinduism is clear. Marriage is for life and once a couple have been joined together in the wedding ceremony they should not be divorced. However, in practice, separation and divorce do take place. Divorce is accepted if there has been cruelty, for men, if their wives have not produced a son and heir within an acceptable time (usually 15 years).

IT'S A FACT

As the Hindu bride and groom take each step around the holy fire they say a special prayer for food, strength, wealth, happiness, children, good health and friendship.

Tasks

1. Write down **THREE** pieces of information about a Jewish wedding.
2. Write down **THREE** pieces of information about a Muslim wedding.
3. Write down **THREE** pieces of information about a Hindu wedding.
4. Describe the teaching of your chosen religion on divorce.

SUMMARY

1 A Jewish couple are married under a chuppah. The signing of the ketubah is central, as is the ring that the man gives to the woman. To divorce, an Orthodox Jewish man gives his wife a get. All Jews wait three months before the divorce is granted.

2 In a Muslim wedding a mahr is given to the bride for her future security. Vows dedicating the marriage to Allah are often made. Divorce is lawful. Attempts must be made to reconcile the couple.

3 Hindu marriages are traditionally arranged. Two families are united through marriage. Birth horoscopes are consulted. Seven steps are taken around the holy fire. The couple are blessed. Hindus are allowed to divorce, though it is discouraged.

3:4 Family life – the facts

What are the different kinds of family arrangement in the UK?

> *As it is the parents who have given life to their children, on them lies the gravest obligation of educating their family ... . It is the duty of parents to create a family atmosphere inspired by love and devotion to God and their fellow-men.*
>
> **... SECOND VATICAN COUNCIL OF THE ROMAN CATHOLIC CHURCH**

In our society, as in almost every other, the family is the most important social unit. The exact form it takes may vary. The 'family' can be described as a group of people, most probably consisting of adults and their offspring, who live together under the same roof or very close to each other. The adults in the relationship are connected to each other either through marriage or cohabitation.

Forms of 'the family'

Broadly speaking, the family can take one of four forms.

1. **The extended family.** The extended family generally consists of at least three generations – grandparents, parents and children living together or very close to each other. This is the form of family life reflected in the various holy books since it is the traditional family arrangement. It is still found in those countries today where it is economically useful and where the State does not take any responsibility for looking after the elderly and so they need to be cared for within the family. There is clear evidence that since the 1950s in the UK the existence of extended families has declined. However, it continues in some UK regions, particularly among Asian communities.

2. **The nuclear family.** This is the modern Western family made up of just parents and children living together. Although there is contact with other members of the family these contacts tend to be spasmodic, often due to distance. Sometimes members of a nuclear family rarely see aunts, uncles, nieces and nephews. The reason for this is that people are much more mobile nowadays and often settle away from their place of birth, there is also less need to rely on members of the family for support and help.

3. **The one-parent family.** This family consists of a single parent, mother or father, and any dependent children. Over 90 per cent of one-parent families are built around a single mother with just 1 in 10 living with their father. In the UK the majority of one-parent families have come into existence because of the rise in the divorce rate; pregnancy outside marriage and the death of a partner.

4. **The re-constituted family.** When someone divorces and remarries they often bring children from their previous marriage with them. These children then gain step-brothers and sisters or half-brothers and sisters. The result is a 're-constituted family'. The number of such families in the UK has increased due to two factors: the increase in the number of divorces and remarriages; the increase in the number of people who change from cohabiting with one partner to living with someone else.

About 50 per cent of children in the UK live in a nuclear family. Apart from one-parent and re-constituted families there are other arrangements that fulfil the functions of family life for those who live in them. There are 'expanded families' in which the elderly, the disabled and the mentally handicapped live together as a family. There is also the 'community family' in which monks and nuns live together. There is also the 'childless family' in which couples choose not to have a family or one of them is infertile.

The importance of the family

Most people believe that family life is extremely important. There are four main reasons for this.

- We gain our sense of identity from our family – our physical likeness, name, values. If a child is adopted they may not take physical characteristics, but they will inherit values, for instance.

- It teaches us what behaviour is and is not acceptable – a process called 'socialisation'. This prepares us for the roles we will be expected to play in later life.

- Our family provides us with our first experiences of 'bonding' – with our parents and siblings.

- Family life is the basic way that society looks after its most vulnerable members – the very young and the very old.

IT'S A FACT

75 per cent of men and 70 per cent of women who divorce are remarried within 5 years. 6 million people live in a re-constituted family. 1 in every 10 children lives with their step-parents.

IMPORTANT WORDS

Extended family; three or more generations of a family living in close contact with each other

Nuclear family; parents and children living together

One-parent family; only one parent living with and bringing up a child or children; this may be as the result of divorce, separation, death or an unmarried parent

Re-constituted family; when two sets of children become one family after their parents become a couple

Tasks

1.a. What are the main functions of a family?

b. What are the main differences between an extended family and a nuclear family?

2. What is meant by:

a. a one-parent family?

b. a re-constituted family?

SUMMARY

1 The family is a very important institution. In the traditional extended family, members support each other with several generations living together. In the modern nuclear family there are just two generations.

2 The one-parent family, usually brought about by unplanned pregnancies or the high divorce rate, is a feature of modern life along with the re-constituted family. Expanded and community 'families' are also very important to those who live in them.

3 We gain our identity, acceptable behaviour pattern, early experiences of bonding and a sense of security from our family membership.

▼ In many communities the extended family still exists.

3:5 Christianity and family life

What are the distinctive characteristics of Christian family life?

> " ... you wives must submit to your husbands ... . In the same way you husbands must live with your wives and with the proper understanding that they are weaker than you. "
>
> **... THE BIBLE (1 PETER 3.1,7)**

Two approaches to family life

There are differences of opinion amongst Christians over the kind of family life that God expects them to lead. There are two main approaches.

1. Those who believe that the Bible gives them a pattern to follow in everything – including the ordering of the family and the roles which should be played by each family member. They go back to the story of creation where God made Adam first and then created Eve. According to the story in Genesis, God realised, after making Adam, that it was not good for man to be without a companion – and created Eve. To many Christians this establishes a pattern. The man in each family has a duty to provide for each family member and the wife has a basic duty to support him in this.

   Some Christians would take it further and point out that it was Eve who first gave in to the serpent's temptations and then encouraged her husband to do so. This shows, they say, that women are weaker than men and need protection. Men and women are given different roles in the family by God. The important decisions have to be made by the man.

2. The much more common point of view is that the above approach may have been appropriate to family life in the past but is hardly applicable today. Both men and women were made 'in the image of God' and were intended to complement each other. Neither is superior in any way to the other. They should have equal opportunities and carry equal responsibilities within the family. Both the mother and father should take equal responsibility for bringing up the children. Both partners should be able to go out to work if that is what they want to do. To justify this viewpoint they point to Bible passages that state that there is no difference in the eyes of God between male and female.

Christians and family life

Christian family life is built upon the relationship between husband and wife although, as the wedding service makes clear, they can expect to be blessed by God with the gift of children.

- Parents are expected to provide a secure and loving environment for their children. They should provide a Christian upbringing within which they introduce their children to such spiritual activities as praying and going to church.

- Children should obey and respect their parents.

- Children should care for their parents when they can no longer look after themselves.

- Christianity believes that the stability of society depends on family life. This is why Christians are very concerned about such features of modern life as cohabitation, a high illegitimate birth rate and a high rate of divorce. They believe that each of these aspects of life today eat away at the importance of family life.

▼ In many families, the father plays a role in the upbringing of his children.

> *So there is no difference between ... men and women; you are all one in union with Christ Jesus.*
>
> **... THE BIBLE (GALATIANS 3.28)**

Churches and family life

Most Christians look upon their local church as a spiritual 'family'. The service of infant baptism encourages members of the church to take some responsibility for the spiritual welfare of the baby. Most churches provide Sunday schools or other similar groups that can help young children to grow as Christians. In the Anglican and Catholic Churches, confirmation is the next stage after baptism in a child's spiritual growth. Family services in most churches provide an opportunity for all members of a family, young and old, to worship together whilst special festivals, such as Christmas and Easter, are times of great celebration. There are also 'uniform organisations', such as Boys' and Girls' Brigades, that operate in many churches.

> *Children it is your Christian duty to obey your parents, for this is the right thing to do. Parents do not treat your children in such a way to make them angry. Instead, bring them up with Christian discipline and instruction.*
>
> **... THE BIBLE (EPHESIANS 6.1,4)**

 Think about ...

Do you think that there are roles in family and work life that are more suited to one gender than the other? Give examples and explain why you have chosen them.

Tasks

1. Explain the two different approaches to family life amongst Christians. Give reasons why they have adopted these approaches.

2. Give **THREE** reasons why Christians believe that family life is very important.

3. Explain how parents and children are expected to behave in a Christian family.

▲ Many babies are introduced to the church family through baptism.

SUMMARY

1 Some Christians believe that the woman's role in a family is to support the man and look after the children. Others believe that marriage should be an equal partnership.

2 Christians believe that parents should provide for their children in a loving and caring environment. They believe that children should respect and obey their parents. Children should also look after parents in times of need – particularly old age.

3 The church is a family – it should be involved in the spiritual welfare of children. Infant baptism and confirmation are important in this respect.

3:6 Judaism, Islam and Hinduism, and family life

How important is family life in Judaism, Islam and Hinduism?

 JUDAISM

> *Honour your father and your mother, that you may long endure on the land that the Lord your God is assigning to you.*
>
> **... THE TORAH (EXODUS 20.12)**

Family life is a central feature of Jewish life. In the wedding ceremony the bride and groom are told that they will be blessed by God with the gift of children and it is their responsibility to set up a home in which the teachings and practices of the faith are followed. A Jewish home is one in which:

- Parents set an example by following all the Jewish dietary laws (kashrut) and teach their children about their faith with its beliefs, prayers, scriptures and moral demands. Within the home shabbat (the sabbath day) will be correctly observed. Parents will also make sure that their children learn the language in which the Jewish scriptures are written – Hebrew. At the appropriate time they will make sure that their children are prepared for their barmitzvah or batmitzvah.

- Children will learn to respect and obey their parents *(see quotation)* as well as caring for them when they grow old.

ISLAM

> *Paradise lies at the feet of your mother.*
>
> **... THE PROPHET MUHAMMAD, HADITH**

The Qur'an teaches that the purpose of married life is that the husband and wife should have children and bring them up as good Muslims. In their home parents and children have their own responsibilities:

- Parents must set their children a good example by respecting the requirements of halal – the Muslim food regulations. In the family, parents have the responsibility of teaching their children how to pray, the beliefs of the faith, the teachings of the Qur'an, which involves learning to read Arabic, and how to live as a good Muslim. They should also make sure that the demands of Salah (prayer rituals) and the fasting of Ramadan are observed in an appropriate way, bearing in mind the age of the child. Muslim children are introduced slowly to the practices and traditions of their religious faith.

- The Muslim husband and wife traditionally have clearly defined roles within a Muslim family. Men must work to provide for their family whilst women must bear and rear the children. Women have the right to study, own property and conduct business whether they are married or not. Men and women have complementary roles – they are not competitors. Yet the Qur'an emphasises that it is the husband who should always take the final decision within the family.

HINDUISM

Traditionally men and women in Hindu families have had very different roles. Hinduism teaches that men and women each have their own dharma (holy duty) and that these are different. A Hindu woman expects to be supported financially by her father until she marries and by her husband afterwards. For this reason the birth of girls into a Hindu family was, in the past, less welcome than the birth of boys. She will work in the home looking after her mother-in-law before she has children and looking after her family afterwards.

The female, as wife and mother, is responsible for looking after the religious responsibilities of each member of the family. She looks after the family shrine that every Hindu household has, making sure that new offerings are laid on it each day. She offers daily puja (worship) at the shrine with members of her family. She also makes sure that any boys in the family receive their sacred thread at the appropriate time. Until this time a mother undertakes the religious education of her sons but afterwards it is entrusted to a spiritual teacher or guru. Motherhood is given a very high priority in Hindu society.

> *May we be happy with our offspring. May we be blessed with dharma. Bless us, protect us, and help us to respect our elders and follow a righteous path for ever. Give us strength to follow the path of the householder, the man to become a gentleman and the woman to be an ideal wife. May our children behave in the same way.*
>
> **... HINDU MARRIAGE HYMN**

Tasks

1. List **THREE** features of Jewish family life.

2. What are the duties of Muslim parents and children towards each other?

3. How do the responsibilities of fathers and mothers differ from each other in a Hindu family?

4. 'Looking after your family is the most important part of being religious.' Do you agree with this comment? Show in your answer that you have considered more than one point of view.

 Think about ...

Look at the Hindu marriage hymn and the hopes that it expresses for the life ahead. Write a paragraph describing what this hymn depicts about Hindu marriage and the ideal relationship for both the husband and the wife in the years ahead.

SUMMARY

1 In a Jewish home the responsibility of parents lies in teaching children about the meaning and customs of their faith.

2 In a Muslim home parents and children have clear responsibilities. Children are taught from an early age about the importance of the Five Pillars of Islam.

3 In a Hindu home the mother's responsibilities are to run the home and organise the religious life of family members. The father must provide for all their physical needs.

▼ A Muslim family pray together in their home in London.

3:7 Contraception

What are the main forms of contraception available and why is family planning so important in the modern world?

> 66 *God blessed them and God said to them, 'Be fertile and increase, fill the earth and master it.'*
>
> ... *THE TORAH (GENESIS 1.28)* 99

It is important to distinguish between:

contraception – any natural or artificial means that people use to prevent conception after sexual intercourse

birth control – any method used to limit the number of babies born either to a couple or within a population

family planning – the deliberate limiting or spacing of births, allowing a couple to choose when to have children

Of course, the same methods are available whether we are talking of contraception, birth control or family planning. The main difference between them lies in the reasons for using them.

Contraception

The main methods of contraception now available are:

1. **The condom or sheath.** Used properly, the condom is a highly effective contraceptive, together with the added benefit of offering real protection against sexually transmitted diseases, including HIV.

2. **The pill.** Over 3 million women in the UK and over 50 million worldwide use the contraceptive pill. By altering the woman's hormonal cycle it renders her infertile while she takes it. The contraceptive pill is 99 per cent effective although some women cannot use it because of their own state of health or its side-effects. The pill was first made available in the 1960s and revolutionised the sexual behaviour of millions of people, especially women.

3. **The IUD or coil.** This is a small plastic and copper device that is placed inside the woman's uterus and left there. It stops sperm reaching an egg. It may bring about a 'spontaneous abortion' (a miscarriage) if an egg is fertilised. Some religious people who feel strongly about abortion object to the IUD.

4. **The diaphragm or cap.** A circular, rubber device that is fitted by the woman over the neck of her cervix before she has sex. This acts as a barrier against the man's sperm.

5. **Sterilisation.** In a woman the fallopian tubes are cut and in a man the tubes which carry the sperm from the testicles to the penis are cut. In both men and women the operation makes the person infertile.

The 'morning after' pill is now freely available and this will stop a fertilised egg implanting in the womb. The male contraceptive pill is still some distance away. So, too, is a reliable 'patch' that can be placed on the arm to release a contraceptive into the body.

Using contraception

Population growth is not a problem in Western, industrialised countries. Sometimes the governments of these countries express concern that the population of their country is at 'zero growth' or even falling below that. The major problems are elsewhere, in those countries where the population is exploding and food supplies are very limited. In some countries, such as Ethiopia, Burundi and Afghanistan there are more than 6 children to an average family. In Somalia and Uganda the figure is over 7. In many parts of the world the population is rising by more than 3 per cent each year. This means that the population in those countries will double every 25 years. Many governments now have huge family planning programmes to persuade their citizens to use family planning – although most of them only meet with limited success.

Religions have traditionally been against the idea of limiting family size, looking on a large family as a sign of God's blessing. Gradually, though, most religious people have come to accept the need to limit the size of the family although some still remain opposed to various methods of contraception. The Roman Catholic Church, however, is the only Christian denomination that is still totally opposed to any artificial means of contraception.

> 66 *Children are a gift from the Lord; they are a real blessing. The sons a man has when he is young are like arrows in a soldier's hand. Happy is the man who has many such arrows.*
>
> ... *THE BIBLE (PSALM 127.3–5)* 99

▲ The Roman Catholic Church is opposed to all artificial forms of contraception, this results in some Catholic couples having many children.

Think about …

Using contraception can be a protection against sexually transmitted diseases and will almost certainly prevent pregnancy. In the light of this, why do you think that many young people still have sex without using any form of contraception?

Tasks

1. Write a sentence to explain the meaning of:
   a. contraception
   b. birth control
   c. family planning.

2. Write down **TWO** reasons why a couple might decide to use contraceptives.

3. Describe **THREE** methods of contraception that are widely used.

IT'S A FACT

It is thought that contraception is used in about 93 per cent of acts of sexual intercourse that take place in the UK.

SUMMARY

1 There are several methods of contraception available – including the condom, the pill, the IUD, the diaphragm and sterilisation. Religious people object to some of them: the Roman Catholic Church objects to all of them as it is against contraception in principle.

2 Contraception is extremely important as a means of limiting family size – especially in countries with a high birth rate. Religion has traditionally looked upon large families as a sign of God's blessing.

3:8 Christianity and contraception

What are the views of Christian Churches on contraception?

Protestant Churches and contraception

Until the 1930s all major Christian Churches were opposed to any attempt to 'regulate birth' – as contraception was then known. The Lambeth Conference of the Anglican Church, held just after the First World War, said that all forms of contraception were morally and spiritually wrong. It was during the late 1920s and early 1930s, however, that the Protestant Churches changed their minds when they saw the effect that too many children had on families struggling to fill empty stomachs. The country was passing through the Depression and poverty in the UK was at an unprecedented level. Contraception is no longer an issue amongst Protestant Christians.

The Roman Catholic Church and contraception

The Roman Catholic Church has been opposed to contraception for centuries and remains strongly opposed today. Pope John XXIII (1958–63) set up a commission to look into this issue but it did not report until after he had died. His successor, Pope Paul VI, was presented with two reports:

- a majority report that recommended that the Church should abandon its opposition to artificial means of birth control

- a minority report that urged the Church remain with its traditional teaching.

The minority report was accepted. In 1968 the encyclical (a document outlining the Pope's thoughts) *Humanae Vitae* was published. It outlawed the pill and the condom, together with sterilisation. It declared that only 'natural' forms of contraception could be used. Roman Catholics in the USA and the UK were deeply upset.

> *Similarly excluded is any action, which either before, at the moment of, or after sexual intercourse is specifically intended to prevent procreation – whether as an end or as a means … it is never lawful, even for the gravest of reasons, to do evil that good may come of it.*
>
> **... HUMANAE VITAE, 1968**

Surveys suggest that as many as 80 per cent of Roman Catholics in these two countries ignore the teaching of their Church on this issue.

Natural family planning

The reasons given by the Pope in *Humanae Vitae* for opposing the use of artificial means of contraception were:

1. The Church has always taught that it is wrong to interfere with the natural processes of conception and birth.

2. 'Natural laws' have been put in place by God to cover all aspects of human behaviour. Any activity against these laws must be resisted. One such law is that every act of sexual intercourse should be open to the possibility of conception and new life.

3. Contraception is unacceptable because it turns an act designed to bring new life into the world into something that is done purely for pleasure.

The Roman Catholic Church teaches that it is permissible for Catholics to take advantage of those times in a month when a woman is naturally infertile to have sex. These infertile days can be worked out by a woman taking her temperature and measuring the consistency of the mucus in her cervix.

> *Each and every married act must be open to the transmission of life.*
>
> **... POPE PAUL VI (1963–78)**

Other Christians and contraception

In the end most Christian couples would say that their choice about whether and what sort of contraception to use should be settled by a combination of: their conscience; the teachings of the Bible; the traditions of the Church; their own thoughts and prayers. This sort of thoughtful approach to the question is often called 'responsible parenthood'.

> **!** **Think about ...**
>
> Some people have said that the 'natural' forms of birth control are, in fact, highly 'unnatural'. What do you think they mean?

Tasks

1.a. Pope Paul VI said, "Each and every married act must be open to the transmission of life". Write a short paragraph explaining what you think he meant.

b. What does the Roman Catholic Church mean when it says that it is against all 'unnatural' forms of birth control?

2.a. What is *Humanae Vitae*?

b. What was the main teaching of *Humanae Vitae* and what reasons were given for its conclusion?

c. Why were *Humanae Vitae*, and its teaching, important for the Roman Catholic Church?

3. 'I believe that contraception is very much a personal matter and the Church should not interfere.' Do you agree with this comment? Refer to the teaching of **ONE** Church in your answer.

SUMMARY

1 The Protestant Churches came to accept the need for contraception during the Depression of the 1920s and 1930s. The Roman Catholic Church, though, has always been against it. It still teaches that only natural forms of birth control are acceptable.

2 Most Christians use a combination of their conscience, the teachings of the Bible and their Church, and thought and prayer to determine their own attitude to contraception.

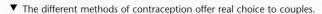

▼ The different methods of contraception offer real choice to couples.

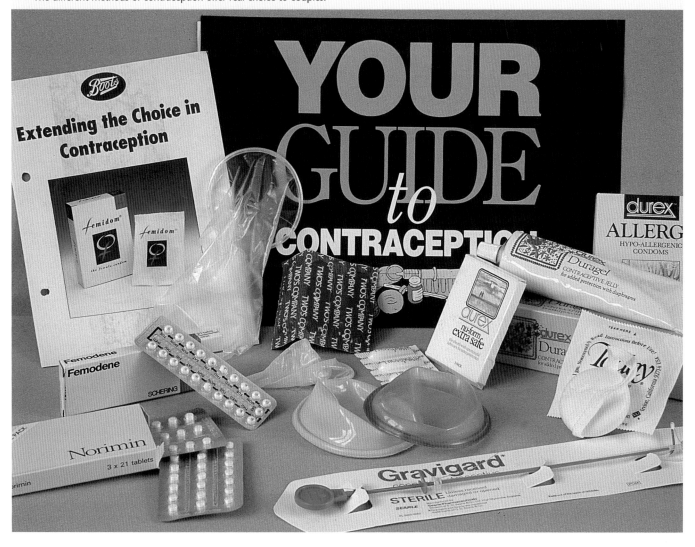

3:9 Judaism, Islam and Hinduism, and contraception

Why are religions against the use of contraception?

■ JUDAISM

The question of contraception is very important in Judaism because sexual relationships within a Jewish marriage are both a duty and a pleasure. It is the Jewish tradition that large families are happy families and that the elderly need to have many children around to look after them when they can no longer look after themselves. Even in a Welfare State the future needs of the elderly can only be met if there is a constant supply of young people to work and pay tax for their care.

Generally, then, Jews are opposed to the use of contraception. In some instances, though, Judaism accepts that running the risk of a pregnancy could be dangerous to the woman and in that situation contraception can be used with a clear conscience. The two principles that should guide a couple in their choice of contraceptive are:

- The contraception should not detract from the pleasure of sex.

- The contraception should not cause an abortion.

■ ISLAM

> He bestows (children) male or female according to His Will, or He bestows both males and females, and He leaves barren whom He will: for he is full of knowledge and power.
>
> **... THE QUR'AN (42.49–50)**

Children are much loved and wanted by Muslim families. Although the use of contraception is not banned by Muslims, their families are large by choice. The birth of a baby is never an accident – it is always planned by Allah. Life is a very special gift. Parenthood is both desirable and rewarding for Muslim couples. The birth of a baby is an event of great joy both within a Muslim family and also in the community generally.

Modern Islam does allow the use of contraception for a married couple if the life of the woman would be put at risk if she were to become pregnant; if there are good reasons for not adding to the family; if there is a risk that any baby would be born with an inherited physical or mental handicap and if the family is so poor that another baby would create real problems.

■ HINDUISM

The vast majority of Hindus live in India and the attitude of this religion to contraception must be seen against the background of the 'population explosion' that has hit that country (see It's a fact). With a high level of poverty in country areas and many slums in the cities it is important that the population is controlled. Even if each family has just two children, India will face a massive population problem in the years to come.

The many Hindu holy books all advise husbands to cohabit with their wife at the right time so that she will conceive many children. In particular, each Hindu family wishes to have at least one son, since sons alone can perform the necessary funeral rituals on the death of a parent. In the past the major concern of most families has been that they will not have enough children to look after them when they grow old. The situation, though, is now very different. Far more children are reaching adulthood as there are better food and medical facilities available. Therefore, the Indian government has encouraged people, with some success, to reduce their family size and Hindu leaders have gone along with this. Most educated Hindus now use contraception. Amongst the uneducated Hindus, living largely in country areas, there is still widespread ignorance and it is here that the population of India is still growing quickly.

> When a man deposits the semen in a woman ... it becomes one with the woman's body as if it were part of her own body.
>
> **... AITAREYA UPANISHAD (2.2)**

IT'S A FACT

India has a population of over 1 billion. Each year this figure increases by some 17 million people – equivalent to the population of Australia.

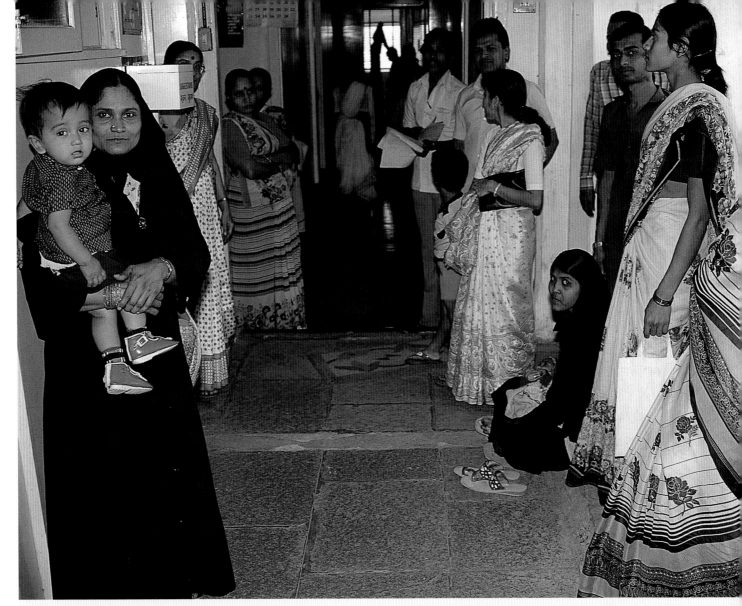

▲ Women queue at a family planning clinic in Bombay, India.

Tasks

1. What is the attitude of Judaism to contraception?

2. If a Jew is going to use contraception, which **TWO** factors should he or she bear in mind?

3. In which FOUR situations is a Muslim justified in using contraception?

4. What is the attitude of Hinduism to contraception?

 Think about ...

Why do you think that even if a religion can accept the use of contraception in certain circumstances, it will almost certainly rule out sterilisation as the method of contraception chosen?

SUMMARY

1 Judaism does not agree with contraception unless a pregnancy would put the life of the mother at risk. Otherwise, a large family is a sign of God's blessing.

2 Overall Islam is opposed to contraception, though many Muslims use it. Parenthood is a great honour and blessing. Islam is strongly against sterilisation.

3 India has a very great population problem and Hindus in India accept that large families are not in the interests of the country as a whole. The desire of each Hindu couple to have at least one son is very strong for religious reasons.

3:10 Homosexuality

How has the legal status of homosexuals changed in the UK?

Homosexuality, from the Latin words meaning 'same' and 'sex'. A homosexual is a person attracted to people of the same sex as themselves. Although known homosexual activity stretches as far back as the ancient Greeks, the word did not enter the English language until 1869. The word 'lesbian' was coined at about the same time to describe female homosexuals. This word was taken from the Greek island of Lesbos where, in the seventh century BCE, Sappho expressed her love and adoration for other women through her poetry. In recent years most male homosexuals have preferred to call themselves 'gay' or 'queer'.

No one knows just how many gay people there are in the UK, but the best estimate is that about 1 in every 15 people in the population is gay – 60 per cent of them men and 40 per cent women. Of this number only about 10 per cent are openly gay – have 'come out' – with the vast majority preferring to keep their sexual orientation secret.

Homosexuality – the law

Until 1967 it was illegal to be involved in male gay sexual activity, although no law has ever existed against female homosexual activity (see It's a fact). In 1967 homosexual activity between men became legal in England and Wales as long as two basic conditions were met:

- all such activity took place in private
- those involved were consenting adults aged 21 or over.

The age of consent was reduced to 18 in 1994. An attempt to reduce this to 16 initially failed, but was later passed. This is important symbolically because it means that the law now treats homosexual sex and heterosexual sex in exactly the same way.

In other ways, though, the law still treats the two groups differently. Homosexual couples in the UK cannot marry and this makes it very difficult, although not impossible, for same-sex couples to adopt a child. On the death of one partner property does not automatically pass to the other. Homosexual couples do not have the same pension rights as heterosexual couples.

Why are some people homosexual?

There is no certain answer to this question. The simple view is that some people are born homosexual, whilst the majority are born heterosexual. If it is part of the genetic make-up of some people, nothing can be done about it.

Homosexuals act in keeping with their nature. Some people try to argue that family background explains homosexuality: it has been suggested that boys who have very strong links with their mothers and weak links with their fathers are more likely to become homosexual – this has not been proved.

In the nineteenth and early twentieth centuries homosexuality was viewed as a disease and it was defined in this way in many medical textbooks. Such stereotyping has now largely disappeared. Doctors tend to agree that homosexuals do not choose the lifestyle as much as it chooses them. They are born homosexual and it is in their genetic make-up.

There is still stereotyping in existence in different forms. Some people are homophobic, which means they fear or hate homosexuals. One of the reasons homosexuals keep their sexual preference a secret is because they are worried about the reaction they will get from those around them. Many groups do not fully accept homosexuality.

IT'S A FACT

No law in the UK has ever been passed to make female homosexual activity illegal. (Although in 2000 an age of consent was introduced.) Such a possibility was raised in the nineteenth century in front of Queen Victoria and she immediately scotched the idea. She simply refused to believe that any member of her own sex would ever bring themselves to do such a thing!

Think about ...

Do you think the time will come when society treats homosexuals and heterosexuals in exactly the same way? Can you envisage homosexuals being allowed, to marry for instance? What is your opinion on homosexual marriage?

Exam tip

In dealing with such a sensitive subject as homosexuality it is very important that you choose your words carefully and accurately. The words 'homosexual', 'lesbian' and 'gay' are acceptable but there are many others that are not.

▲ Graham Norton is openly gay. Homosexual couples in the UK are prevented from marrying by the law and religion.

Tasks

1. Write a sentence to explain the meaning of:
   a. homosexual
   b. lesbian
   c. gay.

2. Describe how male homosexual activity became legal in the UK.

3. What is the current thinking about why some people are homosexual whilst the majority are heterosexual?

IMPORTANT WORD

Homosexual; a person who is sexually attracted to members of their own, rather than the opposite, sex

SUMMARY

1 Homosexuality is a very old sexual activity – for both males and females. Male homosexuals are usually referred to as 'gay', whilst females are often called 'lesbian'.

2 There are several possible explanations for homosexuality. The one supported by most doctors is that it is genetically determined, therefore, homosexuals are born and not made.

3 Male homosexual activity has been legal since 1967 with the age of consent now reduced to 16.

3:11 Christianity and homosexuality

What is the view of Christian Churches on homosexuality?

> *God has given them over to shameful passions. Even the women pervert the natural use of their sex by unnatural acts. ... Men do shameful things with each other and as a result they bring upon themselves the punishment they deserve for their wrongdoing.*
>
> **... THE BIBLE (ROMANS 1.26–27)**

It is generally agreed today that homosexuality is a natural sexual orientation and not a lifestyle choice. It is only comparatively recently, however, that a line has been drawn in the Christian Church between homosexual orientation, which is acceptable, and homosexual activity, which is not.

None of the major Christian Churches condemn the sexual orientation that compels a person to be sexually attracted to someone of their own sex. A homosexual is given the same dignity in the sight of God as a heterosexual. It is pointless condemning someone for being a homosexual – you might as well blame someone for being bald. In the past, Christians have strongly condemned those who are homosexual, taking their lead from the teaching of St Paul in the New Testament *(see quotation)*. It is known that there are a number of Christian priests that are homosexual. The opinion of the majority of Christians appears to be that homosexuals cannot be blamed for their sexual orientation but they must not take part in any homosexual activity.

IT'S A FACT

In the 1980s books were introduced into certain schools that said homosexual relationships, partnerships and the rearing of children within them were normal. In December 1987 Parliament ruled that these books could not be used and this ban has not been lifted.

The Church draws a sharp distinction between what a person is and what a person does. Homosexual activity remains immoral and unacceptable. At this point the Church divides between two views.

1. The majority who believe that all homosexual activity is sinful. Many Protestants and Roman Catholics believe this. The Evangelical Protestants condemn homosexuality because it is contrary to the teaching of the Bible. Roman Catholics condemn it because it is contrary to the teaching of the Church that every sexual act should be open to the possible creation of new life. The Roman Catholic Church condemns masturbation for both males and females for the same reason. This Church also maintains that marriage is the only suitable place for sexual activity.

2. The minority (mainly Protestants) who believe that there is an enormous difference between a casual homosexual relationship and a relationship for life between two men or women who love and are totally committed to each other. Couples in this situation can understand the Bible in the light of modern knowledge, which has given a totally different understanding of homosexuality. In 1964 the Quakers brought out a document entitled *Towards a Quaker View of Sex* in which they argued that the Church must accept homosexuals who are in a serious and committed relationship.

Homosexuality and the Bible

The Old Testament condemns homosexual acts in Leviticus 18.22: "You shall not lie with a man as with a woman" and Leviticus 20.13, which adds the comment that those who do so deserve to be put to death.

In the New Testament Jesus made no comment directly about homosexuality simply saying that the coming together of a man and a woman until they are 'one flesh' is God's ideal for everybody. St Paul, however, condemned homosexual relations in a letter that he wrote to the Romans *(see quotation)*. He also condemned homosexuals strongly in 1. Corinthians 6.9–10 at the same time as attacking adulterers, thieves, drunkards, slanderers and swindlers. These condemnations have not only influenced peoples' opinions down the centuries but have also affected the laws that were passed relating to homosexual activity in many western countries, including the UK.

> *Homosexual persons are called to chastity. By the virtues of self-mastery that teach them inner freedom, at times by the support of disinterested friendship, by prayer and sacramental grace, they can and should gradually and resolutely approach Christian perfection.*
>
> **... CATECHISM OF THE CATHOLIC CHURCH**

Tasks

1. What do the main Christian Churches make of people with a homosexual orientation?

2. Which **TWO** opinions are found in the Christian Church concerning homosexual activity?

3. Briefly describe what the Bible has to say about homosexuality.

4. 'The Christian attitude towards homosexuality does not seem very Christian at all.' Do you agree with this comment?

SUMMARY

1 Most Christians draw a distinction between homosexual orientation and homosexual activity. Nothing can be done about the first – it is a fact of life. No Christian homosexual, though, should be involved in sexual activity.

2 The vast majority of Christians would say that homosexual activity is sinful, including most Protestants and Roman Catholics. There is a minority, however, who distinguish between a casual sexual relationship and a lifelong partnership.

3 Biblical texts – especially St Paul – condemn homosexuality.

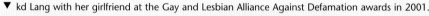
▼ kd Lang with her girlfriend at the Gay and Lesbian Alliance Against Defamation awards in 2001.

3:12 Judaism, Islam and Hinduism, and homosexuality

What are the views of Judaism, Islam and Hinduism on homosexuality?

◼ JUDAISM

> *If a man lies with a male as one lies with a woman, the two of them have done an abhorrent thing; they shall be put to death.*
>
> **... THE TORAH (LEVITICUS 20.13)**

There is nothing in the Jewish holy books to suggest that people may be homosexual by orientation – only that they commit homosexual acts. For Jews, the most authoritative of the holy books are the first five books of the Bible – the Torah. The book of Leviticus in the Torah carries very strong denunciations of homosexual activity – (see quotation). Those who take part in such activity are said to be worthy of death. There is no indication, however, that the death penalty was ever carried out for this particular offence.

It has always been the Jewish custom that men should meet together regularly in pairs to study the Torah as part of their spiritual discipline. The Talmud, a very important holy book, decided that this was acceptable but by the sixteenth century the advice was given that it was not advisable for this to happen.

Today the Orthodox Jewish belief is that homosexual activity is a sin because of its condemnation in the Torah. The only place for sex is within marriage. Reform Jews believe that the teachings of the Torah, including homosexuality, need to be re-interpreted in the light of modern understanding.

◼ ISLAM

Islam forbids homosexual relationships. It looks upon such relationships as unnatural and a departure from the normal behaviour that Allah expects from all believers. Allah has provided males and females for each other and homosexuality is a travesty of His plan. Mention is made of homosexuality in the Qur'an (see quotation). This verse reminds Muslims that the Prophet Lot, the nephew of

Ibrahim, was sent by God to warn His people against the practices of homosexuality. Since the Qur'an is the last and final word of Allah to all Muslims it must be obeyed without question.

> *Of all the creatures in the world, will ye approach males. And leave those whom Allah has created for you to be your mates? Nay, ye are a people transgressing (all limits)!*
>
> **... THE QUR'AN (26.165–6)**

Like Jews, Muslims strongly believe that sex should be confined to marriage. They also believe that sex is the God-given means by which the family is built up and strengthened. The family is at the centre of Muslim religious life and nothing must be allowed to weaken it.

◼ HINDUISM

There is nothing in the Hindu scriptures about homosexuality. The religion teaches that the natural thing for everyone is to marry and have children. Anyone who does not do this is violating their own dharma. Homosexuality is unacceptable to most Hindus. When the AIDS epidemic first hit India in the late 1980s people did not understand the cause and wrongly believed it was a disease that only affected homosexuals; as a result homophobia (fear of homosexuality) was very high.

Some people believe that homosexuality goes back a long way in Indian culture and religion. There are some carvings on Hindu temples that show men and women indulging in homosexual sex. There is also a special Hindu caste of religious devotees in which men are castrated and dress as women.

> *When the tip of a hair is split into a hundred parts and one of those parts further into a hundred parts – the individual soul, on the one hand, is the size of one such part, and, on the other, it partakes of infinity. It is neither a man nor a woman, nor even a hermaphrodite [neither man nor woman]; it is ruled over by whatever body it obtains.*
>
> **... SVETASVATARA UPANISHAD (5.9–10)**

Tasks

1. What is the teaching of the Torah on homosexuality?
2. How do Orthodox and Reform Jews differ in their approach to homosexuality?
3. What is the teaching of the Qur'an about homosexuality?
4. What is the approach of Hinduism to homosexuality?

✓ Exam tip

In dealing with the attitude of Judaism, Islam and Hinduism to homosexuality it is not always possible to see clear differences between them. Concentrate, therefore, on any differences that you find and the difference of views within each religion, such as between the Orthodox and Reform Jewish points of view.

SUMMARY

1 The Jewish scriptures condemn homosexual behaviour. Orthodox and Reform Jews have different approaches to the issue.

2 Islam condemns all homosexual behaviour because it is condemned in the Qur'an. Muslims believe that all sex must be confined to marriage.

3 Hindus believe that 'normal' behaviour is to marry and have children. Some Hindus, though, find homosexuality acceptable.

▼ Protest outside Islamic conference in Wembley, London, 1994. Many gay men refer to themselves as 'queer'.

In this section we have looked at arrangements that affect the lives of everyone, that is marriage and family life. The way that a religion looks at marriage is reflected in its wedding service. Here there are important differences between the different religions and you must be aware of them. The same is also true of family life. All religions agree that family life is extremely important. It is through the family that children are taught religious traditions. There are also important religious principles involved in the use of contraception and the practice of homosexuality.

1.a. What is cohabitation?

  b. What is the Christian teaching on cohabitation and sex outside marriage?

  c. Describe the teaching of **ONE** religion, other than Christianity, on marriage.

  d. 'Family life is at the heart of religion.' Do you agree? Your answer should refer to the teaching of at least **ONE** religion.

1.a. Cohabitation is when two people live together whilst they are unmarried.

  b. There are many reasons why two people might choose to live together without being married. It might be seen as a preparation for marriage; a couple might want to have children but not the legal commitment of marriage or they might see marriage as unimportant to their happiness together. 30 per cent of all couples between the ages of 25 and 34 now cohabit.

- Most Christian couples feel unhappy about cohabiting. They see marriage as given by God and the only suitable place in which to bring up children. The vows at the heart of the marriage service sum up their commitment to each other.

Sex before marriage.

- Many Christians take a strong line against sexual relationships before marriage.

- They look upon sex as a sign of commitment towards each other – in the Bible God's place for sex is marriage.

- The commitment of a couple cannot be complete without marriage. What if one person leaves the other?

continued ...

- Roman Catholics believe that sexual intercourse is designed to lead to the conception of children. This is why they believe it is wrong to use contraception.

- Responsible sex and parenthood are ideas that most Christians would support – the only place where these can be guaranteed is within marriage.

  c. The chosen religion is Judaism.

- Marriage and family life are at the heart of Judaism.

- A Jewish wedding does not have to take place in a synagogue but the couple must marry under a chuppah – which is a wedding canopy. This symbolises the home that they are going to set up together.

- The signing of the ketubah (wedding contract) is at the heart of a Jewish wedding. This is the document in which the groom promises that he will always love and provide for his wife. It also states the penalty he will have to pay if he divorces his wife.

- The promise that the man makes as he gives his bride the ring indicates that their marriage will always be lived according to the rules of Moses and Israel.

- The groom crushes a wine glass beneath his feet. This reminds the bride and groom that their marriage is fragile and needs protecting.

  d. The chosen religion is Judaism.

- Family life is at the heart of the Jewish faith. In the wedding ceremony the bride and groom are told that God will bless them with the gift of children. Every Jewish person is brought up to expect to have a family of their own.

- Many Jewish rituals and festivals are celebrated in the home and not the synagogue. It is mainly at home that children learn about the beliefs, prayers and scriptures of their faith.

- The important Jewish laws about diet and food (kashrut) are learned and carried out within the family.

continued ...

The importance of family life is also stressed in other world religions. In Hinduism, for instance, each family has its own shrine in the home. Some Hindu families rarely go to the temple for worship – all of the necessary prayers are performed at home. In most religious families it is the mother who is responsible for religious life and teaching.

2. What are the different kinds of family?

2. There are four main kinds of family arrangement that are found in the modern world.

- The extended family: where three generations, or more, live in the same house or very close to each other. This is the traditional family arrangement and is reflected in the holy books. It is still found to be economically useful for looking after the young and old – especially where there is no Welfare State. This family unit is still found in the Asian community in the UK.

- The nuclear family: where two generations – parents and children – live together. There is often only infrequent contact between the nuclear family and other family members such as parents and grandparents. This family unit has come about because people move away to seek work and to go to university.

- The lone-parent family: a single parent, most likely to be the mother. The rise in the divorce rate and pregnancy outside marriage is most likely to be the cause of the lone-parent family.

- The reconstituted family: which is formed when someone with children remarries.

- There are also other 'family' arrangements. The elderly and the disabled often live together in an 'expanded' family. Monks and nuns live together in a 'community' family. There are also childless families.

3. Describe the attitude of ONE religion, other than Christianity, towards divorce.

3. The chosen religion is Islam.

- Divorce is allowed in Islam although it is discouraged.

- However, only a man can initiate divorce in Islam. A three month cooling-off period is required to ensure that the wife is not pregnant before divorce is allowed. This also allows time for an attempt to be made to sort out the couple's problems.

- Muhammad is the supreme example for all Muslims. He had a very happy family life and was blessed with several children by Allah. Muhammad was opposed to divorce.

4:1 The sexes

How are men and women treated in the UK and is the situation changing?

Out of every 100 babies born in the UK, 52 will be boys and 48 girls. At the moment of birth boys and girls are treated equally, but from that moment onwards the situation changes. Many people, especially in certain cultures, feel that the sex of a child is very important. The expectations we have of boys and girls are often different and this can be shown by the words we use to describe the different sexes. Boys are described as strong, tough or 'little rascals'. Girls are described as sweet, pretty or angelic. These descriptions reveal our expectations.

As children grow up these same basic expectations remain. Females are supposed to be more caring and to demonstrate this by the way they behave. Males are expected to be forceful and successful at whatever career they choose to follow. They will both discover that sexism exists and that they are growing up into a very unequal world.

> Times have changed. Today women no longer expect to just be a mother and housewife – they have aspirations. They can see just what they would like to achieve. Although they can see where they would like to go, however, they rarely get there. Women today face a glass ceiling – they can see the top jobs, but they just cannot get there.
>
> ... **THE GUARDIAN, OCTOBER 1998**

The battle of the sexes

There are important inequalities between men and women in the UK today. Here are some of them:

- Women are likely to do most of the housework. This is true even though today woman are often working full-time. Women are much more likely to give up work to look after the home and bring up the children. Although there are exceptions, this is a still a role that would make most men feel uncomfortable.

- Parents are likely to lay down different rules for boys and girls – and to treat them differently.

- Women are much more likely than men to be the victims of domestic violence.

- After a divorce women are more likely than men to gain custody of the children and this affects their chances of finding paid employment.

- Although more and more women are in paid employment their salary levels are significantly lower than those of their male equivalent. Women earn, on average, 75 per cent of what men earn. Women are more likely than men to work part-time. Nine out of every 10 part-time workers are women. Women are also more likely to be in the most lowly paid occupations and are less likely to obtain promotion.

- Women are more likely than men to experience poverty. One of the poorest groups in society is single mothers. There are about 1 200 000 of them in the UK.

- In politics there are far fewer women than men in Parliament.

There are two explanations often used for this inequality.

1. Men and women are different biologically and so they will act differently. Women are naturally the ones to stay at home and care for the children because they are genetically programmed to do so.

2. Men and women carry out their different roles in society because they have been taught to do so. Take a simple example. Young girls help their mother around the house whilst boys often spend time with their fathers participating in more 'masculine' roles. In this way girls learn that their principal role in life is as a home-maker, whilst boys are taught that their role is to get somewhere in life, to earn enough to support a wife and family, to solve problems and make things happen.

The law and inequality

The law in the UK has often helped to maintain a difference between the sexes and prevent equality.

Until 1882 married women could not own property in their own name and it was only in 1892 that they were allowed to vote in local elections and stand as councillors. In 1918 women over the age of 30 were allowed to vote in parliamentary elections, but it was not until 1928 that the age was reduced to 21 – the same age as for men at the time.

▲ Women's rights march, Kathmandu, Nepal.

In 1970, for the first time, it was made illegal for women to be paid less than men for doing the same job. Five years later it was made illegal to discriminate against women in the workplace because of their sex. However, whilst most people would now accept, in theory, that men and women are equal it is not so easy to bring about true equality in practice.

IT'S A FACT

Nearly all of Britain's 6 million carers are women. This form of work is known as 'invisible' as it is generally unpaid – although now some state benefits are paid to carers. Many of these women would like to return to work, but there is no one else to look after the people for whom they are caring.

IMPORTANT WORDS

Equality; being equal, treating men and women in the workplace and elsewhere on an absolutely equal basis – in pay, career opportunities, for example

Sexism; a bias against one sex or the other meaning that one of the sexes is treated unfairly

✓ **Exam tip**
There are often articles in the newspapers showing up the inequality between men and women in the UK – collect some examples to use in your work. Do the same for other social topics. You need to be up to date with your information and this will be reflected in the quality of your exam answers.

Tasks

1. Give **FOUR** examples of changes in the law in the UK to make men and women more equal.

2. Give examples from **THREE** different branches of modern life to show that men and women are treated unequally.

3.a. Which **TWO** explanations have been put forward to explain this inequality?

b. Which explanation do you favour? Give reasons for your answer.

SUMMARY

1 The two sexes are expected to grow up differently. They are expected to show different characteristics in their adult life. One possible explanation is that the two sexes are different genetically. The other explanation is that they are treated differently from birth onwards – and so act and feel differently.

2 There are many examples of inequality between the sexes in the UK – covering such areas as life-styles, education and employment. Although steps have been taken to create a fairer society it still favours men.

4:2 Christianity and the sexes

What does Christianity have to say about the roles of men and women in modern life?

> *I do not allow them [women] to teach or have authority over men; they must keep quiet [in a place of worship]. For Adam was created first and then Eve. And it was not Adam who was deceived; it was the woman who was deceived and broke God's law. But a woman will be saved through having children, if she perseveres in faith and love and holiness, with modesty.*
>
> **... THE BIBLE (1 TIMOTHY 2.12–15)**

Christianity has often been accused of discriminating against women because of the way that it has traditionally seen them and their place in society. Its teaching on this matter has had a huge effect on the whole of Western society over the past 2000 years. In church life women have often been expected to perform the most lowly tasks, such as making tea, arranging flowers, scrubbing floors and polishing pews and to be subordinate to the authority of men. The above quotation, which refers to a letter from St Paul, shows support for this subordination.

Men and women in the New Testament

Jesus and St Paul seem to have had very different attitudes towards women.

- **Jesus.** Jesus chose 12 men to be his disciples and close companions, helping him in his work of teaching and healing. Women were there to 'wait on him' as Mark tells us in his Gospel (15.41). Yet, in many ways, Jesus did break the mould in his attitude towards women, even though this does not seem to be particularly 'mould-breaking' today. Many of Jesus' closest followers and supporters were women and some of them were wealthy benefactors who supported him with their gifts as well as their love. His friendship with Mary and Martha, two sisters, was clearly very important to him and he stayed with them and Lazarus, their brother, in Bethany on more than one occasion. Women were the earliest, and most important, witnesses to the resurrection of Jesus, although they did have some difficulty persuading the male disciples to believe and act on their incredible story. At the time women were not considered to be trustworthy enough to be criminal witnesses.

- **Paul.** It was St Paul, rather than Jesus, who reflected the ideas of his time about women. Paul wrote that "The man is head of the woman, as Christ is the Head of the Church" as well as teaching that a wife should 'obey' her husband whilst it was her responsibility to 'love' her husband. You can find out what Paul said about women leading public worship in the quotation shown from the Bible. He would not allow women to play any public role in the churches he established.

Christians today and women

In recent years many things have changed in the Christian Church and one of the most important of these is its attitude towards women. In most Churches women now play a role, if not the leading role, in worship. The Methodist, Baptist and United Reformed Churches have had female ministers for much longer. There have been female officers in the Salvation Army since the beginning of the movement in the nineteenth century and it has, from time to time, been led by a woman. The Church of England allowed women to become deacons and priests for the first time in 1994, although there have not, as yet, been any elected to be bishops. In the wider Anglican Church, however, there have been women bishops for a long time.

The Roman Catholic and Eastern Orthodox Churches are firmly against admitting women to the priesthood. The main reason for this is that Jesus chose only men to be his disciples and priests today are the successors of the apostles of Jesus. As you can see from the quotation from the Catechism of the Catholic Church, this is still the firm teaching of the Church today.

> *The Lord Jesus chose men to form the college of the 12 apostles, and the apostles did the same when they chose collaborators to succeed them in their ministry ... for this reason the ordination of women is not possible.*
>
> **... CATECHISM OF THE CATHOLIC CHURCH, 1994**

 Think about ...

Why do you think that some Christian Churches have given women a leading part in church life whilst others have found it very difficult or impossible to involve them in positions of leadership?

▲ Female priest taking communion.

Tasks

1. Write **THREE** things that the following said and did to show their attitude towards women:
    a. Jesus
    b. Paul.

2. Name:
    a. **TWO** Churches that have always had women ministers.
    b. **ONE** Church that has had women officers since its beginning.
    c. **TWO** Churches that refuse to ordain women priests.

3. Describe **TWO** ways in which parts of the Christian Church have tried to improve the way in which they treat women.

4. Why does the Roman Catholic Church believe that the ordination of women to the priesthood is impossible?

SUMMARY

1 Although Jesus chose only men to be his disciples he had an enlightened attitude towards women for his time. Paul, though, believed that women should not play any part in the leadership of the churches that he established.

2 Some Churches have given leadership positions to women for a long time, although the Church of England only ordained women in 1994. The Roman Catholic and Eastern Orthodox Churches do not have women priests. The Salvation Army has given leadership responsibilities to women since it began.

3 The Roman Catholic and Orthodox Churches rule out the possibility of women priests – because they believe Christian tradition and the Bible make it impossible.

4:3 Judaism, Islam and Hinduism, and the sexes

How do Judaism, Islam and Hinduism differ in their teachings on men and women?

▌ JUDAISM

Orthodox and Reform Jews both accept that men and women are equal, but they believe that they have different roles within the worshipping community and at the synagogue.

Orthodox Jews. Women have absolute authority in an Orthodox Jewish home. This is where the children are mainly taught; shabbat is observed and festivals celebrated. Men have absolute authority in the public aspects of religious life, in the synagogue and in the Jewish courts. Woman cannot form part of a minyan – 10 people who need to be present before a Jewish service can be held in an Orthodox synagogue. Women sit separately from men in the synagogue and play no part in the services. Orthodox women cannot demand a divorce nor can they remarry unless their husband grants them a get (a bill of divorce).

Reform Jews. Reform Jews are those who believe that the old scriptures, laws and traditions of the Jewish faith need to be understood in the light of modern life. Men and women from this strand of the faith share domestic and religious responsibilities whereas only men can read from the Torah in an Orthodox synagogue, this privilege is also enjoyed by women in Reform synagogues. Reform synagogues can have a female or a male rabbi.

▌ ISLAM

> ❝ Whoever works righteousness, man or woman, and has Faith, verily [in truth], to him will We give a new Life, a life that is good and pure; and We will bestow on such their reward according to the best of their actions. ❞
>
> **... THE QUR'AN (16.97)**

Islam does not accept that men and women are equal in all respects. They have different roles. Women are called by Allah to be mothers; to care for the home and to bring up the children. Men are called by Allah to be protectors; to earn a living and take overall responsibility for decision-making. Men should also make sure that their children are sent to the madrasah, where they will learn to read the Qur'an. Men and boys should worship in the mosque but women can only attend for prayers when it is only women praying. Children often attend single-sex schools. Women only inherit 50 per cent of what men inherit, reflecting the Muslim tradition that men take on full financial responsibility for looking after the family with women being supported by male relatives.

▌ HINDUISM

The traditional Hindu view was that procreation was all-important and that only women could guarantee this. Women, therefore, were more important than men in traditional Hinduism. Modern Hinduism, however, sees men and women as equal partners both in religious and also home life. This means that modern Hindus often find themselves in conflict with the ancient texts of their faith (*see quotation*). Hindu men, however, often feel that they still need to protect the women in their family. Some Hindu females are discouraged from going out to work by their husband or other men in their family. Older girls in the family are usually kept under very strict supervision. It is often hard for young female Hindus to balance the demands of their faith with Western ways. This can cause many problems when living in a country such as the UK where there are about 500 000 Hindus. One clear consequence of this is a strong preference in the Hindu community for their children to attend single-sex schools.

▼ Hindu gods and goddesses.

▲ Female rabbi reading from the Torah scroll in a Reform synagogue in Bristol.

 Her father protects a woman in childhood, her husband protects her in her youth, her sons protect her in old age; a woman is never fit for independence.

... THE LAWS OF MANU

Tasks

1. Write down **THREE** ways in which men and women are treated differently in the Orthodox Jewish community.

2. Compare the different ways that women are treated in the Orthodox and Reform Jewish communities.

3. Describe how the Qur'an sees the different roles played by men and women in the Muslim community.

4. Why do women in the Muslim community only inherit half as much as men?

! Think about ...

Describe where and why there might be conflict between parents upholding traditional religious values and their children observing how friends from non-Hindu or non-Muslim homes are treated.

SUMMARY

1 Orthodox and Reform Jews have different approaches to the part that women can play. Orthodox Jews believe that the woman is supreme in the home and men in the synagogue. Reform Jews take a more equal approach.

2 Muslims believe that women are primarily called to be mothers, whilst men are called to be protectors. Women rarely attend the mosque for prayers. Their prayers are usually said in the home whilst they are attending to their domestic duties.

3 Hindus struggle to apply their ancient books to modern ways of life. Women are allowed an independent lifestyle but many Hindu men are reluctant to grant it to them.

4:4 A multi-ethnic society

What is meant by describing the UK as a multi-ethnic society and how has this come about?

> *I believe deeply that all men and women should be able to go as far in our country as their talent, ambition and effort can take them. There should be no barriers of religion and no barriers of race. I want ... a society that encourages each and every one to fulfil his or her potential to the utmost ... let me say here and now that I regard any barrier built on race to be pernicious and wicked.*
>
> ... **JOHN MAJOR, BRITISH PRIME MINISTER, 1991**

Due to the mix of different cultures, the UK is often described as multi-ethnic, multi-racial or multi-faith. The UK has always had a mixed population. For centuries its population has included people from many different backgrounds. People living in the UK today can trace their ancestors back to people descended from Celts, Romans, Angles, Saxons, Jutes, Danes, Vikings and Normans – amongst others. The UK has a long tradition of personal and religious freedom. It has offered shelter to people suffering persecution in their own country. In the 1930s many Jews, for instance, fled to the UK to escape persecution in Hitler's Nazi Germany.

Towards a multi-ethnic UK

The move towards the UK becoming a truly multi-racial society began after the Second World War ended in 1945 when there was a great shortage of workers in essential occupations like running public transport. The UK government deliberately set out to find extra workers from Commonwealth countries. Many people were recruited from India, Pakistan, Bangladesh, Africa, Hong Kong and the West Indies. Many of these people had fought for the UK in the war. There were more people from the Commonwealth than from Britain involved as soldiers in the Second World War. This country owed them a tremendous debt. Until the 1960s people were allowed freely into the UK to work. Men often came ahead of their families, found work and somewhere to live and then sent for their wife and children.

Race and politics

As more people came to settle in the UK – especially in the inner-city areas – so the problem of racism began to rear its ugly head as people were often prejudiced against those coming from abroad for work; so the problem of discrimination soon set in. The Labour, Conservative and Liberal Democrat parties all declared themselves to be totally against racism in any shape or form. The most important law against racism was the Race Relations Act 1976. This made it illegal in England, Scotland and Wales to:

- discriminate against anyone because of their race, colour, nationality, ethnic or national origins (this law covered housing, employment and education)
- use threatening or abusive language that could stir up racial hatred
- publish anything that is likely to create racial hatred.

The law was extended to Northern Ireland in 1997. This law is still a very important part of our social fabric but this does not mean that racial hatred, prejudice and discrimination do not exist. They still do and no way has yet been found to create a society in which everyone, irrespective of their racial origins or religion, is treated with absolute fairness.

In 1976 the Commission for Racial Equality (CRE) was established. This was to make sure that the Race Relations Act was working and it was given three tasks:

- to fight against all racial discrimination
- to show people the importance of giving everyone a fair chance in life
- to monitor the way in which the law is working.

The Commission for Racial Equality continues its very important work today.

IT'S A FACT

In a total UK population of about 59 million people there are:

53 million white people, 1.3 million black people, 0.7 million from Pakistan, 1 million from India, 0.3 million from Bangladesh, 0.2 million of Chinese origin and 0.8 million from other nationalities.

This means that only about 1 in 15 people in the UK belongs to an ethnic minority. Over 50 per cent of these people were born in the UK.

The benefits of a multi-ethnic society

Benefits of living in a multi-ethnic society include:

* it brings a wide variety into everyday life in the areas of music, culture, food and clothes

* it helps people from very different backgrounds and cultures to know and understand each other

* it brings new ideas and ways of doing things into the everyday lives of people living in this country.

IMPORTANT WORDS

Discrimination;	putting prejudice into practice, treating people unfairly because of their race, religion, gender or class
Multi-ethnic society;	a society in which people from different racial backgrounds live together
Racial harmony;	a society in which people from different racial and ethnic backgrounds live together happily and peacefully
Racial prejudice;	believing that one race is inferior, intolerance of or dislike for people of a specific race or religion
Racism;	the belief that one race is better than another and acting as if this is true

Tasks

1. Why has the UK become a multi-ethnic society since the end of the Second World War?
2. What became illegal in the UK after the implementation of the Race Relations Act 1976?
3. Write down **THREE** things that the law says about racial discrimination.
4. Which of the **THREE** tasks of the CRE do you think is most important and why?

SUMMARY

1 The UK is a mixed society. The UK has always given shelter to those fleeing from persecution.

2 The main immigration to the UK happened after the Second World War due to the shortage of labour in key industries and occupations.

3 All the main political parties are against racism. The Race Relations Act 1976 outlawed racism. The Commission for Race Equality was set up at the same time.

▼ The UK is a multi-ethnic society. Revellers celebrate the Hindu Rath Yatra festival on Park Lane, London.

4:5 Christianity and racial harmony

What insights can Christians bring to the issue of racial harmony?

> 66 *God loved the world so much that He gave His only Son, so that everyone who believes in Him may not die but have eternal life.* 99
>
> ... **THE BIBLE (JOHN 3.16)**

Christians believe in one God, the creator and father of humankind. They believe that the love of God for the whole human race was demonstrated in the life, teaching and death of Jesus. Differences of race, sex, colour and physique are found amongst all the nations and peoples of earth, they are part of the richness that goes to make up humanity. To Christians these differences are irrelevant compared to the fact that everyone is a child of God. Racism is wrong because it denies the richness of God's creation.

The unity of humankind

Almost all Christians believe in the basic unity of humankind. However, there have been some very serious exceptions. Here are two examples:

- When African-Caribbean people came to the UK in large numbers in the 1960s many of them were religious. They sought to find a home in the Church of England and other churches in this country, but found the atmosphere cold and unwelcoming. They soon left to start their own churches in which they were free to express their Christian faith in a way that made them feel comfortable. There are now hundreds of these churches in large towns and cities such as London, Birmingham and Leicester. Many of these churches are thriving today and are attracting hundreds of people, white and black, to their services.

- A significant supporter of the policy of apartheid in South Africa during the 1970s and 1980s was the Dutch Reformed Church – a Church whose membership was totally white. This Church claimed that white people were superior to black people and all other races. Other Christians opposed this as totally un-Christian. Without question the apartheid regime in South Africa would have fallen much more quickly than it did if it had not been supported by the Dutch Reformed Church.

Some of the most important figures who took part in the fight for personal and political freedom in South Africa and elsewhere were Christians. There were people like Martin Luther King in the USA, Bishop Desmond Tutu in South Africa and Father Trevor Huddleston (who was born in the UK and spent time in South Africa campaigning against apartheid).

Racial harmony and the Bible

The tone and inspiration for the Christian understanding of racial harmony comes from the Bible. It takes its lead from the story of creation in the early chapters of the book of Genesis where the human race is said to have been created 'in the image of God'. This simply means that the whole human race has a spiritual likeness to God that no other part of the created order shares. This view was shared by Paul who believed that questions of race, colour and national identity were irrelevant in the Church.

Jesus also seemed to be in favour of racial equality. In the parable of the Good Samaritan (Luke 10.25–37) it is a member of a hated race, the samaritans, who helps a Jewish traveller in need. Jesus also broke barriers of sex and race by talking to a Samaritan woman by a well (John 4) and healing the servant of a Roman centurion whilst his cross was carried by Simon of Cyrene (Cyrene was located in Africa so many believe Simon was black). St Peter had a vision from God to make sure that he understood that God had no favourites among the many races on earth.

Christianity teaches that any form of racism or discrimination based on racial differences is wrong. Christians should be at the forefront of those working to bring about racial harmony in a divided society. In recent years most of the Christian Churches have released statements identifying themselves with this position. They are in a position to make their voice heard on this issue because there are churches at the heart of the communities that suffer most from racism.

> 66 *There is no difference between Jews and Gentiles, between slaves and free people, between men and women; you are all one in union with Christ Jesus.* 99
>
> ... **THE BIBLE (GALATIANS 3.28)**

Tasks

1. Write down **FOUR** things that Christians believe, which affect the way in which they understand racial harmony.
2. Describe **TWO** instances of the Christian faith failing to show in practice that it believes in racial harmony and tolerance.
3. Find examples from the Bible that show racial and colour differences are not important.
4. 'The Church is in a good position to make its voice heard on racial issues.' Do you agree with this comment? What do you think the speaker was thinking about when it was made?

Think about ...

Can you think of **THREE** positive things that the Christian Church could do to improve relationships between members of different racial groups in this country?

SUMMARY

1 Christians believe that their God is the Father of humankind. Human differences are irrelevant.

2 Two past examples show that Christians have been misguided in their attitude towards different ethnic groups: the lack of welcome given by many churches in the UK to African-Caribbean Christians and the attitude of the Dutch Reformed Church to apartheid in South Africa.

3 The Bible teaches that race and colour are unimportant. Some Christians believe that their faith is the only way to God but others believe that there are many ways.

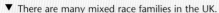

▼ There are many mixed race families in the UK.

4:6 Judaism, Islam and Hinduism, and racial harmony

Where do Judaism, Islam and Hinduism agree in their attitudes towards racial harmony?

◼ JUDAISM

Judaism recognises that all people are different and that differences in colour are God-made. People with a disability, a different skin colour or born into a different religious community should not be looked down on in any way. It is the duty of every human being to make sure that no one is disadvantaged by any of these differences. The teaching of the old rabbis was that every person is descended from the same human father – Adam. They used to say that when God created Adam he used dark, light, red and yellow earth so showing that He intended his descendants to be varied in colour. No single person can claim to be more original or pure than any other. The experience of the Jews under Hitler means that they could never support any form of racial discrimination or any attempt to eradicate racial differences by creating a 'pure' race.

Judaism strongly teaches that any form of racialism or racial discrimination is wrong. Jews should be at the forefront of those working to achieve real racial harmony. They believe this because:

- The Torah, the most important of all holy books, strongly forbids the mistreatment of any foreign people living within Israel's borders.
- Jewish teaching emphasises that we are all children of God and so should receive equal rights.
- The Holocaust was a racist attack on the Jewish people and for many Jews this prevents them carrying out the same inhumanity on others.

◼ ISLAM

> O mankind! We created you from a single (pair) of a male and a female, and made you into nations and tribes, that ye may know each other (not that you may despise each other) Allah has full knowledge and is well acquainted (with all things).
>
> ... THE QUR'AN (49.13)

The unity of Allah (tawhid) is a basic Muslim belief and this acknowledges that God is the Creator of all creation and that humanity is one. The different colours, races and languages of humanity are a clear sign of God's wonderful work of creation. These differences should enrich everyone. Equal respect should be given to each man and woman. All Muslims form a single world community – the ummah – and this is expressed by the complete mix of people who join the Hajj to Makkah each year. People of different races and colours express their unity as children of Allah.

In accepting that all people are equal in the sight of Allah, Muslims are following the example of Muhammad the Prophet. He chose Bilal, an African former slave, to be his first muezzin – the man who began the tradition of calling the faithful to prayer. In his last sermon, which he delivered on his final pilgrimage to the holy city of Makkah, Muhammad told his listeners that they belonged to a community in which everyone should treat everyone else as their brother. In the eyes of Allah no one race, or people, is superior to any other.

◼ HINDUISM

> I look upon all creatures equally, none are less dear to me and none more dear.
>
> ... BHAGAVAD GITA (9.29)

Hindus see the world as one interconnected whole in which many different races and colours intermingle. India, though, is a country that has been divided for centuries with very little mixing between the different castes. Even though the caste system has been abolished, marriage between members of different castes is uncommon. Even in the UK, where there is a large Hindu population, certain groups of Indians have tended to settle in particular cities and in certain localities within cities. Many Hindus view the caste system as a way of treating everyone with respect because everyone has their own place in society.

Hindus are opposed to all racism and discrimination because of the way their ancestors suffered in the past at the hands of the Mogul emperors and of the British in the days of the Empire. If every soul is a part of the Divine, then everyone should be treated equally.

▲ Over 2 million Muslims from around the world make the pilgrimage each year to the holy city Makkah in Saudi Arabia.

 Think about ...

Christianity, Judaism and Islam are all monotheistic faiths believing that there is only one God. Does it surprise you that there has been so much tension between religions over the centuries when they start from the same basic belief about God?

Tasks

1. Upon what does Judaism base its belief that everyone is made in the image of God?

2.a. What is tawhid?
 b. What is ummah?
 c. What do ummah and the Hajj teach Muslims about racial harmony?

3. Why do Hindus believe that everyone is entitled to receive equal treatment and respect?

4. 'Religious people have a duty to work against racial prejudice.' Do you agree with this comment? Give **TWO** reasons to support your answer, and show that you have considered more than one religious point of view.

SUMMARY

1 Judaism teaches that all people are equal having come from the same root – Adam. Judaism recognises that it has much in common with Christianity and Islam.

2 Muslims all belong to one world community (ummah) living in a world created by God. The differences between peoples and nations are intended to enrich the human family.

3 Hindus believe that the world is one although there is often little mixing between the different Indian groups. Hindus do not seek to make converts and they are upset when other religions do so.

4:7 A multi-faith society

Would it be true to describe the UK as a truly multi-faith society?

> *Britain is now truly a multi-faith society for the first time in its history. There may, from time to time, be friction among members of the different faiths but when people come to terms with the multi-faith nature of our society they will find their own spiritual lives greatly deepened and strengthened.*
>
> *... BRITISH POLITICIAN, 1970s*

The UK has a very strong spiritual heritage related to the Christian religion and this remains the dominant religion in the UK. At the same time the UK is more of a multi-faith community than any other country in the European Union and the religions within it show a remarkable strength and vigour.

From single faith to multi-faith

Prior to the Second World War there were comparatively few people who followed a religion other than Christianity in the UK. The first wave of immigrants after 1945, mainly from the West Indies, were largely Christians who soon formed their own churches. Then, in the 1960s and 1970s, there was a large influx of people from India, Pakistan, Bangladesh and Hong Kong followed later by people from Tanzania, Uganda and Kenya. This led to the growth of significant communities of Hindus, Muslims and Sikhs in the UK.

▼ Hindus worshipping.

To begin with, most immigrants concerned themselves with the task of finding somewhere to live; settling into a new job and sending money back to help their families. Then attention was given to arranging for their families to join them in this country. This led to the growth of religious communities and places of worship to support the new communities. Mandirs, gurdwaras and mosques sprang up and these became increasingly important in the local communities. Although some purpose-built places of worship were put up, in the majority of cases either houses or redundant churches were converted.

Concentration

Some religions have their members scattered throughout the UK but it is more usual for them to be concentrated in certain urban areas.

- The most concentrated Jewish population is in the Greater London area whilst there are also large Jewish populations in Glasgow, Leeds and Manchester. There are also sizeable Jewish populations in Birmingham, Bournemouth, Brighton, Southend and Liverpool. The oldest synagogue still in use is the Bevis Marks synagogue in London, which was opened in 1701.

- Most Muslims are found in Lancashire, Greater London, the West Midlands, West Yorkshire and parts of Scotland. The first known mosque in the UK was opened in Cardiff in 1860.

- The largest Hindu communities are to be found in Greater London, Birmingham and Leicester.

- The most substantial Sikh communities are found in Greater London (especially Southall), Cardiff, Birmingham, Bradford, Coventry, Wolverhampton, Glasgow, Leeds and Leicester. The first Sikh gurdwara in the UK opened in Putney, West London, in 1911.

The size of the communities

There are no totally reliable figures to indicate the size of the different religious communities. There are many who feel they belong to a faith whom do not appear in statistics because they do not attend worship regulary. The estimated active faith memberships are as follows:

- Christians 6 000 000
- Muslims 665 000
- Hindus 165 000
- Sikhs 400 000
- Jews 95 000
- Buddhists 50 000

It is very interesting to compare these figures with those for the different Christian Churches. There are slightly

▲ Muslims at prayer in a mosque.

more members of the Roman Catholic Church (1 768 000) than belong to the Anglican Church (1 654 000). There are more Presbyterians, largely in Scotland, (at almost 1 million) than there are Methodists (400 000); Baptists (200 000) and Pentecostalists (250 000) combined. In all, though, the Christian Church has twice as many members in the UK as belong to all the other main religious faiths combined. About 1 in 5 people belongs to a religious group.

One other interesting piece of information relates to the number of places of worship in the UK. There are about 45 000 churches, 1000 mosques, 300 synagogues, 140 mandirs, 200 Sikh gurdwaras and 100 Buddhist monastries and temples. There are also 385 places of worship belonging to other groups.

IMPORTANT WORDS

Multi-faith society; society in which many different religious faiths are represented and practised

Religious freedom; freedom for members of any religious faith to meet and worship together

Religious pluralism; society in which there are many different religions

IT'S A FACT

It must be remembered that not everyone follows a particular faith. According to the 'British Social Attitudes Survey 1998':

- 21 per cent said 'I know God exists and I have no doubt about it'
- 23 per cent said 'While I have doubts, I still feel that God exists'
- 14 per cent said 'I believe in God some of the time'
- The remainder said they did not believe in God.

 Think about ...

Imagine that you were amongst the first wave of immigrants entering the UK from your chosen religion. Make a list of your first **FIVE** priorities as you settle into your new home.

Tasks

1. How did the UK move from being a largely single-faith country to being multi-faith?

2. What led to the formation of different religious communities and the growth in the number of places of worship in the UK?

SUMMARY

1 Until the end of the Second World War the UK was largely a single-faith country. Then, with the large influx of immigrants, it became multi-faith. The largest religious groupings in the UK, apart from Christians, are of Muslims, Jews, Hindus and Sikhs.

2 Most multi-faith communities are found in large city areas. It is there that they have built their own places of worship or converted houses or redundant churches for religious use. There are about 47 000 places of worship in the UK. Twice as many people belong to the different Christian Churches as belong to the various other religions.

4:8 Christianity and other religions

What attitudes are found in the Christian Church towards other religions?

Christians are committed to religious freedom. They believe that everyone should have the freedom to express their religious beliefs in any way they choose. It is Christian teaching that people should not suffer from any form of religious discrimination against them. All Christian churches agree on these principles. Within this framework, however, there is more than one approach within the Christian community towards people who belong to other religions. There are three main approaches.

1. **Exclusivism.** This expresses the belief held by many Christians that there is only one approach to God – and that is through Jesus. These Christians often use the text in which Jesus is recorded as saying: "I am the way, the truth and the life" (John 14.6). Until recently this was the main Christian point of view and during the nineteenth and early twentieth centuries missionaries were sent out to other countries so that people there had the opportunity to become Christians. It was expressed in the Roman Catholic phrase 'outside of the Church there is no salvation' – a phrase that was also applied by many Catholics to those Christians who belonged to Churches that were not part of the Catholic Church.

2. **Inclusivism.** People who follow this approach often refer to the incident in the New Testament when Paul is visiting Athens. He recognises that in their search for the Unknown God to whom they have built an altar, the Athenians are following a genuine spiritual search (see quotation). These Christians believe that people can come to God through different religious paths but only Christianity has the full truth. Those who live a moral life, however, are known as 'anonymous Christians' who will be saved in the end.

3. **Pluralism.** This approach is more modern than the previous two. It says that all religions focus on reality. By following a religious path people become more reality-centred and less self-centred – and that is a very good thing. If we look at all the main religions, including Christianity, they have produced both good and bad people. All religions are equal to each other and, in their best moments, they help people to find God. One is not better, or superior, to the others. What suits one person will not necessarily suit another. The Bible is one of several 'words of God'. It is not, as many Christians believe, the only 'word of God'. God is out there waiting to be discovered and it is up to each individual to make that discovery for themselves. They are totally free to choose which path they take.

There is a great difference between these three approaches. Exclusivism claims that the Christian religion is the only way and that a person can never know God unless they come through the Christian door. Inclusivism claims that many people have, in fact, entered through the Christian door without realising it. They may think that they are being good Hindus or good Muslims but they are actually 'anonymous Christians' who are worshipping God through Jesus all the time. Pluralisism claims that the twentieth century brought a much greater understanding of the different world faiths and the insights that they bring. From this position of understanding Christians can take part in interfaith dialogue bringing their own understanding of God whilst, at the same time, listening to the insight that others are able to shed on the spiritual pathway. People come to this dialogue from very different positions. Dialogue, though, is relatively easy compared to shared worship between people of different faiths and this remains comparatively rare.

> *Paul stood up in front of the city council and said, 'I see that in every way you Athenians are very religious. For as I walked through your city and looked at the places where you worship, I found an altar on which is written "To an Unknown God". That which you worship, then, even though you do not know it, is what I now proclaim to you.'*
>
> **... THE BIBLE (ACTS 17.22–23)**

> *Differences of race, sex, colour, physique and capacity undoubtedly exist within the human race but they are all seen by Christians as part of the richness of humanity. For they are all insignificant in comparison with the fact that everyone is related as a child of God.*
>
> **... TREVOR SHANNON, THEOLOGIAN**

Tasks

1. Write down **ONE** reason why many Christians believe that they have the total truth and that members of others religions are misguided.

2. Look at the quotation from the Acts. Sum up what Paul is saying about God and the search for spiritual truth.

3. What are the differences between the 'exclusivist' and the 'inclusivist' approaches adopted by many Christians in their attempts to understand other religions?

Think about ...

Why do you think that it is much easier for people to talk about the differences that separate them than it is for them to engage in worship together? What do you think are the main problems of common worship?

SUMMARY

1 The exclusivist approach, adopted by many Christians, believes that Christianity alone provides a way to God. Based on John 14.6, followers believe that the sole truth is to be found in the Christian Church.

2 The inclusivist approach insists that many people, living a moral and religious life, are Christians without realising it. They are anonymous Christians.

3 The pluralistic approach insists that any way to God is valid. All are leading to reality. A reality-centred life is infinitely preferable to a self-centred life.

▼ Many Christians believe that any worship of God is valid regardless of faith. The photo shows Jewish men praying at a synagogue.

4:9 Judaism, Islam and Hinduism, and other religions

How do Judaism, Islam and Hinduism agree, and disagree, in their attitudes to other religions?

■ JUDAISM

Judaism teaches that all religious believers have the right to worship freely and openly. Jews have suffered too much at the hands of other religious believers in the past to deny this basic human right to others. Traditionally, Judaism has divided other religions into two categories:

1. **Idolatrous religions.** By this the rabbis of old were referring to those faiths that taught their followers a way of behaving that was contrary to the teaching of the Ten Commandments.

2. **God-fearing religions.** By this the rabbis were referring to the other two great monotheistic religions – Christianity and Islam. Both of these religions believe in one God and encourage a way of behaving which is close to the Ten Commandments. At the same time it must be recognised that Jews have suffered greatly at the hands of Christians and Muslims in the past.

Jews make no attempt to convert others to their religious faith. At the same time they expect other religions to respect their own desire to be allowed to practise their own faith in their own way.

■ ISLAM

> **"** *We believe in Allah, and the revelation given to us, and to Abraham, Ishmael, Isaac, Jacob and the Tribes, and that given to Moses and Jesus, and that given to the Prophets from their Lord, we make no difference between one and another of them.* **"**
>
> **... THE QUR'AN (2.136)**

The safety of those people who live in a Muslim community but do not belong to a religion is guaranteed under Islamic law. These people are under the protection of Allah, the Prophet Muhammad and the Muslim community. Those who are Christians and Jews, however, have been given a special guarantee of protection in the Qur'an since they are, along with Muslims, 'people of the Book'. Christians and Jews are also promised that they will be rewarded by Allah on the Day of Judgment.

On the other hand, the Qur'an clearly teaches that Islam is the only true religion. The Prophet Muhammad was given the final revelation from Allah and this revelation superseded every other given to the earlier prophets – including Abraham, Moses and Jesus. This is why Islam is a missionary faith. Muslims believe that they have a God-given duty to share this final revelation with everyone else in the world.

■ HINDUISM

Hinduism does not have a problem in accepting that everyone has the right to worship freely. Hinduism itself does not have a strict definition of its own religious beliefs and so it does not see other religions as offering a threat. God, they believe, is One and is found through the teachings of different religious figures and gurus. This is why you will often find pictures of such religious leaders as Jesus and Buddha in Hindu temples. All of them can inspire the person who is searching for God.

Followers of other religions, however, might do things that upset Hindus. For instance, a Hindu would find the eating of beef in their presence particularly upsetting. This means that non-Hindus must be careful in their social and religious contacts with Hindu believers if they do not want to give offence.

▼ Muslims believe that Christians and Jews are also 'people of the Book'.

BIRMINGHAM CENTRAL MOSQUE

▲ Hindus accept the right of everyone to worship as they choose.

Tasks

1.a. Which religions are, according to the Qur'an, 'religions of the Book'?

b. What do you think makes these religions distinctive?

c. What special protection does the Qur'an guarantee those who belong to the 'religions of the Book'?

2. Why do Muslims believe that their religion is the only true one?

3.a. Into which two groups does Judaism divide other religions?

b. What is the main difference between these two groups?

4. What is the attitude of Hinduism towards other religions?

5.a. Summarise the quotation from Mahatma Gandhi.

b. Do you think that Gandhi is right when he suggests that the different religions are 'different roads converging to the same point'?

c. Give **TWO** reasons why you think that most religions would disagree with him on this point.

6. Clearly there are major differences between the different religions. How do you think members of the different religions could try to make sure that they do not give offence to followers of other religions?

> *Religions are different roads converging to the same point. What does it matter that we take different roads as long as we reach the same goal? In reality, there are as many different religions as there are individuals.*
>
> *... MAHATMA GANDHI, HINDU REFORMER*

SUMMARY

1 Judaism divides other religions into two groups – idolatrous religions and God-fearing religions. It recognises the dangers of those religions that teach a way of life that is contrary to the Ten Commandments. It respects the teachings of Christianity and Islam.

2 Islam guarantees freedom of worship to other religions. It also believes that it alone is the true faith and that the Qur'an is *the* Word of God.

3 Hinduism teaches that all religions are attempts to reach the truth. God is One and every way of trying to worship Him is acceptable.

4 There are some people who believe that the differences between the different religions are far less important than those issues that unite all religious believers.

Exam help ...

This section has introduced us to important issues in modern society. We have looked at sexism – the relationship between men and women. We have also looked at the growth of the multi-ethnic and multi-racial society. You must be aware of the attempt to outlaw racial discrimination and how successful/unsuccessful this has been. The attitude of the main religions to each other is important. Is it going to be possible for the different religions to exist happily alongside each other in the future?

1.a. What is a multi-faith society?

b. What are the advantages of living in a multi-faith society?

c. What is the attitude of Christians towards other religions?

d. 'Religious people should not try to convert others to their faith.' Do you agree?
Give reasons for your opinion, showing that you have considered another point of view. In your answer you should refer to at least ONE religion.

1.a. A multi-faith society is one in which many different faiths are openly practised.

b. The UK has become increasingly multi-faith after widespread immigration took place since the 1950s. Living in a multi-faith society has many advantages for those who are willing to see them.

- People from different backgrounds and religions bring their own beliefs and cultures with them, as well as a variety of different foods. This introduces people to ideas they have not met before. These beliefs are reflected in schools. Children grow up knowing far more about other people and their cultures. They particularly become aware of them at festival times.

- Intolerance is usually based on ignorance. Religious education in schools informs children about religious differences. Television programmes and newspapers spread information about different faiths. People become more aware of the beliefs of others. Hopefully this will lead to a more tolerant society.

continued ...

- Learning about the faith of others and coming into contact with them should make people think more about their own religious faith. The minds of many people have been broadened by meeting people from other religions.

c. Since 1945 the UK has increasingly become a multi-faith society. Followers of other religions now make up 5 per cent of the population. This has forced many Christians to re-think their attitude towards other religions. There are three attitudes:

- The 'exclusive' approach. Those who maintain that Christianity is the only way – all other religions are false. Based on John 14.6. Led to missionary movement in nineteenth century. Still the attitude of many. Expressed in Roman Catholic phrase – 'Outside the Church there is no salvation.'

- The 'inclusive' approach. Those who maintain that people may use many different ways to reach God – but only Christianity has the full truth. People who worship in other religions are called 'anonymous Christians'.

- The 'pluralist' approach. Those who maintain that there are many different faiths and all are acceptable. By following a religion a person looks away from themselves to God – and that is what religion is all about. All religions are of equal value. All religious books are of equal value.

All three attitudes are found in the Christian Church. Only one, the pluralist, can lead to the different religions really talking to each other. Even then shared worship rarely takes place.

d. Religions can be divided into two groups – those that set out to make new converts (Christianity and Islam) and those that do not (Judaism and Hinduism). Seeking to make new converts can cause conflicts.

continued ...

- Jews find it difficult to understand why Christianity and Islam should target their faith. Jews have suffered in the past from Muslim and Christian attention that has often involved the use of force. Many Jews were forced to convert to Christianity, but practised their faith secretly. These Jews are known as 'Marranos'. A person's Jewishness comes through their mother and it is impossible to lose it. It is very difficult for a person to convert to Judaism and for a Jew to join another faith.

- Both Christianity and Islam teach that they are 'the Way'. Their holy books are called 'the word of God'. Both religions believe that they are called to share their faith with others. They are both 'evangelistic'. In the past this has led to many disasters. Amongst these have been the Crusades. Both faiths insist that conversion must be by gentle persuasion, but this has not always happened.

2. What does Christianity teach about the relationship between men and women?

2. Christianity has often been accused of discriminating against women. Much of this discrimination has come from the teaching of Paul in his letters in the New Testament. One example is that Paul said women should not speak in church and should be subservient to their husbands. Jesus, though, had an enlightened attitude towards women for his time. There are many examples that can be quoted from Paul and Jesus.

- The Christian Churches have had a mixed attitude towards women. The Roman Catholic and Orthodox Churches do not allow women priests. The Anglican and Free Churches have women priests and ministers.

- Influenced by Paul, some Christians believe that women should stay at home and have no public ministry in the church. Other Christians maintain that men and women are equal in the sight of God.

- In many Churches the role played by women has changed. Anglican Church – women priests and bishops. Free Churches – women ministers. Salvation Army – women leaders. Yet in others, such as the Roman Catholic Church, women's role has not changed. This Church believes that women cannot be priests as Jesus only chose men to be his disciples.

3. Outline how ONE religion, other than Christianity, approaches other religions.

3. The chosen religion is Islam.

- The Qur'an guarantees religious freedom and safety to non-Muslims living and worshipping in a Muslim country. They are guaranteed this because they are under the protection of Allah, the Prophet Muhammad and the Muslim community.

- Special respect is given by Muslims to Christians and Jews – the followers of the three religions are all described as 'people of the book'. All will be rewarded by Allah on the Day of Judgement.

Yet Muslims believe that Islam is the one true faith. There can be no compromise on this. The revelation given by Allah to the Prophet Muhammad superseded that given to all the other prophets – including Abraham, Moses and Jesus. Islam is a missionary faith. All Muslims are given the responsibility of making new converts to the faith – wherever they come from.

5:1 Wealth and poverty – the facts

What do we mean when we speak of the divide between rich and poor countries in the world?

As far as wealth and poverty are concerned today the world can be clearly divided into two significant parts.

The Northern or economically developed world. This consists of areas that have a high standard of living and includes North America, Western Europe, including the UK, and Australasia. These areas only have about 25 per cent of the world's population (about 1 500 million people) but they consume 75 per cent of the world's wealth and resources. Sometimes these are called 'First World' countries.

The Southern or economically developing world. These are countries that have a low standard of living. Although 75 per cent of the world's population lives in the developing world (about 4 500 million people) they use just 25 per cent of the world's resources. These are often called 'Third World' countries. Some developing countries are very poor, like Somalia and Bangladesh, whilst others, such as Peru and Bolivia, are less so.

Countries like the old Communist ones in Eastern Europe are referred to as 'Second World' countries because they are not as rich as Western countries but are not as poor as those in the developing world.

The developed and developing countries

'Absolute poverty' means that people do not have the basic necessities to sustain life. 'Relative poverty' means that people are poor compared to those living around them in the same country. 'Absolute poverty' is determined by using the following tests.

1. **A high level of malnutrition.** In the world's poorest countries up to 75 per cent of the people try to make a living out of agriculture, compared with fewer than 5 per cent in the UK. This is largely 'subsistence' farming with people desperately trying to grow enough to meet their own needs and those of their family. They have little left to sell or buy the things they cannot grow.

2. **A low level of education and literacy.** There is a direct correlation between the level of poverty and the level of literacy in poor countries. People who are illiterate (at least 850 million in the world) can find no way out of the poverty trap. Their lack of education keeps them where they are.

3. **A high level of illness and disease.** If children living in poor countries survive the hazards of birth and infancy they find that their living conditions leave them vulnerable to illness and disease. At least 25 per cent of the world's population does not have access to clean drinking water; this problem has created major health hazards in today's world.

4. **A high rate of infant mortality.** Children are most vulnerable in the first years of their lives. Over 15 million children under the age of 5 die of malnutrition each year. Malnourished mothers are unable to provide milk for their underfed babies and so the cycle of poverty continues.

5. **A low life expectancy.** In the UK, on average, men can hope to reach the age of 75 and women 80. In many developing countries there is a low life expectancy. In Rwanda men can expect to live to the age of 39 and women to 40.

Short and long-term aid

Most countries accept that they either need to give or to receive help. This aid can come in the form of food, shelter, medical help and supplies or loans of money.

Short-term aid. Short-term aid is given when a natural disaster hits a poor country, as it frequently does in the form of earthquakes, floods, typhoons or other extreme weather. At such times, poor countries need the speedy provision of the right kind of help – shelters, food and people-power.

Long-term aid. Long-term aid is given to help poor countries overcome their underlying problems. Help might be given to build hospitals or schools; advice to improve the fertility of the soil; expertise to build irrigation projects and so on. Rich countries are often very slow to provide this kind of help. The UK, for instance, only gives 0.3 per cent of its wealth each year to help poorer countries – and this amount is going down. This is in spite of Britain's declared aim to give three times this amount to help the neediest countries.

 Think about ...

Clearly the world's wealth is very unevenly distributed. Do you think the world's wealthiest countries should be prepared to share more with the poorer countries – and cancel their debts? Think of **TWO** arguments to support your answer, whatever it is.

> *Many hundreds of millions of people are preoccupied solely with survival and elementary needs. For them work is frequently not available or, when it is, pay is very low and conditions are often barely tolerable. Homes are constructed of permeable [non-waterproof] materials and have neither piped water nor sanitation. Electricity is a luxury … . Primary schools, where they exist, may be free and not too far away but children are needed for work and cannot easily be spared for schooling. Flood, drought or disease affecting people or livestock can easily destroy livelihoods without hope of compensation.*

... THE BRANDT REPORT, 1977

Tasks

1. Describe **THREE** differences between countries in the developed world and those in the developing world.
2. What is the difference between absolute poverty and relative poverty?
3. Explain the difference between short-term and long-term aid.
4. '1 per cent of everything we earn as a country does not seem to be much to give to help the poorest people in the world.' What do you think? Show in your answer that you have thought about more than one religious point of view.

SUMMARY

1 There is a sharp difference between the standard of living of people living in the rich Northern and those living in the poor Southern countries of the world.

2 The difference can be seen when comparing the malnutrition levels, the levels of literacy and education, the illness and disease, the rates of infant mortality and the life expectancy of people in these countries.

3 Poor countries need both short-term and long-term aid and a reduction in their debt.

▲ The accommodation in which a person lives is often the clearest indication of their wealth – or poverty.

5:2 World debt

Why is debt one of the most important obstacles to world development?

> *O God, to those who hunger give bread; and to those who have bread give the hunger for justice.*
>
> **... LATIN AMERICAN PRAYER**

The developing countries of the world are heavily in debt. They owe vast sums of money to the countries of the developed world. These sums of money are growing all the time as high rates of interest are demanded on the money that is lent. One area, sub-Saharan Africa, pays back four times as much money on the loans that it has from the USA as it spends on health and medicine. This area, not surprisingly, is one of the poorest in the world.

Servicing debts

The International Monetary Fund (IMF) says that over 40 countries in the world today are heavily in debt. They owe over £150 billion. Much of this money was lent in the 1970s for various projects but a series of corrupt governments and wars meant that the money was wasted and not used for the purpose for which it was lent. Instead of being used to build schools and hospitals, it was wasted. These poorest developing countries have no alternative but to use valuable land and resources to grow crops that are for export only, to pay off the debt. Meanwhile people at home go hungry and starve to death.

Developing countries can only pay their debts in 'hard currency' and not goods. This means that they have to exchange their currency for dollars, pounds or euros. If the value of their currency goes down then their debts increase correspondingly. It is a vicious circle. Offers by developing countries to pay off some of the debts in goods, such as cereals or oil, have always been rejected. Some developing countries try to borrow more money to pay their existing debts but they find that this just increases their problems in the long term: they are caught in a 'debt spiral', which makes their situation even worse. Often the new debts also come with conditions attached – such as abandoning new health or educational projects. They may also be obliged to buy certain products from the country that is lending them money, making it more difficult for them to become truly independent.

There is, of course, a solution to the problem of world debts – cancel them. The developing countries have paid back their original debts many times over. It is not the original debts that are causing the problems – it is the interest that has built up on them. Each year the developing countries may spend more money servicing their debts than they receive in aid – a great deal more. Until this situation is changed the developing countries will remain poor and become poorer. This is what is happening in the world. Today, the rich countries, the 'haves', are getting richer all the time. The poorest countries, the 'have-nots', are falling further and further behind.

Jubilee 2000

> *The question to be asked is not what we should give to the poor, but when we will stop taking from the poor. The poor are not our problem; we are their problem.*
>
> **... JIM WALLIS, AMERICAN CHRISTIAN ACTIVIST, 1986**

As the new millennium dawned, a coalition of voluntary organisations and societies banded together to call on the major developed countries to cancel all world debt. This pressure group was named Jubilee 2000. Rallies and meetings were held throughout Northern Europe and the USA to call for the breaking of the 'debt cycle'. People linked arms and lit candles to show that the world was united in calling for a world in which the light of freedom from debt would dawn. Pressure was brought to bear on the delegates at the G8 conference in Genoa in July 2001. Unfortunately, this meeting was marred by violent demonstrations by people protesting at what they saw as increasing 'globalisation'. The chance to take a significant step forward was not made.

IT'S A FACT

Almost 150 organisations and charities have decided to work together as the UK Coalition Against Poverty. The aim of the coalition is to work together to eliminate poverty in the UK and to work for the cancellation of world debt.

▲ Bono, of U2, feeds an 11-month-old at a prenatal HIV clinic in Soweto, May 2002. Many celebrities are active in calling on governments to do more to help Third World countries.

Tasks

1. Give **ONE** reason why poor countries borrowing money from rich countries might not be a good idea.

2. Why do so many of the poorest countries in the world find themselves in great difficulties today because of the money they borrowed in the past?

3.a. What is the 'debt spiral'?

  b. Why do poor countries find it very difficult to escape from the 'debt spiral'?

4.a. What is Jubilee 2000?

  b. What were the objectives of Jubilee 2000?

5. 'The rich countries should allow debts of the world's poorest countries to be cancelled.' Do you agree or disagree with this statement? Give reasons for your answer.

SUMMARY

1 The debts owed by the poorest countries of the world are the main reason for their poverty. Much of the money borrowed was wasted but the interest on the debts is still being paid.

2 Debts have to be paid in the currency of the country owed the money. This is very costly. These countries will not accept payment in kind. Countries borrow more money to pay off their debt – this leads to a debt spiral.

3 Jubilee 2000 was a pressure group to force rich countries to cancel the money owed to them. Little was accomplished.

5:3 Christianity and wealth

What different attitudes towards wealth and poverty are found in the Christian Churches?

> 66 The Church should concern itself first, and indeed second, with the poor and needy, whether in spirit or in body. 99
>
> **... FAITH IN THE CITY, A CHURCH OF ENGLAND REPORT ON POVERTY IN BRITAIN**

There are two main attitudes in the Christian community towards wealth and poverty. There is great wealth in some Churches, like the Roman Catholic Church and the Church of England. Many Christians have personal fortunes. There is a segment of the Church, particularly in America, that preaches that a belief in God and amassing personal wealth go together. Yet there have always been Christians who have chosen to live in poverty in some of the poorest parts of the world. They believe that this is what Jesus himself, their great example, would have done.

Wealth

Christians believe that the world, and everything in it, has been created by God for them to enjoy. Nothing in the world is evil in itself. Money is neither good nor bad – what matters most is the use to which the money is put. It can be used to help the needy or it can be squandered. They turn to the Bible for support and find that:

- Jesus lived in a world in which some people were very rich and others very poor. Jesus announced at the beginning of his ministry that he had been sent by God to preach good news to the poor (Luke 4.18). We are told that Zacchaeus, a cheating tax-gatherer, gave away 50 per cent of his ill-gained wealth after he had met Jesus. Jesus told the rich young man who wanted to know how he could enter God's kingdom that he must sell his possessions first.

- Christians cannot ignore the poor. In the classic statement by Jesus on caring for the poor, he told his followers that when they feed the hungry, clothe the naked, visit the criminal in prison and help the sick they are helping each person as if it were him they were helping (Matthew 25.31–46). Jesus identified himself with those at the bottom of the ladder. The parable of the sheep and goats encourages Christians to see Christ in all people. It also explains why people like Albert Schweitzer and Mother Teresa spent their lives working in Africa and India amongst those who had none of this life's wealth.

- The parable of the Good Samaritan (Luke 10.25–37) suggests that no Christian should ignore the needs of others when they see people around them in great need. That help should be extended to all – friend or enemy, fellow countryman or foreigner.

> 66 It is much harder for a rich person to enter the Kingdom of God than for a camel to go through the eye of a needle. 99
>
> **... THE BIBLE (MARK 10.25)**

▼ Christians believe that people need 'spiritual' food as well as food to eat.

▲ The parable of the Good Samaritan shows that human need should not be ignored.

Christians and poverty

All Christians have a responsibility to care for the poor. For some this has meant living as the poor live and sharing their struggle. Some have followed the example of St Francis of Assisi, in the thirteenth century, who gave away everything that he had. They, too, have taken a voluntary vow of poverty and lived as a monk, nun or friar. This is not the way of life that all Christians are called to follow: all have a duty to help the poor and needy according to their own means. They should give their charity to the poor secretly (Matthew 6.2–4). Christians living in wealthy and affluent societies have a two-fold responsibility:

- not to succumb to the many temptations that making and spending money bring
- to think with compassion and love about the needs of those who are denied life's basic essentials.

> God blesses those who come to the aid of the poor and rebukes those who turn away from them ... . Love for the poor is incompatible with immoderate use of riches or their selfish use.
>
> **... CATECHISM OF THE CATHOLIC CHURCH**

 Think about ...

In his ministry Jesus seems to have concentrated almost wholly on the poor and to have spent little time on the rich. Can you think of **TWO** reasons why Jesus might have placed this emphasis in his teaching?

Tasks

1. Which **TWO** attitudes towards wealth and poverty have always been found in the Christian Church?
2. What do Christians believe about money?
3. Describe **THREE** examples from the Bible that show what the Christian attitude towards wealth and money should be.
4. How did Jesus show that his followers in helping others were actually helping him?

SUMMARY

1 There are many wealthy Christians and some Christian Churches are wealthy. Some Christians have chosen a life of poverty and helping the needy.

2 Christians believe that God has created everything and this should be shared. Jesus taught that wealth can be a great spiritual obstacle. He advised a rich young man to sell everything – and to enter God's kingdom.

3 Christians must not succumb to the temptations that wealth brings. They must act with compassion to those in need.

5:4 Judaism, Islam and Hinduism, and wealth

What are the teachings of Judaism, Islam and Hinduism on poverty?

■ JUDAISM

The Hebrew word for charity also means 'justice'. Giving money to help the poor, in Judaism, is to do with fairness – the 'haves' giving to the 'have-nots' because that is the only fair thing to do. Moses Maimonides was a great Jewish teacher in the twelfth century and he taught that there are eight different levels at which one can give charity – including the lowest level which is unwillingly giving less than you can afford and the highest level which involves working alongside a needy person to bring them into a partnership with yourself. This helps them to move out of poverty altogether. This level of giving means that not only are poor people helped but they retain their dignity and stand a fair chance of moving beyond their poverty.

It is not a sin for a wealthy Jew to look after their own needs and those of their family first. That is the right and proper thing to do. Only after doing this can they be expected to put their wealth at the service of the wider Jewish community. The Jewish tradition is that a wealthy person should try, if possible, to meet all the needs of the poor but if this is not possible then they should give away up to 20 per cent of their wealth. Jewish homes and synagogues have charity boxes so that young members of the family get into the habit of giving to the poor. This establishes the strong link, which is at the heart of the Jewish tradition, between giving to the poor and worshipping God.

■ ISLAM

> Fair in the eyes of men is the love of things they covet: women and sons; heaped-up hoards of gold and silver; horses branded [for blood and excellence] and [wealth of] cattle and well tilled land. Such are the possessions of this world's life; but in nearness to Allah is the best of goals [to return to].
>
> **... THE QUR'AN (3.14)**

It is human nature to love wealth and possessions – houses, land, money and valuables – yet Muslims are expected to keep their lives in perspective (see quotation). All wealth is created by Allah and so belongs to Him. All human beings can do is work hard, but any reward that comes their way is from Allah. All wealth is a gift and trust from Allah. For this reason, wealth is to be spent both on one's own family and also on those who are needy in the Muslim community.

Two ways of distributing wealth are mentioned in the Qur'an – zakat and sadaqah. Zakat is one of the Five Pillars of the Muslim faith – a kind of 'religious tax' that all Muslims are obliged to pay. This requires every Muslim to give 2.5 per cent of their income to the poor. This is not seen as a charity payment to all poor Muslims but is seen as their 'right' to receive money and an obligation on every believer. Sadaqah is a voluntary gift which should be made secretly to relieve the problems and sufferings of fellow human beings. In giving sadaqah no distinction is to be made between Muslims and non-Muslims. Generosity in giving brings true happiness and contentment. Much of the money is channelled through Muslim charities such as Islamic Relief and Muslim Aid, which work extensively in developing countries.

■ HINDUISM

Pursuing wealth is one of the four aims of a Hindu's life. This pursuit must not, however, be allowed to dominate a person's life. It is legitimate because during the householder phase many people, including children, spouse and older members of the family, are dependent on one person's ability to earn. There is only one restriction that the holy books place on this activity and that is that the wealth must be earned in a righteous way. During the Hindu festival of Divali, Hindu businessmen pray to Lakshmi, the goddess of wealth, for her blessing on them and their business.

In Hinduism wealth does not belong to one person but to a family – four living generations and three generations of ancestors. The present family members enjoying the wealth are trustees of the fortune. Hindus are expected to give away the wealth they do not need. This explains why begging is such a strong Hindu tradition. Giving money away means that a person gains merit in the next life. As a person grows older, and moves beyond the householder period, they need their wealth less and less. The giving is often done through temples in very needy areas or though such organisations as the Swaminarayan Hindu Mission in the UK.

▲ The cow was traditionally a symbol of wealth in Hinduism. It is considered by Hindus to be a sacred animal.

Exam tip
When you are giving more than one example to illustrate a point make sure that they are really different. Do not try to fool the examiner.

Tasks

1.a. What does Judaism teach about wealth and giving to the poor?

b. Write down **ONE** reason for these teachings.

2.a. Where do Muslims believe that all wealth comes from and what implication does this have for the way that they use it?

b. What are zakat and sadaqah?

3.a. What is a Hindu expected to do during the householder phase of life?

b. How is it expected that this will be done?

SUMMARY

1 In Judaism, charity – giving to the poor – is to do with fairness to all. The best form of charity is to give so that the needy can work to relieve their own poverty.

2 For Muslims all wealth is God-created and must be spent on the family and the wider community. Zakat and sadaqah are the two appointed ways of distributing wealth.

3 Acquiring wealth is a major aim of Hindus in the 'householder' phase. This wealth must be acquired in a righteous way. Wealth that is not needed must be given away to those in need. Begging is a common activity in Hindu countries.

5:5 Christian organisations

What is distinctive about the work of CAFOD and Christian Aid?

There are many Christian organisations at work amongst the poor and needy of the world. Here we look at just two of them, CAFOD and Christian Aid, and the work that they do.

CAFOD

> The goal of CAFOD is to promote human development and social justice in witness to Christian faith and Gospel values.
>
> **... CAFOD MISSION STATEMENT**

In 1962 the Catholic bishops in England and Wales set up CAFOD (the Catholic Fund for Overseas Development). From its beginning CAFOD has always tried to help the poor and disadvantaged throughout the world by helping them to help themselves. Projects financed by CAFOD attempt to tackle the causes, as well as the symptoms, of disease and poverty. To this end CAFOD now supports well over 500 different projects in more than 75 countries.

Tackling world development

CAFOD sets out to tackle many of the world's most pressing development issues by working along three lines.

1. **Fundraising.** CAFOD holds sponsored fasts during Lent and October each year in this country. Church congregations and individuals are encouraged to go without food for a day and to give the money raised to CAFOD projects. Each year more than £20 million is raised in this way.

2. **Providing aid.** CAFOD is often able to provide short-term aid quickly to refugees in response to a war or natural disaster. The organisation is able to gather food, medicines and shelter so that it can respond within days. Often a number of charities such as CAFOD and Christian Aid launch a joint appeal to the public for money. The organisation also works on long-term projects. Help is often channelled through Caritas, a subsidiary international Catholic organisation. Amongst other projects, irrigation, food production, educational and health projects are financed.

3. **Education.** Educating people in the UK about development issues is an important part of the work of CAFOD. The organisation spends 5p in every £1 raised on educational work in churches and schools. It considers this to be a very important part of its work as it tries to build a better world through the help and support of the next generation.

Christian Aid

Christian Aid began in 1945 when churches in the UK helped refugees in Europe after the Second World War. This work was later extended to serve the needs of the poor throughout the world. Christian Aid does not initiate projects of its own but prefers to work through local people on the ground. It believes that they have the best understanding of what the needs of people in the area are.

Each year in the UK a special week is devoted to fundraising for the organisation. Door-to-door collections are part of this and they raise over £10 million each year. Around £30 million is raised each year by other means and is used to fund many projects, such as sinking wells to provide clean drinking water, financing irrigation projects, organising family planning education and so on. Christian Aid also has an emergency fund to deal with natural disasters such as floods, earthquakes and hurricanes. Often Christian Aid joins with other charities in launching a combined appeal to raise as much money as possible to meet these needs when a sudden emergency takes place. Also, just as CAFOD does, Christian Aid spends a proportion of the money it receives on raising the awareness of the people in the UK about development issues.

> I hope that, despite all obstacles, the generosity of your hearts will never weaken. I hope that through programmes such as CAFOD you will continue to help the poor, to feed the hungry and to contribute to the cause of development. Always keep alive your Gospel tradition.
>
> **... POPE JOHN PAUL II, SPEAKING IN LIVERPOOL, 1982**

> ✔ **Exam tip**
> If there is a charity working in an area in which you are particularly interested then refer to it it in your answer – as long as it meets the basic requirement of being a religious organisation.

Tasks

1.a. What do the letters CAFOD stand for?

  b. Why was CAFOD set up in the first place?

2.a. How does CAFOD raise a large amount of its money?

  b. Why do you think that this way of raising money is particularly appropriate for an organisation concerned with world development?

  c. In what kind of projects does CAFOD involve itself?

3.a. Why was Christian Aid set up and how did its work expand?

  b. How does Christian Aid raise much of its money and for what kind of projects is this money used?

 Think about ...

CAFOD and Christian Aid place a great emphasis on educating people in the UK about the needs of developing countries. Why do you think this work is given such a high priority?

SUMMARY

1 CAFOD, the main UK Catholic charity working in world development, seeks to fundraise, support projects in developing countries and educate people in this country.

2 Christian Aid supports local projects aimed at helping developing countries. It has a special week each year for fundraising.

▼ Education is given a high priority in developing countries, as many parents feel it is the best chance for a better future for their children.

5:6 What are the media?

What do people mean when they speak of the media?

> *Britain's poorest households are being left behind in the digital revolution because they cannot afford access to the Internet. Figures released yesterday reveal that a 'digital divide' has opened up between the poorest households and the better off.*
>
> *... THE GUARDIAN, 11 JULY 2000*

The media (or 'mass media') is a very important aspect of modern life. It refers to all forms of written communication – such as books, newspapers and magazines; and transmitted or oral communication – such as radio, television, cinema and the Internet.

The mass media

The 'mass media' refers to any means of communication that is designed to reach a large number of people (the 'mass') at the same time. The most effective aspects of the mass media are inventions of the twentieth century.

The first medium of mass communication came with the invention of the printing press in the fifteenth century. This was not developed on a large scale until the seventeenth century and it only became really important when mass literacy arrived in the twentieth century. It was during this century that a large growth in the mass media took place with the beginning of BBC radio (1926), talking films (1920s), television (1936), commercial television (1955), commercial radio (1972), cable television and satellite broadcasting (1985).

In the 1990s there was a growth in personal computers and mobile phones with access to the Internet. These items moved very rapidly from being luxury items owned by a small minority to being available to the large majority who considered them to be necessities. They have ushered in a great revolution in the mass media and have completely altered the way in which we now look at communication.

In the last 20 years there have been many changes in broadcasting and printing, brought about mainly by new technology.

- **Broadcasting.** Cable, satellite and digital technology make it possible for many more stations to be on the air. Digital TV allows viewers to interact with those doing the broadcasting. 99 per cent of UK homes now have a TV set and by 2010 the majority of these should be digital.

- **Video and DVD.** 85 per cent of homes now have a video or DVD player but this has not led to lower attendance at cinemas – quite the reverse. Over 150 million visits are made to the cinema each year in the UK. Films shown in the cinema today become available for personal viewing in the home within a few months.

- **Print.** The developments in information technology allow newspapers and books to be produced by fewer staff, at lower costs and in a shorter time. The result has been an explosion of publications with more books, magazines and newspapers printed than ever before. The three most popular UK newspapers each sell more than 2 million copies a day. Over 10 million newspapers are sold daily in the UK.

- **The Internet.** This has been the largest growth area in the media since the 1990s. The Internet now offers access to a huge range of sites and information. Many companies now offer services directly to the customer, such as booking train and theatre tickets. Most churches and religions, together with individual churches, now have their own website. The latest mobile phones are linked to the Internet allowing advertisers and broadcasters to communicate directly with people. As there are now about 700 million mobile phones worldwide this is clearly a method of communication set to explode in the coming years.

The mass media and religion

The increase in mass communication offers the different religions great challenges for the future. There are many religious websites giving information about services, beliefs and so on. Religious groups are also free to bid for the franchises of local radio stations and there is already more than one Christian radio station in the UK. As these stations are local they can reflect the tastes and interests, including religious, of the people living around them.

> **IT'S A FACT**
>
> One of the first films ever shown included a train coming into a station. The audience could not understand what was happening. Several people were injured when the crowd made a mad rush for the exit to avoid being run over by the train!

Tasks

1. Explain what you understand by the term 'mass media'.
2. Describe **THREE** aspects of the mass media.
3. The quotation on this spread hints at a major problem of the mass media. What is that problem?

SUMMARY

1 The term mass media refers to all forms of written and transmitted communication. These had become very sophisticated by the end of the twentieth century.

2 The digital revolution has made information readily available to most people – but the poorest are likely to miss out.

▼ The electronic revolution has totally changed how we look at the mass media.

5:7 Religious broadcasting

What are the key components of religious broadcasting in the UK?

> *Information is power, more valuable than oil, more precious than gold. And most of it is created, stored and distributed in rich countries.*
>
> **... THE GAIA ATLAS OF PLANET MANAGEMENT**

The media exist to educate, inform and entertain. They also reflect what is important in the lives of those who use them and this includes religious worship. In the UK this invariably means acts of Christian worship.

Religious worship

For a long time religious worship has been part of the staple diet of radio and television. The *Daily Service* is the oldest running programme on BBC radio, having started in 1927 in the old *Home Programme*. It is still transmitted for 15 minutes each weekday on Radio 4. Another Christian religious service is included in the schedules each Sunday morning with extra services during Christian festivals, such as Easter and Christmas, together with special State occasions which are usually broadcast from Christian Churches. There are also short *Prayer for the Day* and *Thought for the Day* spots included in different programmes on Radio 4. Religious worship on television is largely covered by the long-running *Songs of Praise*, although other programmes have come and gone over the years.

These worship programmes are almost exclusively Christian. They provide an opportunity for people, such as the elderly, to worship in their own homes. On the odd occasion when an attempt has been made to move them to another time, or even end them, there have been strong protests.

Education and information

For a long time both BBC and ITV operated a 'God slot', which kept time on Sunday free for religious programmes. That has long since gone. The television remains, however, a very useful medium for educating and informing its viewers about religious matters. In 2001, ITV showed the *Alpha Course* in a series of ten hour-long programmes late on Sunday evenings. These are popular courses run to introduce people to the Christian faith. At about the same time on BBC television a four-part series called

The Son of God used modern computer-generated graphics to re-create events in the life of Jesus, especially his death and resurrection. Other series in recent years have looked at the world of Islam and the history of the world's religions. In March 2002, Channel 4 began a series of programmes looking at the Muslim community in the UK and the challenges that it is facing.

There are also many programmes on television on a wide range of topics of social interest: programmes on the environment, natural disasters such as floods and earthquakes, marriage and divorce, homosexuality, abortion and many more. These same issues, are also covered on Radio 4. A long-running series, *The Moral Maze*, examines social topics from a moral perspective. Most religious people feel that it is important for them to know what is going on in the world so that they can pray about it and find ways of helping those in need. Newspapers, in particular, respond to important topical issues by carrying reports and in-depth articles. The choice of a new Archbishop of Canterbury in 2002, to lead the Anglican Church worldwide, led to many articles being published.

Discussion is a very important way of interesting people in spiritual matters and issues. From time to time, programmes bring people together from different religions to discover what unites and separates them. A programme broadcast on Radio 4 each Sunday morning, called *Sunday*, does this on a variety of topical issues. To take just one example: on 8 March 2002, a Muslim educationalist and a Jewish rabbi were brought together to discuss whether multi-faith or one-faith schools offered the best hope for the future. One of the most important features of the mass media is that they can respond quickly to world events of immediate importance, educating and informing viewers, listeners and readers.

Televangelism

The law in the UK does not allow religious groups to bid for terrestrial television licences. Radio, though, is different and there is, for example, a Christian radio station, Premier Radio, operating from London. In America, the situation is different and evangelists are able to preach on cable and satellite television and appeal for donations to support their work. These people are known as 'televangelists'. Most Christians, and members of other faiths, would not like to see a similar situation arise in the UK. It would allow all kinds of fringe religious groups and preachers to gain a wide audience for their message.

▲ Jimmy Swaggart is a televangelist who preaches on American television.

BBC Religion exists to ask the big questions that underlie all human life and explore the different ways in which people try to answer them, whether through worship, prayer, or simply giving food for thought.

... THE AIMS OF RELIGIOUS BROADCASTING, BBC

Tasks

1. Write a paragraph to explain how radio and television cater for those who want to use programmes to help them worship.

2. Explain what religious broadcasting is about.

3. Give **TWO** examples of how television seeks to educate and inform viewers about religion.

! Think about ...

Have a look at the variety of religious programmes that are broadcast on any one Sunday. Choose one programme to study in detail. Why do you think it could be popular or unpopular?

SUMMARY

1 There are many programmes of Christian worship and hymn-singing on UK radio and television. These include *Songs of Praise* on BBC television.

2 Documentaries and discussion programmes also cover topics of religious and social interest.

3 There is little in the mainstream media relating to faiths other than Christianity.

4 In the UK, religious groups can own their own radio stations but not terrestrial television channels.

5:8 Soaps and moral issues

How closely do the soaps on television mirror real moral and religious issues in society?

> *The television violence debate re-ignited yesterday with the revelation that children and teenagers are more disturbed by violence in soap operas such as EastEnders than in Hollywood action movies. The difference was that violence in soaps occurred in a real-life setting.*
>
> **... THE INDEPENDENT, 13 DECEMBER 1996**

We live in a media-saturated world. On average, people in the UK spend between three and four hours each day watching television. There is a bewildering array of choice as terrestrial, satellite and cable delivery systems give us the possibility of watching hundreds of different channels. One thing, though, seems to remain constant about our television viewing habits – the most popular kinds of programmes are those that we now know as 'soaps'.

The soaps

'Soap operas' take their name from the fact that the earliest examples of this kind of programme in America were sponsored by the manufacturers of soap powders. Targeted at a mainly female audience, 'soap operas' are serials that are screened several times a week and contain various interlocking story lines and characters based in a small community. Each programme is broken down into many episodic events that have followed each other rapidly.

▼ Soaps have an enormous impact on the lives of viewers.

The most popular soaps, *Coronation Street* and *EastEnders*, are broadcast four times a week in the early evening. These soaps average about 13 million viewers each episode. Both of them are set in 'typical' working-class communities – one in the north of England and the other in the East End of London. The focal point for both of them is the local pub, the *Rover's Return* and the *Queen Vic*, with an amazing number of dramatic incidents taking place within a very small geographical area. Every episode ends with some kind of cliff-hanger that is designed to entice viewers to switch on for the next episode. The emphasis is placed on 'realism' so that viewers will identify with the different characters and feel at home in the community in which they are set.

> **IT'S A FACT**
>
> In the 1970s the viewing time for *Crossroads*, a popular soap at the time, was changed from 6pm to 4.30pm. Female factory workers in Devon were so upset that they would no longer be able to see their favourite soap that they went on strike!

Soaps and real issues

The producers of the soaps pride themselves on the realism that they bring to their programmes. Because they thrive on drama, however, the stories have to be exaggerated and contain a higher number of incidents, such as marriages, than is realistic. Sometimes the public becomes really involved in an issue that is at the heart of a soap – there was a campaign to free 'the Wetherfield One' when Deidre Rashid, a character in *Coronation Street*, was wrongly imprisoned. A question was even asked in Parliament about the case. Around the same time there was concern that there had been more than one 'miscarriage of justice' in the real world.

Soaps often tackle real, significant issues and raise public awareness more effectively than a factual or documentary programme. Storylines in soaps in recent years have covered topics such as living with AIDS, homosexual love, teenage pregnancy, domestic violence, drug addiction, transsexuality, adoption, the use of euthanasia and the influence of religious cults, to name but a few. Look at the following two examples from *EastEnders*:

- In 2002 the issue of domestic violence was tackled. Little Mo Slater was systematically abused by her husband, Trevor, culminating in a brutal episode in which she responded violently out of sheer desperation. The producers were able to stretch this theme out for several months.

▲ All religions recognise the influence that soaps have on the majority of people. *EastEnders,* for example, has had over 17 million viewers for some episodes.

- In 2001 the issue of euthanasia was tackled on Eastenders. Dot Cotton helped her oldest friend, Ethel, to end her life when pressure was put on her to do so. Dot, who makes a great play of her Christian convictions in the series, battled long and hard with her conscience before she agreed to help Ethel.

One important feature of soaps must be noted. Often the violent and highly unpleasant characters seem to come out on top, but evil characters are rarely allowed to emerge victorious in the end. Soaps are, in fact, the modern equivalent of the old morality tales in which good will almost always triumph over evil in the end. At the same time, as the quotation shows, they are taken very seriously by viewers and have a great influence on many people.

Tasks

1. What is a soap opera?

2. Write down **THREE** characteristics of a soap.

3.a. Write down **THREE** important issues that have recently been tackled by your favourite soap.

   b. Are there any issues that you think should be tackled, but which have not been, to the best of your knowledge?

   c. Are there are any issues that you think would be unsuitable to include in a soap? Why do you think they are unsuitable?

 Think about ...

Why do you think that so many viewers identify so closely with many of the characters in the most popular soaps?

Do you think that soaps are an important way of introducing people to controversial issues and getting them to think about these issues?

SUMMARY

1 The name 'soap opera' derives from America where such programmes were originally sponsored by the manufacturers of soap powders. In the UK, they are serial programmes, usually centred on a small working-class community.

2 They are intended to be realistic using common everyday experiences such as weddings, teenage romances, arguments and so on. They also have a 'cliff-hanger' ending to entice viewers to watch again.

3 Soaps tackle many controversial and important moral issues. Sometimes evil appears to triumph although, in the end, good usually wins through.

 **Exam help ...**

In the main part of this chapter it is the world, rather than the UK, that is focused upon. Make sure that you understand the differences between the rich and the poor parts of the world. World debt plays a very important role. Look at the work of CAFOD and Christian Aid as examples of a practical Christian response and similar organisations within other faiths. It is important to understand the teachings of the different religions on wealth and poverty. We have also looked at the mass media and the effect that they have on the lives of people in the UK. Particularly important are the areas of religious broadcasting and the impact that soaps have.

1. Why is the problem of world debt important to many countries?

1. Many developing countries in the world are heavily in debt to the rich, developed countries. Unable to pay back the money that they first borrowed, the debt of these countries is growing all the time. Some countries pay back far more money in debt payments than they spend on hospitals and schools each day. This means that they are becoming poorer and poorer all the time.

   - Over 40 countries are heavily in debt. Much of the money borrowed was wasted or stolen by corrupt leaders. Often the country did not benefit. Now countries have to use valuable resources and land to grow crops to earn money and pay their debts. At the same time, people are going hungry and starving to death.

   - Another problem faced by poor countries is that they have to pay their debts in hard currency – the currency of the country they owe. If their own currency goes down in value then it is worth fewer dollars, pounds or euros. It is a vicious circle: as the poor countries get poorer they borrow more money to pay off their debts. This is the 'debt spiral' into which poorer countries are drawn.

   - World debts should be cancelled or reduced considerably. This would be a significant way of helping poor countries. Jubilee 2000 was a campaign designed to bring this about. It called for the rich countries to break the 'debt cycle' and cancel world debts, but it failed.

2. Outline the Christian teaching on wealth and poverty.

2. Christians believe that the world, and everything in it, was created by God – for all people to enjoy. Nothing is evil in itself, but everything can be misused. This includes money. It can be used to help those in need or it can be squandered.

   - Jesus identified himself with the poor and their needs throughout his ministry on earth. Zacchaeus, a highly unpopular tax-gatherer, gave away much of his wealth when he became a follower of Jesus. Jesus said that anyone who wanted to enter God's kingdom must sell their possessions first.

   - Jesus made it clear that his followers must care for the poor in order to be accepted into God's kingdom. Many of the followers of Jesus have spent their lives working amongst the very poorest people (Mother Teresa, for example).

   - In the parable of the Good Samaritan, Jesus showed his followers must take time to help those in need – even if the needy are not those one would naturally help.

   - Wealthy Christians are called to avoid the temptations that wealth brings. They must also help those in need to the best of their ability.

3. Explain the teaching of ONE religion, other than Christianity, about wealth and poverty.

3. The chosen religion is Islam.

   - Islam teaches that it is human nature to love wealth – yet the Muslim life tries to keep everything in perspective. Muslims start from the belief that all wealth belongs to Allah. If God rewards hard work then the wealth is a trust from Allah. It must be used to help members of one's own family and those in need in the Muslim community.

continued ...

- The Muslim community provides two ways of distributing wealth to those who need it:

  Zakat – one of the Five Pillars of Islam. This is a 'religious tax' paid by all Muslims that amounts to 2.5 per cent of their annual income. Every poor Muslim has the 'right' to share in this wealth and so it is not charity.

  Sadaqah – a voluntary gift made in addition to zakat. Given to Muslims and non-Muslims. Generosity brings spiritual contentment to the giver.

- Many of the donations made by Muslims are channelled through Muslim relief agencies such as Islamic Relief and Muslim Aid. They are then used to help those living in developing countries.

4. Describe the work of ONE Christian relief agency.

4. The Catholic Fund for Overseas Development (CAFOD) is the leading Roman Catholic relief agency in the UK. It was set up in 1962 to help the poor in developing countries help themselves. It now works in over 75 countries and supports more than 500 projects at any one time. There are three parts to the work undertaken by CAFOD.

   - **Fundraising.** Mainly through specially sponsored fasts. Apart from raising money, these provide people with a small experience of hunger and so gives them an insight into the experience of others.

   - **Providing aid.** CAFOD provides short- and long-term aid in developing countries. CAFOD works with other charities in meeting need when disasters strike. It also works with Caritas, an international Catholic organisation. The organisation finances irrigation, food production, educational and health projects.

   - **Education.** Seeks to educate people in the UK about development issues. This is a very important part of its work.

5. What makes up the main elements of religious broadcasting in the UK?

5. Religious broadcasting in the UK relies on the broadcasting of acts of worship. This goes back to the earliest days of radio with the *Morning Service* – the longest running BBC programme. There is also a Christian service broadcast every Sunday morning, together with special services during religious festivals.

   - In addition to services there are *Thought for the Day* spots in most programmes on Radio 2. Although most of these programmes are Christian some are given by members of other religious faiths.

   - On television *Songs of Praise* is the longest-running Christian worship programme. Occasional services are also broadcast on BBC and ITV, especially at Christmas and Easter. These are very popular, particularly with the elderly and housebound.

   Apart from worship programmes, both radio and television have religious documentaries designed to inform and educate. ITV has shown a ten-part series based on the *Alpha Course* – a course of Christian instruction. BBC has shown a four-part series *The Son of God* based on the life of Jesus. The BBC broadcast *The Long Search,* which covered different world religions and Channel 4 showed a series in March 2002 that looked at the Muslim community in the UK.

6:1 Making moral decisions

How do Christians make moral decisions?

> *Do for others what you want them to do for you: this is the meaning of the Law of Moses and of the teachings of the prophets.*
>
> ... **THE BIBLE (MATTHEW 7.12)**

Christians have four basic beliefs about the world.

- The world was made by God.
- The world is essentially good, since God Himself is good.
- The people who live in the world are important and valuable to God.
- By sinning against God, human beings have disobeyed God's commands.

Creation and its aftermath

These four beliefs are expressed in the story of the creation of the world (Genesis 1–3). The world did not happen by chance – it was created by a good God who was pleased with His work. Existence is a good thing: the world and being alive are gifts from God to the human race and should be treasured. The story in Genesis says that human beings were made like God and in His image. They were given the freedom to think and act; they have free will. Humans were blameless before sin entered the world and the first man and woman lost their innocence. People chose the path of disobedience, turned away from God and learned to commit evil, sinful acts. Christians believe that God rescued the world from the consequences of sin by sending Jesus. Through his death and resurrection He made it possible for human sin to be forgiven.

How, then, do Christians decide what is the right thing for them to do? There are two main branches of Christianity in the UK, Roman Catholic and Protestant, and they have different ways of answering this question.

The Roman Catholic approach

The Roman Catholic Church believes that God reveals His will in two ways: through the Bible and through the teachings of the Church. The Gospels tell us that Jesus gave his authority to teach to his 12 apostles and promised that the Holy Spirit would lead them into truth. Roman Catholics believe that this has happened over the centuries and that this truth has been transmitted through the bishops of the Church. Bishops are seen as following in the footsteps of the original disciples of Jesus. Occasionally the bishops meet together in a General Council of the Church and it is thought that the Holy Spirit has prevented them from making any wrong decisions. The Pope has had a special role, as the successor of St Peter, to play in this.

When Roman Catholics want to know whether something is right or wrong they turn, first of all, to the teaching of the Church. They then look to the teaching of the Bible. Finally they look to 'natural law' – the laws of God that are clearly visible in the world. God does not have to tell us everything, some things are obviously wrong because they contradict the way the world was made. These natural laws work through our consciences so that we are able to know what God wants us to do. Think about the act of adultery, for example. To commit adultery is against God's natural law that the only place for sexual relations is within marriage. No one who wants to comply with the will of God can hope to commit adultery with a clear conscience.

IT'S A FACT

Councils of the Catholic Church are very rare. Only 21 have been held since the Church began – roughly one every century. The last one was held between 1962 and 1965 and this is referred to as the Second Vatican Council (Vatican 2).

The Protestant approach

The Protestant belief is that God speaks to the world and individual Christians through the Bible. Protestants refer to the Bible as 'the word of God' and the way in which God has made His will known to us is called 'revelation'. The Protestant Churches broke away from the Catholic Church during the Reformation in the sixteenth century. When Protestant Christians want to know whether something is right or wrong they ask themselves:

- What does the Bible say?
- How should the teachings of the Bible be applied today?

Moral problems are always with us. The most important set of moral laws in the Bible is the Ten Commandments (Exodus 20) although the Sermon on the Mount (Matthew 5–7) is of equal importance for Christians. The Golden Rule in the quotation is often taken as the most basic statement of the teaching of Jesus. When Christians are confronted with modern problems that are not mentioned in the Bible they try to work out what their approach should be from biblical principles. Both Roman Catholic and Protestant Christians also look to the guidance of God's Holy Spirit when making their moral decisions.

Many modern Christians adopt a more radical approach to decision making. They do not believe that there are any principles that apply to each and every situation. Each situation must be judged on its merits. This is called 'situation ethics'.

Tasks

1. What are the four basic beliefs that Christians hold about the world?

2. Why is the Bible very important to many Christians when they have a moral decision to make?

3. 'All Christians arrive at their moral decisions in the same way.' Do you agree with this comment? Show in your answer that you have considered more than one point of view.

IMPORTANT WORDS

Bible;	holy book sacred to Jews and Christians; Protestants and Roman Catholics believe that the Christian Bible contains important moral teaching, Catholics believe that the Church alone is able to interpret the Bible faithfully
Church;	the organisation begun soon after the death and resurrection of Jesus; Roman Catholics believe that the Church alone can interpret the Bible faithfully, its teaching on moral matters must be followed by Catholics
Conscience;	an 'internal voice' recognised by Christians and non-Christians alike; to Christians this represents the 'voice of God', a way of distinguishing between right and wrong
Situation ethics;	flexible way of deciding the right thing to do, takes into account each situation before deciding the correct course of action

▲ Prayers play an important part for Christians in reaching moral decisions.

SUMMARY

1 Christians believe that the world was made by God and so is good. Human beings are valuable to God. Human beings have disobeyed God by sinning. These beliefs are found in the creation story.

2 Roman Catholics make their moral decisions by referring to the teachings of the Church, the Bible and natural law.

3 Protestants depend on the teaching of the Bible to make their moral decisions.

6:2 The electoral system

How does the electoral system in Britain work?

The British political system is a democratic monarchy. There are elected parliaments in London and Edinburgh with an unelected Queen as the Head of State. There are also elected assemblies in Wales and Northern Ireland.

Parliament

In a representative democracy, such as we have in Britain, elections have to be held every five years or sooner. It is up to the government to decide when an election will be held. Everyone in the UK over the age of 18 has the right to vote and they cast their vote for the political party they prefer. At the same time each voter is choosing a person to represent them in Parliament as their Member of Parliament (MP). Each area where candidates run for election is called a 'constituency'. The winner is chosen by the first-past-the-post system. This means that the person who gains most votes in each constituency wins. The political party with the largest number of MPs forms the government and the leader of this party becomes the Prime Minister.

There are two branches of Parliament.

The House of Commons. 659 MPs are elected to the House of Commons. In 2002 there were 118 women MPs; this translates as just 18 per cent of the total MPs. This figure is lower than in most other EU countries. Of 419 Labour MPs, 239 went to university and 68 of these attended Oxford or Cambridge. MPs are mainly white, male and middle class with very few being drawn from ethnic groups.

The central government makes policy decisions covering all the basic areas of life – taxation, defence, social security, housing, education and health. To do this it is assisted by the Civil Service, which numbers over 600 000 staff and is not elected. Ministers and governments come and go, but the members of the Civil Service remain in their jobs – some say this helps give the UK stability.

The House of Lords. This is known as the 'Second Chamber' and is not elected. Until recently most of its members came from the aristocracy: wealthy families that often owned a lot of land, but now many of its members are appointed by the government. The long-term future of the House of Lords was open to debate in 2002.

In addition there is an European Parliament which meets in Strasbourg. Members (MEPs) are elected to Parliament by proportional representation, which reflects more accurately the number of votes cast for them. At the same time it means that constituencies have to be much larger and, consequently, few people know who their MEP is.

Local elections

Local elections are held in the UK every four years. These elect councillors to serve on local councils. The local elections are conducted on political lines although alongside the familiar Conservative, Labour and Liberal candidates there are also candidates from smaller parties and Independents. Local councils are responsible for specifically local issues, such as refuse collections, planning applications and street lighting. Each householder in the borough has to pay a Council Tax based on the value of their property. Part of this tax goes to County Councils, which are responsible for matters that go across local council borders such as the building of roads.

Voting

It is not compulsory to vote in the UK, although it is in many other countries. A large number of people do not vote in elections. In a general election there is usually a 75 per cent turn-out for voting, although when a by-election is held, due to an MP resigning or dying, the voting figure usually goes down significantly. The voting figure for local elections is much lower still. For most local elections it barely reaches 30 per cent. Non-voting is highest in those areas where people are socially disadvantaged. This suggests a widespread feeling among the people that politicians do little to improve their situation.

Think about ...

In most UK elections one out of every three people does not vote.

a. Think of **TWO** reasons why someone would choose not to vote.

b. Think of **TWO** ways that more people could be encouraged to vote.

c. Do you think that voting should be made compulsory, with fines being imposed on those who do not vote?

Tasks

1. How are MPs chosen in the UK?

2. Write down **FIVE** pieces of information about the House of Commons.

3. What are the main differences between national and local government?

4. Describe **ONE** difference between the House of Commons and the House of Lords.

5. The UK has a first-past-the-post electoral system. Explain what this means.

6. 'It is very important for everyone to vote.' Discuss this with other members of your group and try to work out why so many people do not vote. Will you vote when you have the chance?

IMPORTANT WORDS

Electoral system;	the system by which people elect (vote for) their national and local representatives
First-past-the-post;	system in the UK used to elect national and local representatives, the person who gets most votes in a constituency is elected
Local government;	councillors elected in local elections to take decisions on local matters
National government;	government ministers, including Prime Minister, drawn from the political party that has most MPs after an election
Proportional representation;	a system that gives parties seats in parliament in proportion to the number of votes cast for them

▲ To encourage more people to vote, the government is trialling a scheme in local elections allowing people to cast their vote by mobile phone text messaging.

SUMMARY

1 The House of Commons is the most important Parliamentary house. MPs are elected at a general election. The party with most MPs forms the government. The government makes important decisions for the country. Members of the House of Lords are not elected.

2 MEPs are elected to the European Parliament. This election is by proportional representation.

3 Local elections elect local councillors. They are responsible for local affairs such as refuse collection and street lighting.

6:3 Christianity and politics

What are the different Christian attitudes to involvement in politics?

Christians can, and do, belong to any of the political parties. There is no religious reason for a Christian to feel more comfortable in any particular party. There is nothing in the teaching of Jesus that would rule out belonging to any of the parties or would point towards any particular political affiliation. Over the years Christians have shown two very different approaches to involvement in political issues.

Involvement in politics

There are many Christians in politics – national and local. The Prime Minister, Tony Blair, has been open about his own Christian beliefs. Many Christians believe that their faith is concerned with working out its implications in every avenue of life – including the political. Christians are usually very concerned with helping others – especially those in the greatest need. To improve the way of life of others, Christians feel it is necessary to bring about changes in society and they are aware that in order to do this they must have access to power – and that means being involved in politics.

> *I submit that Christians ought not to be scared of a moral issue just because someone has stuck a political flag on it.*
>
> **... GERALD PRIESTLAND,**
> **BBC RELIGIOUS AFFAIRS CORRESPONDENT**

Many Christians believe that religion and politics need each other. In the Sermon on the Mount (Matthew 5–7) Jesus warned his disciples about the dangers of many things, but he did not suggest to them they should not be where the action is! Political action is the only way of bringing about real change in society and that is what the Christian Gospel is all about. When Jesus threw the money-changers out of the Temple he was carrying out a political rather than a religious act. He knew that this was how it would be seen by the religious and political leaders of the time.

> *My brothers and sisters, what good is it for people to say that they have faith if their actions do not prove it. Can that faith save them? Suppose there are brothers or sisters who need clothes and don't have enough to eat. What good is there in your saying to them, 'God bless you! Keep warm and eat well!'*
>
> **... THE BIBLE (JAMES 2.14–16)**

Separation from politics

Some Christians believe that religion and politics should be kept firmly apart – in separate compartments. One reason for this is that society is made up of many different kinds of people – including those with no religious faith as well as those who belong to religions other than Christianity. Politicians must take decisions in the interests of everyone and this is very difficult for someone who is a committed believer in one faith. There appear to be two justifications in the Christian scriptures for keeping religion and politics firmly apart:

- The occasion when Jesus was asked by some Pharisees and Herodians whether it was lawful to pay taxes to Caesar or not (Mark 12.13–17). In his answer Jesus seemed to suggest that there was a part of our life that fell into the political domain and one that was strictly spiritual. "… pay the Emperor what belongs to the Emperor and pay God what belongs to God."

- The advice of Paul to the Christians in Rome – "Everyone must obey the state authorities, because no authority exists without God's permission, and the existing authorities have been put there by God." (Romans 13.1) This is interpreted to mean that as the political authorities have been put in place by God they must be obeyed. No one is to be encouraged to doubt or question the decisions that the political authorities make.

In the UK the Church of England is the established church. This means that this Church, and its leaders, almost act as spiritual advisers to the political leaders. The political leaders have a say in choosing the leaders of the Church of England. Since both know the limits of their power, Church and State can be kept firmly apart. Others, though, argue that the Church and State should not be joined as this involves the Church in making too many compromises.

▲ Prime Minister, Tony Blair, and his wife are both Christians. Some Christians feel it is essential to be involved in the political process.

> No government can expect to be wholly at ease with the church since the church serves the kingdom which is not of this world.
>
> ... **MARK SANTER, BISHOP OF BIRMINGHAM**

Tasks

1. Give **THREE** reasons why:
   a. Some Christians argue that they should be involved in politics.
   b. Some Christians argue that they should not be involved in politics.
2. Summarise the argument of James (*see quotation*) for Christian political involvement.
3. What is meant by describing the Church of England as the 'established church'?

SUMMARY

1 There is no indication in the scriptures or elsewhere as to how Christians should vote. Christians support various political parties.

2 Some Christians argue that they should be deeply involved in politics, to change things that need changing.

3 Some Christians argue that religion and politics should be kept separate.

6:4 The Welfare State

What is the Welfare State and why was it set up in the first place?

> *The critics of the Welfare State may have some valid points, but a glance back to life in Britain before its existence shows a dreadful level of poverty, disease and misery, which the Welfare State has undoubtedly relieved.*
>
> *... STEPHEN MOORE, SOCIOLOGY ALIVE, 1987*

The Welfare State describes those government departments and other organisations that take responsibility for the health and welfare of the population in the UK.

The birth of the Welfare State

In 1942 the Beveridge Report was published which showed that levels of poverty and ill-health in the population were so bad that the government had to intervene to help. After the war the Welfare State was put into place.

Although some help had been given to the elderly and sick since 1908, the government did not take any responsibility for the unemployed or for hospitals. Beveridge said that there were five great evils that the Welfare State must tackle as it provided care and support for everyone in the country 'from the cradle to the grave'. These evils were:

1. **Want.** The government must provide state benefits to prevent extreme poverty. This led, in 1948, to the introduction of social security payments for the unemployed and the sick, as well as pensions for the elderly.

2. **Disease.** The government must build, finance and staff hospitals and GP surgeries, for people to attend without paying. Looking after the nation's health became the main task of the Welfare State.

3. **Ignorance.** The government must build more schools and pay for teachers. This led, in 1944, to free secondary schools and the raising of the school leaving age from 14 to 15. It was later raised to the age of 16.

4. **Squalor.** The government had to make sure that everyone could afford to buy or rent suitable accommodation; this meant a large house-building programme.

5. **Idleness.** The government must take steps to make sure that unemployment is kept as low as possible.

Today, the Welfare State has many critics. Some people argue that it is far too extensive and costly and has created a vast and wasteful bureaucracy that runs and supports it. It has weakened the family, the local community and voluntary organisations. It does not get help to those who most need it. It makes people too dependent on welfare help when they should be helping themselves – a state of living known as 'welfare dependency'.

Others, though, point out that the Welfare State is still the envy of the world as many other countries have failed to copy it successfully. It does not keep people in luxury but it provides a safety net to stop people falling into real poverty.

The Welfare State today

Through its collection of taxes and National Insurance contributions, the Welfare State still manages to touch almost every aspect of life in the UK today.

- It funds a health service that is free of charge to anyone who is ill.

- Financial benefits are paid to those who are unemployed, disabled or in very poorly paid employment.

- An educational system of schools and colleges is funded: there is free education to the age of 18 and some help with studying afterwards.

- Local councils are able to run social services departments that employ social workers to care for the elderly, children and anyone else needing help.

- Housing associations are supported that provide accommodation at affordable prices for those in need.

- Child benefit is paid for everyone up to the age of 16 and up to the age of 19 for those receiving full-time education.

This is a very wide-ranging and heavy commitment. To deliver these amenities the government, local authorities, voluntary organisations and commercial companies all need to be involved. In addition a great deal of welfare support is often supplied to the needy by family members, individual friends and neighbours. These activities can range from a person helping an elderly neighbour, caring for a disabled relative or a friend lending someone money to tide them over. This is called 'informal welfare'.

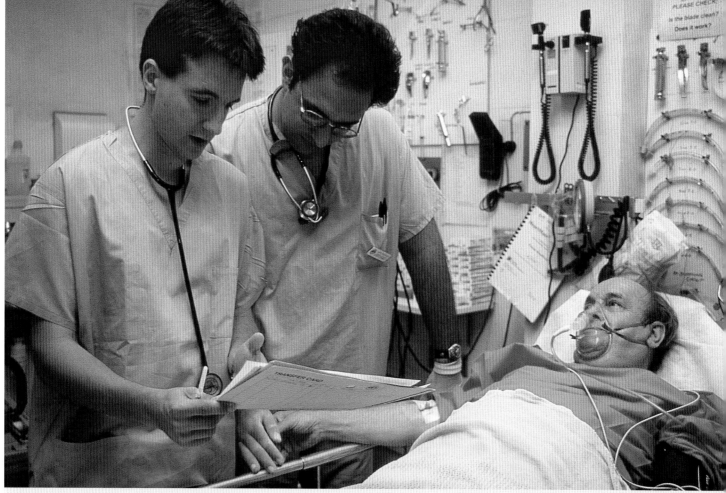

▲ The National Health Service is a very important part of the Welfare State.

Tasks

1.a. What is the Welfare State?

b. Why did the government feel the need to introduce the Welfare State?

c. List **THREE** ways in which the Welfare State is likely to affect the lives of all of us.

2.a. Describe the five evils that were outlined in the Beveridge Report.

b. Which **TWO** of these evils do you think are the worst? Give a reason for each of your choices.

 Think about ...

Most people think that the Welfare State has been the most important part of life in the UK since the Second World War. Some people argue, however, that it creates a 'dependent culture' making people lazy about looking after themselves and their relatives. Give TWO examples of how this might happen. Do you think that the Welfare State is a good or a bad thing?

SUMMARY

1 The Welfare State looks after everyone from the cradle to the grave. It was formed fully in 1945, after the 1942 Beveridge Report drew attention to the five evils of life in the UK – want, disease, ignorance, squalor and idleness.

2 Today the Welfare State provides a free National Health Service, unemployment and sickness benefits, education to the age of 18, social services and child benefit.

3 Although the Welfare State has many critics most people support it.

6:5 Christianity and the Welfare State

Why do most Christians support the Welfare State?

 I thank God for the Welfare State.

... *DONALD SOPER, METHODIST LEADER, 1953*

There was a great deal of poverty and squalor in the UK in the nineteenth century and the first half of the twentieth century. Many of the voices that were raised in concern about this came from different parts of the Christian Church. Some Christian denominations, such as the Salvation Army, worked largely in inner-city areas helping the needy. Officers of the Salvation Army were a familiar sight on city streets with their distinctive uniform and were well known for their work amongst alcoholics, the sick and the homeless. An evangelical Christian, Thomas John Barnardo, set up an orphanage in 1870 to help homeless children in the East End. By the time Thomas Barnardo died in 1905, the charity he had founded ran 96 homes. Today, Barnardo's is one of the biggest children's charities in the UK.

Despite all the good work that was being done by charities many Christian churches believed that it was the responsibility of central government to be involved in combating the problems that were destroying people's lives. Voluntary work alone could only scratch the surface. Christians look to the Bible for their inspiration on such social matters.

The Ten Commandments

Also known as the Decalogue, the Ten Commandments are the most widely respected code of laws, the influence of which has gone far beyond Judaism and Christianity. The first four of the laws, covering the relationship of the worshipper with God, may seem out of date to many but most people respect the other six commandments, covering social relationships between human beings. Many Christians argued that honouring parents, not stealing or committing acts of violence and not wanting the goods of other people needed government support in some way. In particular, this support should strengthen the family relationship, encouraging people to look after and honour their parents by taking away the most obvious signs of poverty. The introduction of the State pension in 1908 was a good start in this direction but more needed to be done. That is why Donald Soper and other church leaders enthusiastically welcomed the Welfare State *(see quotation)*.

The Golden Rule

Jesus firmly placed himself on the side of the poor and deprived throughout his ministry. He gave his disciples what was later described as the 'Golden Rule' *(see quotation below)*. As a simple guide to living it has probably not been bettered – we should treat other people just as we would like them to treat us. The Welfare State is based on the principle that those who are working and earning should support those who are too old or ill to work. The sub-text is that those who are working today will, one day, become too old or ill to work – and then they themselves will need supporting. This is the basic principle that underlies the Welfare State. The same principle is found in many Jewish books, although it is usually put in a negative form – 'do not do to others what you do not want them to do to you.'

Parable of the sheep and goats

The parable of the sheep and goats has inspired much social action by the Christian Church. It depicts everyone appearing before Jesus, as their judge, at the end of time. The people are divided into two groups – the sheep and the goats. The sheep are invited to enter into God's kingdom because, Jesus tells them, they have fed and clothed him when he needed it. The sheep wonder when this happened and are told that on those occasions when they did it for anyone in need they were doing it for Jesus himself.

This is a responsibility that the Christian Church has always taken seriously. For a long time it has fed the hungry, given water to the thirsty, befriended the stranger, clothed the naked, nursed the sick and visited prisoners. The Church recognises that the Welfare State cannot possibly do everything and that there will always be people still in need.

 I was hungry and you fed me, thirsty and you gave me a drink; I was a stranger and you received me in your homes, naked and you clothed me; I was sick and you took care of me, in prison and you visited me. The righteous will then answer him, 'When, Lord, did we ever see you hungry and feed you, or thirsty and give you a drink? When did we ever see you a stranger and welcome you in our homes, or naked and clothe you? When did we ever see you sick or in prison, and visit you?' The King will reply, 'I tell you, whenever you did this for one of the least important of these members of my family, you did it for me!'

... *THE BIBLE (MATTHEW 25.35–40)*

Tasks

1.a. What is the 'Golden Rule'?

b. Explain why the Golden Rule might have led a Christian to support the setting up and the work of the Welfare State.

2. Explain the relationship between the teachings of the parable of the sheep and goats and the provisions of the Welfare State.

3. Why did many Christians believe in the 1920s and 1930s that the government needed to be involved in meeting human need?

Think about ...

Read the Golden Rule quotation carefully. Do you think that this provides a good rule for life? Can you think of any situations in which it does not apply?

SUMMARY

1 The Christian Church has always taken its responsibility to meet human need very seriously. Before the Welfare State was set up, the Church tried to meet the needs of many people but it was clear that government help was essential.

2 The Ten Commandments lay out the responsibilities that human beings have towards each other. The Welfare State tries to support these responsibilities.

3 The Golden Rule summarises the teachings of Jesus – we should treat others as we expect them to treat us.

4 The parable of the sheep and goats explains that in helping others the followers of Jesus are doing such things for him.

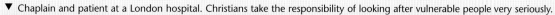

▼ Chaplain and patient at a London hospital. Christians take the responsibility of looking after vulnerable people very seriously.

 **Exam help ...**

This important chapter asks you to look at three areas: how Christians make moral decisions; the attitude of Christians to involvement in politics and the link between the Christian faith and the Welfare State. Concerning the first of these notice the different approaches in the Roman Catholic and the Protestant traditions. Concerning the second there is a marked difference between those who believe that Christians should be heavily involved in politics to change society and those who believe that Christians have more important work to do. Concerning the Welfare State the Christian input into this has been considerable since it was first introduced after the Second World War. You should be aware of this.

1.a. What is the Welfare State?

b. What do you think is the relationship between the parable of the sheep and the goats and the Welfare State?

c. Explain how Christians make moral decisions.

d. 'Christians are in the world to change it for the better. They cannot hope to do this unless they are politically involved.' Do you agree? Explain your answer

1.a. The term 'Welfare State' is used to describe all the services in the UK – such as education and medical – which are provided for everyone by the State.

b. In the parable of the sheep and goats, told by Jesus, everyone appears before Jesus. Jesus is their judge. The sheep are those who enter heaven after judgement. The goats are those sent to hell after judgement. The test of the judgement is whether people helped those in need: fed the hungry; gave water to the thirsty; clothed the naked; helped the sick and visited those in prison.

- Christians understand the tests set out by Jesus to apply to the work that the modern Welfare State carries out. The Welfare State feeds the hungry by providing social security payments. The National Health Service looks after the sick and the elderly and funds education. The Welfare State helps with the rehabilitation of prisoners.

continued ...

- In modern society, the Church recognises that the Welfare State cannot meet the needs of all people. The Church works to supplement the provisions of the Welfare State – particularly by its work amongst the young and the old, the most vulnerable people in modern society.

c. Christians believe four things about the world in which they live: it was made by God; it is good; the people who live in it are valuable to God and sin is an offence against God. These four principles are found in the Genesis creation story.

- There are two traditions about how moral decisions are made in God's world – the Roman Catholic and Protestant approaches. The Roman Catholic approach stresses the Bible and the teachings of the Church. The Church is important because there is a link between the disciples of Jesus and the bishops of the Church today. God has also given us 'natural' laws in the world that show us how things should be.

  The Protestant approach places the Bible at the heart of everything. The Bible gives us the principles by which we should live – the Ten Commandments, the Sermon on the Mount and the Golden Rule are the basic guides.

- Some Christians believe that every moral decision must be approached individually. There are no rules that cover everything. This approach is called 'situation ethics'.

d. National and local politics are about changing the world for the better. The Christian faith also wants to do this. Christians can only affect the world for the better if they are deeply involved in politics. There are many Christians involved in politics. They include some very well-known people. They want to improve the everyday lives of people. They claim that Jesus would encourage them to be involved.

2. Why do many Christians believe that Christianity and politics should be kept separate?

2. There are a number of Christians who believe Christianity and politics should be kept separate.

- Politicians serve people of many faiths – and atheists. Decisions must be made in the interests of everyone, regardless of faith. This is difficult for a person who is deeply committed to one faith.

- Jesus told his disciples that we should give to Caesar what belongs to Caesar and to God what belongs to God. This means that there are practical and political issues that have little to do with God. These are the matters that politicians should concern themselves with.

- Paul said that the authorities should be obeyed without question. Political beliefs and convictions divide people.

- The Church of England is the established church. The Church carries the spiritual responsibility for the whole nation. The Church carries the spiritual responsibility and politicians carry the political responsibility. The two roles are kept apart.

- The Church has enough to do looking after the spiritual needs of the people. It does not have the time to fully involve itself in politics.

3. Why is the Bible helpful to Christians who are trying to decide what to do in difficult moral situations?

3. Christians have different attitudes towards the Bible. Clearly those who regard it as the 'word of God' will give it a higher priority than those who do not.

- All Christians look to the Bible for advice to guide them in their everyday lives. The New Testament is particularly important as this contains the teachings of Jesus in the four Gospels. Only parts of the Old Testament are taken to apply to Christians.

- The teachings of the Bible need to be applied to modern situations. The world of the Bible is very different from the world today. So, for instance, there is no direct teaching in the Bible about modern issues such as cloning and methods of fertilisation. Christians look to the Bible to find principles that they can apply to an issue.

4. 'I take my conscience to be my most reliable guide to what is right and what is wrong for me personally.' Do you agree with this statement?

4. The conscience is like an internal guide indicating what is right from what is wrong for a person. Many different factors feed into a person's conscience – their upbringing, the influence of their friends, the influence of the mass media and the influence of their religious beliefs. The conscience is a complex mixture of all these things and others.

- The conscience is stronger in some people than others. It may be stronger or weaker depending on the issue. It may not always be possible to be sure what our conscience is telling us. It may not be easy to put what our conscience tells us into practice, especially if we do not want to follow its prompting.

- Christians believe that their conscience is a very important guide. Some look upon it as 'the voice of God'. Most Christians see it, though, as something they must always take into account. They set it alongside the teachings of the Bible and the Church to guide them when they are making a moral decision. God speaks in many different ways and they all have to be taken into account: together they provide a Christian with the most important guide to deciding how to behave.

CHAPTER 7: RELIGION AND THE ENVIRONMENT

7:1 Pollution

How much are we damaging our planet by the way that we live?

 We have not inherited the earth from our fathers, we are borrowing it from our children.

... LESTER BROWN, AMERICAN ENVIRONMENTALIST

The environment is the world in which we live and the atmosphere that surrounds it. The environment is suffering from the effects of pollution, brought on by misguided human activity.

Deforestation

Deforestation refers to the permanent clearing of forests, particularly rainforests, for agriculture, building projects or other uses. Between 1985 and 1995, forest areas were cleared worldwide at the rate of 40 million acres a year – 100 per cent faster than the previous decade. Since then one million acres – an area the size of the UK – is being cleared each week. This has very serious consequences.

- Although rainforests only cover 10 per cent of the earth's surface they contain 50 per cent of the world's species. Many have not yet been named.

- Deforestation is a major factor in global warming. Carbon dioxide is the most important of the greenhouse gases that build up in the atmosphere to cause global warming and over 20 per cent of this comes from forest burning.

- Rainforests help to regulate the climate. In the Venezuelan mud-slides (which killed at least 30 000 people in 1999) deforestation was a major factor. Trees bind the earth together and when they are destroyed the effect can be disastrous.

Global warming

Our planet is surrounded by a blanket of gases that insulate it and provide a fairly stable temperature. This blanket acts like a greenhouse around the earth and, because of global warming, the greenhouse is becoming too warm (this is known as the greenhouse effect). If this trend continues the ice-caps in the Antarctic and Arctic Oceans will melt and water levels will rise by 1.5 metres – flooding low-lying areas with sea water.

The ozone layer

Ozone in the atmosphere forms a layer above the earth to filter out lethal ultraviolet rays from the sun. CFCs (chlorofluorocarbons) released from aerosols and refrigerator compressors have led to the destruction of ozone molecules in the upper atmosphere and holes appeared in the ozone layer. These may take a century or more to repair. In the meantime people are at risk from a whole range of health hazards including eye cataracts and skin cancer.

Pollution

Pollution of the atmosphere presents the greatest threat to the future of our planet. Here are three examples:

- **Traffic pollution.** In 1955 there were about 40 million cars on the road worldwide, now there are over 400 million. By 2025 the figure will reach 1000 million. Hydrocarbons are released from petrol, when sunlight acts on them dangerous low-level ozone is produced. This can cause cancer and breathing problems.

- **Waste.** Each family in the UK disposes of a tonne of rubbish each year. Most of this is placed in landfill sites, but the bulk of it is not biodegradable. Although 30 per cent of rubbish is now recycled this is not enough.

- **Water pollution.** For thousands of years humans have consigned most of their waste to rivers and seas. When settlements were small and the amount of waste limited, little harm was done. As cities have grown and the toxicity of waste has increased, many rivers have lost the ability to cleanse themselves. On the land, pesticides and nitrates have been used to make the ground more productive. Rain has washed these into local rivers and streams. Fish have been killed in their thousands and drinking water has often been badly affected.

The human race cannot hope to continue to rush headlong down this path and survive. The whole of the world's fragile future life depends on maintaining a careful balance between the health of the planet and the needs of the human race.

> *Species that are important to human welfare are not just wild plants or animals. Species such as earthworms, bees and termites are important in terms of the role they play in a healthy and productive ecosystem. It would be a grim irony indeed if just as new genetic engineering techniques begin to let us peer into life's diversity and use genes more effectively to better the human condition, we looked and found this treasure sadly depleted.*

... THE BRUNDTLAND REPORT, OUR COMMON FUTURE, 1987

IMPORTANT WORDS

Acid rain;	rainfall containing pollutants released into the atmosphere by coal smoke and other fossil fuels
Greenhouse effect;	the warming of the earth's surface due to the long-term effect of the trapping of radiation by carbon dioxide and other greenhouse gases
Natural resources;	essential materials or substances that occur in nature, such as water and wood; these can be destroyed by human action and many of them are irreplaceable
Pollution;	the poisoning and contamination of the environment and atmosphere, such pollution harms plant, animal and human life

 Think about ...

Are you optimistic or pessimistic about the future of the planet? Explain your answer.

Tasks

1. Describe **THREE** major causes of pollution.
2.a. What is global warming?
  b. Why does global warming present a great threat to the future?
3.a. What is the ozone layer?
  b. What does the ozone layer do?
  c. How is the ozone layer under threat?
  d. What will happen if we continue to damage the ozone layer?

▲ Raw sewage can destroy fragile marine life.

SUMMARY

1 The environment is under great threat. Deforestation is contributing to a change in the climate and to the destruction of many species. Global warming means that the Earth's temperature is rising with possibly disastrous consequences.

2 Pollution from traffic fumes, the accumulation of waste and water pollution represent a major threat for the future.

7:2 Christianity and the environment

Why do Christians feel concerned about what is happening to the planet?

> *I believe in one God ... Maker of heaven and earth and of all things visible and invisible.*
>
> **... NICENE CHRISTIAN CREED**

Christians and non-Christians are often concerned with looking after the environment. Their reasons for doing so may be very different. Christians are often involved in conservation – taking steps to preserve the natural environment. Christian attitudes toward the environment reflect the basic belief that the whole universe, of which we are just a very small part, is the special creation of God *(see quotation above)*. Looking after it, therefore, is a spiritual and not only a practical responsibility.

Christian principles

The story of the creation of the universe and all forms of life is told in the opening chapters of the book of Genesis. The description that is given of God creating the world in six days is a poem, not a factual or scientific account. The poem speaks of the essential goodness of God's creation: "God looked at everything he had made and he was very pleased" (Genesis 1.31). The creation was perfect and God was satisfied with everything that He had accomplished. On the seventh day He rested, after six days of work.

The poem speaks of humanity's God-given responsibility in the task of 'ruling' over creation: "Have many children, so that your descendants will live all over the earth and bring it under their control. I am putting you in charge ..." (Genesis 1.28). These words have always caused problems for Christian believers – what exactly does it mean to bring the world of nature 'under control' and what is involved in being 'in charge'?

Certainly people in the past believed that they had been given a free licence to use the earth, and its many resources, as they pleased, and we are now paying the price for this. Christians have become increasingly aware that the universe has not been treated responsibly in the past and this teaching from Genesis is partly responsible for this. Christians believe that the world has been misused in the past because human beings are sinful by

nature and this shows in their relationships with each other and the world in which they live.

Jesus and reconciliation

Christians believe that the coming of Jesus was intended to reconcile (bring together) human beings with God. He also came to reconcile human beings with the world of nature. When the world ends, and Jesus returns to rule, this reconciliation will be complete. In the meantime, human beings must treat this planet with great respect and care *(see quotation from Hildegard of Bingen)*. The universe is waiting to be restored to the glory that God intended for His work of creation. Paul wrote about this:

> *... there was the hope that creation itself would one day be set free from its slavery to decay and share the glorious freedom of the children of God. For we know that up to the present time all of creation groans with pain, like the pain of childbirth. But it is not creation alone which groans; we who have the Spirit as the first of God's gifts also groan within ourselves, as we wait for God to make us his children and set our whole being free.*
>
> **... THE BIBLE (ROMANS 8.21–23)**

Christians believe that human beings have been called by God to be 'stewards' of the world of creation. This means that each generation is responsible for passing on God's good gifts to the next generation. Clearly they are expected to hand these gifts on in a satisfactory condition. Our children, and their children, have the right to expect nothing less. In practice, this means that this generation needs to take adequate steps to deal with the problems of pollution and the depletion of invaluable resources. Many Christians join with others to engage in this struggle. Many of them belong to movements like Friends of the Earth and Greenpeace, to put into practice the principles that Christians believe go to the very heart of their faith.

> *All of creation God gives to humankind to use. If this privilege is misused, God's justice permits creation to punish humanity.*
>
> **... HILDEGARD OF BINGEN, TWELFTH-CENTURY CHRISTIAN MYSTIC**

1. What is the difference between the way in which Christians look at the world in which they live and the way in which other people might do so?

2. Describe **TWO** things that Christians could take from the story of creation in the book of Genesis.

3.a. What word do Christians use when they speak of human responsibility for the environment?

   b. What do you understand this word to mean?

4. Read the quote from Hildegard of Bingen. Produce **TWO** examples from recent years that show how pollution or destruction of the habitat causes nature 'to punish humanity'.

> When I look at the sky, which you have made, at the moon and stars, which you set in their places – what are human beings, that you think of them; mere mortals that you care for them?
>
> ... *THE BIBLE (PSALM 8.3–4)*

IMPORTANT WORDS

Conservation; protecting and looking after the natural resources in the world and the environment that sustains them

Creation; the universe or the world that God has created and the act of creating it

Environment; conditions that influence the development or growth of plants, animals and people

Stewardship; the act of looking after something, the world and all that is in it, with which human beings have been entrusted

Think about ...

Why have people not taken much greater care of the world in which they live? Is it, as Christians would say, because of human sinfulness? Is it that human beings do not understand the serious consequences of their actions? Is there some other reason? What do you think?

▲ Many Christians support recycling as an important way of looking after God's creation.

SUMMARY

1 The Christian approach to the problems facing the planet begin with the belief that the universe was created by God and that human beings have a special responsibility to look after it.

2 In the Christian understanding human beings are 'stewards' – entrusted with receiving, caring for and passing on the planet in perfect condition.

3 Christians believe that Jesus came to reconcile human beings, and the universe, to God.

7:3 Judaism, Islam and Hinduism, and the environment

Why do Jews, Muslims and Hindus feel concerned about how the environment is treated?

▮ JUDAISM

Looking after nature. The Jewish holy books, especially the Torah, emphasise the importance of looking after the world that God has made. Both Jews and Christians share the same creation story in Genesis 1 and 2, with emphasis upon the activity of God in creation culminating with God pleased with everything that He had made. The land created by God must be looked after. The Torah stipulates that the agricultural land of Israel must be allowed to lie fallow for one year in every seven to allow it to recover *(see It's a fact)*.

There were other laws in Israel to safeguard the land and its produce. Fruit could not be taken from a tree, for instance, which was less than two years old whilst the owner could not profit from the tree in the third year. It was only in the fourth year after planting that the fruit from the tree could be sold. Today trees are planted in Israel by Jews from all over the world to celebrate such events as weddings and barmitzvahs.

Creation is good. Rabbis highlight that the Genesis account of creation continually notes that God's work is 'good'. The only part that is not described in this way is the creation of 'man'. In his activities, man is told to always think about the effect of what he is doing on the environment. This is particularly true when a battle is going on; the Torah states that great care must be taken not to damage the trees around a city that is being besieged.

▮ ISLAM

> *It is He who hath made you (His) agents, inheritors of the earth.*
>
> **... THE QUR'AN (6.165)**

Creation is Allah's gift. Muslims believe that Allah made the world and everything that is in it. Human beings are the most important part of this creation and they have been given the responsibility of looking after the creation, acting as its guardians *(see quotation)*. The world has been given to the human race to use, but they must do this responsibly. Muslims must use their skills to make sure that responsible use is made of the planet's natural resources with neither waste nor extravagance. Nature is a resource that Allah, in His great love, has bestowed on mankind but He remains the owner of all that exists. On Judgement Day, Muslims will be questioned by Allah about the way they have used all the natural resources He has liberally given to them.

Tawhid. The responsibility of looking after nature has been given to the ummah – the worldwide community of Muslims. It is the responsibility of the ummah to make sure that, when damage takes place to the environment, compensation is paid by the person responsible. This is because of the Muslim belief in tawhid, the unity of all creation. Under the unity of Allah, all creation exists in perfect balance and this must be respected. It is a serious matter to upset this balance in any way.

▮ HINDUISM

> *The Earth is our mother and we are all her children.*
>
> **... HINDU SAYING**

Respecting all life. Respect and reverence for the natural world are basic parts of Hindu thinking. The belief of ahimsa mean that harming any living thing is the same as hurting a friend or relative. Many plants are regarded as holy, whilst animals, such as the bull and tiger, are used to represent the different gods. The most sacred of all animals in Hinduism is the cow. Showing a reverence for it is an expression of gratitude for the whole of life. This is because the cow is a great source of nourishment. Even the dung of the cow is valued as manure as fuel as well as being used for plastering floors.

Vegetarianism and conservation. Hindus do not eat beef for religious reasons. Some Hindus eat mutton and chicken. Since Hindus regard the whole universe as a manifestation of God, protecting it is a religious duty. The well-being of mankind is seen as depending on the proper and careful use of natural resources. One Hindu organisation that has had a considerable influence in recent years has been the Chipko Movement; members use non-violent resistance to influence natural resources policy in India. Women in India have linked hands around trees to stop them being felled.

Tasks

1.a. Describe **TWO** ways in which the Torah encourages Jews to look after the environment.

b. Why do you think rules were developed relating to the treatment of trees in Israel?

2. How do Muslims try to put into practice the idea that they are guardians, appointed by Allah, to look after nature?

3.a. How do Hindus show that they respect all life?

b. What is the Chipko Movement?

SUMMARY

1 The Torah emphasises the need to look after nature. Land was allowed to lay fallow for one year in seven so that its strength could be renewed. Every human must bear in mind the effect on nature of their actions.

2 Muslims believe that nature is Allah's gift and that they are its guardians. Human beings must treat it responsibly. They will be held to account on the Day of Judgement for their actions.

3 The Hindu belief in ahimsa means that nature must be treated with great respect. The cow is a sacred animal and beef is not eaten. Many Hindus are vegetarians. Natural resources must be used with great care.

▲ The Torah, which this man is reading, emphasises the importance of looking after God's creation.

7:4 Animal rights

Do animals have rights?

> *The greatness of a nation and its moral progress can be judged by the way its animals are treated.*
>
> *... MAHATMA GANDHI*

Animals and human beings have had a very long association. In the past, animals were used as transport, hunting assistants, for protection, companionship, food and clothing and also, more recently, in medical research. Human beings have also used selective breeding for hundreds of years to provide varieties of animals that are most suitable for different purposes and to satisfy the fancies of their owners. As a result most domestic animals would now find it very difficult to survive in the wild.

Animal rights

Towards the end of the nineteenth century, Henry Salt introduced the term 'animal rights' when he wrote a book of that name. Since then many charities and organisations have been set up to safeguard the rights that we now believe animals should have. They seek to guarantee that:

- animals can live in a way that is in keeping with their nature
- animals can live free from harm and unnecessary danger
- animals are protected from abuse and cruelty
- animals are not be exploited by human beings.

Animals are protected by many of the rights that apply to human beings. In addition, there are particular abuses against which animals need to be protected. Amongst these are factory farming, vivisection, the use of animals for cosmetic testing and the use of animals for entertainment. In amongst these issues are questions which divide animal rights supporters. Two important issues are often raised.

- Should animals be used in experiments that will, ultimately, benefit the human race? Can experiments that harm animals ever be morally justified?
- Should there be a limit on the amount of violence and civil disobedience that is justified to defend animals?

IT'S A FACT

The number of animals in the UK is astonishing – including over 130 million chickens, ducks and geese, 9 million pigs and 58 million sheep and cows.

Blood sports

When discussing the relationship between human beings and animals the question of blood sports is probably the most controversial issue. A bill was passed in Scotland in 2001 banning fox hunting. In 2002 the government in England and Wales affirmed its intention to ban fox hunting and other blood sports elsewhere in the UK.

There are fewer than 200 fox-hunts in Britain and they kill about 25 000 foxes each year. Farmers argue that the fox is a major pest in the countryside killing lambs, poultry and other wildlife. Opponents of fox hunting argue that the fox is chased and killed for sport and excitement and not merely to keep down the number of foxes. Opponents of fox hunting claim that killing foxes cruelly should not be allowed as a sport. The debate continues.

Animal experimentation

It is generally accepted in the UK that animals should not be used for experiments to produce better cosmetics. Their use in medical research, though, is far more complex as an issue. Some of the great medical advances in the past – including the development of insulin to treat diabetes and vaccines against whooping cough and diphtheria – involved the use of animals. These discoveries have saved the lives of thousands of people. The use of animals in such experiments is called 'vivisection'. Opponents of vivisection argue that animal experiments are becoming increasingly unnecessary. More speedy and satisfactory results can now be obtained using other methods. However, research is being carried out to see whether animal organs can be successfully transplanted into humans in the future.

Vegetarianism

Many people choose to be vegetarians (not eating meat) or vegans (not eating or using any animal products). They may do this for religious reasons – many Hindus and Buddhists are vegetarian – or because they are against factory farming.

> *Every year in Britain tens of thousands of wild animals are chased, terrified, and brutally killed in the name of sport.*
>
> *... THE NATIONAL ANTI-HUNT CAMPAIGN*

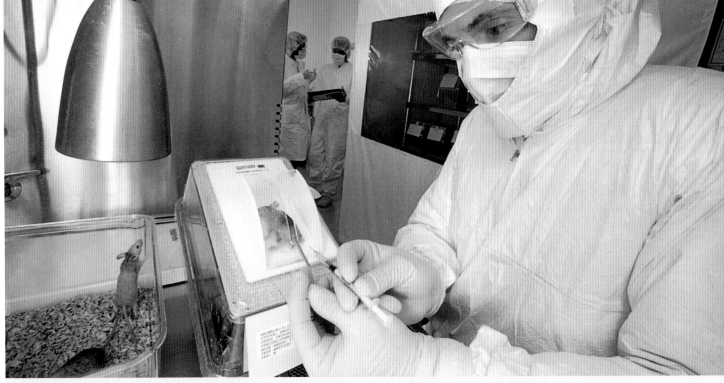

▲ People are divided over whether experiments on animals for medical purposes are justified or not.

Think about ...

Jeremy Bentham (1748–1832), a philosopher, insisted that since animals can feel pain human beings have moral responsibilities towards them. What responsibilities do you think humans have towards animals?

IMPORTANT WORDS

Animal rights; many people believe that animals have the right to be treated humanely

Tasks

1.a. What is a vegetarian?

b. What is a vegan?

c. Do you think that animals should be used for food? Present **TWO** arguments in favour and **TWO** against.

2. 'For too long we have misused animals for our own needs and pleasure. It is now time to stop doing this.' Do you agree? Produce **TWO** arguments in favour and **TWO** against the comment.

3. Record arguments for and against the use of animals in medical research.

SUMMARY

1 The idea that animals have rights is comparatively new. It means that animals should be able to live natural lives, free from harm and danger and protected from abuse and cruelty. Animals should not be exploited by human beings.

2 Fox hunting is a controversial issue. Supporters believe that they reduce the fox population. Opponents believe that hunting foxes for fun is very cruel.

3 Experiments on animals in the past have led to the development of many drugs and vaccines. With genetic engineering this will become less necessary.

4 Some people are vegetarian or vegan for religious or personal reasons.

How do Christian attitudes to animals differ from attitudes to human beings?

> In the end, a lack of regard for the life and well-being of an animal must bring with it a lowering of man's self-respect, and it is important to our Christian faith that this is God's world and that man is the trustee and steward of God's creation.
>
> **... DR ROBERT RUNCIE,**
> **FORMER ARCHBISHOP OF CANTERBURY**

Christians believe that human beings are different from animals. Human beings alone are made 'in the image of God', as the story of creation in the book of Genesis teaches, whilst animals are made for humans to rule over and control. The implications of this difference are very important. The main difference between the two forms of life is that whilst human beings have a soul and so are 'spiritual' beings, animals do not. The Roman Catholic Church does not believe that animals have any 'rights' as such, although this does not mean that human beings can mistreat or exploit them in any way.

The Jewish and Christian scriptures describe a vision in which humans and animals coexist in a harmonious world where animals are not exploited. In this perfect world animals that are natural enemies will also exist peacefully alongside each other.

> Wolves and sheep will live together in peace, and leopards will lie down with young goats. Calves and lion cubs will feed together, and little children will take care of them. Cows and bears will eat together, and their calves and cubs will lie down in peace. Lions will eat straw as cattle do. Even a baby will not be harmed if it plays with a poisonous snake.
>
> **... THE BIBLE (ISAIAH 11.6–8)**

In the New Testament, Jesus taught that God's covenant (agreement) Jesus brought was with all forms of life. Even the death of a single sparrow does not go unnoticed by a God, who cares for the whole of creation.

Christians and vivisection

Most Christians are happy to eat animals for food, although there are some vegetarians who refrain from eating meat for religious reasons. There is not a long Christian tradition of concern for animals although, in recent years, the feeling has grown that all animals, as part of God's creation, deserve respect. God may have given humans authority over them but that authority must be exercised with care. Often that has not happened in the past.

Vivisection, the use of animals in scientific experiments, raises problems. The different Christian Churches have decided that experiments carried out on animals for essential medical research are acceptable. As the quotation from the Church of England Board of Social Responsibility points out, the value of animal life has always been considered by Christians to be less than the value of human life. If one has be sacrificed to save the other then that is the way things must be. Clearly any form of experimentation to aid the development of better cosmetics, or for some other trivial reason, is not covered by this. Even if an experiment is considered to be medically necessary every step must be taken to reduce the amount of suffering involved for the animal.

The Roman Catholic Church agrees with this teaching. It teaches that experiments on animals can be justified from a Christian point of view as long as human lives will be saved as a result. As long as there are people who are suffering in the world, animals should not be given an exaggerated degree of importance. In today's world many people bestow far more love and attention on their animals than they should. Christians should take a sensible but unemotional attitude towards animals and pets. Cruelty towards animals, though, is entirely unacceptable. This is why many Christians feel distinctly unhappy about blood sports, factory farming and the transportation of live animals across countries to be slaughtered. It is almost impossible to do any of these without subjecting the animals involved to inhumane conditions, often for no valid reason.

> Christian tradition asserts that animals have been created by God and that they have an intrinsic value for that reason. Nevertheless, the value of animals has always been seen as secondary to that of human beings made in God's image and placed in a central position in creation. Human beings have both an affinity with and an obligation to animals.
>
> **... CHURCH OF ENGLAND BOARD OF SOCIAL RESPONSIBILITY**

▲ Christians believe that caring for animals is part of their stewardship of the natural world.

 For only a penny you can buy two sparrows, yet not one sparrow falls to the ground without your Father's consent ... you are worth much more than many sparrows!

... THE BIBLE (MATTHEW 10.29–30)

Tasks

1. **What is the basic motivation of all groups working to secure animal rights?**

2.a. **Why do Christians believe that animals are different from human beings?**

b. **What is the Christian vision for the relationship between animals and human beings?**

3. **What is the basic Christian attitude towards experiments being carried out on animals?**

! Think about ...

Christians maintain that whilst animals should always be treated with respect, their lives are not as important as a human life.
a. Do you agree with this?
b. Do you think this view makes experiments on animals as part of medical research acceptable?

SUMMARY

1 Christians believe that animals are an essential part of God's creation but are not equal to human beings. Only human beings are made in God's image. Christians believe human beings and animals should live together harmoniously. Jesus said that not even the death of a sparrow goes unnoticed by God.

2 Christians accept that experiments on animals may be necessary in the search for cures to human diseases.

7:6 Judaism, Islam and Hinduism, and animal rights

How does the attitude of Jews and Muslims towards animals differ from that of Hindus?

> Teachers must see that children respect the smallest and largest animals, which, like people, have feelings. The child who gets enjoyment from the convulsions of an injured beetle will grow up to be insensitive to human suffering.
>
> ... RABBI HIRSCH

■ JUDAISM

Permission to eat meat. In the Jewish scriptures human beings are given permission to eat meat. At the same time they are given laws about which animals they can, and can't, eat. Animals and birds can only be eaten if they are killed in a certain way and the blood totally drained out of their carcasses. Animals must be killed by a speedy slitting of the carotid artery – called 'shechita'. Although some Jews choose to be vegetarian, the majority only eat food which is 'kosher' – 'fit' to be eaten and killed in accordance with the regulations in the Jewish scriptures.

Treatment of animals. The rules about how animals are to be killed underline the Jewish teaching that animals should always be treated with kindness and respect. It is also believed that working animals are entitled to a day of rest. In the story of creation, humans were given 'dominion' over animals since they were intended to be of use to the human race. Animals must never be treated cruelly although Jews accept that they can be used in medical research and that their organs can be used for transplantation into the bodies of humans.

■ ISLAM

> A good deed done to a beast is as good as doing good to a human being; while an act of cruelty to a beast is as good as an act of cruelty to a human being.
>
> ... THE PROPHET MUHAMMAD, HADITH

Muslims and animal rights. The starting point for a Muslim understanding of animal rights is the belief that Allah created all life for human beings to treat with great respect and care. Muslims are allowed to hunt animals, but only for food, not for sport. If someone has killed an animal unnecessarily then that animal will testify against that person on the Day of Judgement and the person will be refused entry into heaven. Experiments on animals are allowed as long as they are important in the battle against human disease. In this case every attempt must be made to limit the animal's suffering. Experimentation for cosmetic or any other purpose is strictly forbidden.

Ihram

Ihram is the practice of undertaking a Hajj (pilgrimage to Makkah), which is one of the Five Pillars of Islam. The pilgrimage ends with the celebration of the festival of Eid-ul-Adha at which animals are slaughtered and their meat distributed to everyone. Concerning the slaughter of animals, two rules are laid down:

- an animal must not be slaughtered in front of other animals
- a person must not slaughter an animal that they have bred themselves.

■ HINDUISM

The Laws of Manu, an important holy book, expresses the belief that all forms of life are sacred – insects, fish, birds, animals and human beings. As a result, all forms of life must be treated with equal respect. The faith expresses this respect by frequently placing its gods in the company of animals. Siva is often linked with a bull; Vishnu frequently took the form of animals; whilst Ganesha has an elephant head. When Krishna came to earth he looked after cows and spoke to the birds in their own language. Following these examples most Hindus are vegetarians since ahimsa – a belief in non-violence – is a very important Hindu belief and extends to animals as well as human beings.

The cow enjoys the respect of all Hindus and is never slaughtered – it provides so much that is basic to life in India in the way of food (milk, cream, cheese), transport and fuel (dung).

> No person should kill animals helpful to all. Rather by serving them, one should attain happiness.
>
> ... YAJUR VEDA (13.47)

Tasks

1. a. What is the Jewish attitude towards eating meat?

  b. How are Jews told that they should treat animals?

2. a. What is the Muslim attitude towards the treatment of animals?

  b. What is the link between the festival of Eid-ul-Adha and the sacrifice of animals?

3. Explain the attitude of Hindus towards animals.

4. 'Hindus believe that animals are as sacred as human beings.' Do you agree with them? If so, why?

SUMMARY

1 Jews are given permission by their scriptures to eat meat – but only if animals are killed in a certain way. Jews must only eat kosher food. Human beings have dominion over animals but they must always treat them kindly.

2 Muslims believe that Allah created all life – human beings have dominion over animals but must treat them respectfully. Animals are slaughtered and eaten during the festival of Eid-ul-Adha.

3 To Hindus, all forms of life are sacred. Hindu gods and animals are frequently shown together. The doctrine of ahimsa covers all forms of life. The cow is a sacred animal.

▼ The cow is a sacred animal in India and never killed by Hindus.

Exam help ...

This chapter asks you to explore the relationship between the different world religions and the problems confronting our use of the environment. All of them stress that all life was created by God, that human beings are God's stewards and that responsibility for the environment is part of this stewardship. Animals are a central part of God's creation. Most religions recognise that animals have rights although you need to be aware that those rights are not the same as those enjoyed by human beings. You also need to be able to show that even within the same religion, believers do not necessarily hold the same views about animal rights.

1.   Explain the teachings of Christianity that could be applied to the modern problem of pollution.

1.   Christians look upon pollution as the result of human behaviour, as a spiritual rather than a purely practical problem. This gives the problem another dimension. The spiritual nature of the problem stems from the Christian belief that the whole of creation is a special work of God. This is God's world.

*   The poem of creation found in the Bible emphasises that God created the world: it was seen by God to be good and God was pleased with His handiwork. By resting after the six days of creation, God was showing that the work of creation was perfect and finished.

*   Human beings were given the responsibility of 'ruling' over creation. They were to be the 'stewards' of creation, inheriting it from the last generation and handing it over the next.

*   Jesus came to reconcile (bring together) human beings and the world of nature. This reconciliation will be completed when Jesus returns at the end of time. In the meantime, human beings must treat the world of nature with immense care.

*   Christians must work with others – fellow Christians and non-Christians – to keep the universe in as good a condition as possible.

2.   Explain the teaching of ONE religion, other than Christianity, on the need to look after the world.

2.   The chosen religion is Islam.

*   Muslims believe that they have been called by Allah to maintain the balance of creation and follow the way of life set out for them by Allah. Anyone who upsets this balance has sinned and must pay for any damage they have caused.

*   The most basic Muslim belief is in tawhid – the unity of all things under Allah. Pollution upsets this. The world that Allah has created is fragile and the balance is easily upset. The responsibility for looking after the world has been given to the ummah – the worldwide community of Muslim believers.

*   The world is Allah's gift to the human race. Natural resources are part of that gift. It is wrong to treat them wastefully or with extravagance. Allah remains the owner of the world. On the Day of Judgement all human beings will be held to account.

3.   'Animals do not have any rights of their own. They simply exist to meet the needs of human beings.' Do you agree with this comment?

3.   The association of human beings with animals goes back a long way. Often animals have been exploited by humans. In the past, people did not believe that animals had rights. The term was first introduced in the nineteenth century.

*   Many people today accept that animals have rights but not the same rights as human beings. They have a right to live in a way that is in keeping with their nature. Wild animals should be able to live in the wild. They should not be exposed to unnecessary harm or danger. They should not be treated with cruelty nor should they be exploited by humans.

continued ...

- Most people agree that animals need to be protected from practices such as factory farming, aspects of vivisection (experiments carried out on animals) and the use of animals for entertainment. Surveys show that the majority of people in this country are against the hunting of wild animals – especially hares, deer and foxes. There are regularly calls, supported by many MPs, to ban blood sports.

- Religion has encouraged the idea that animals exist for the benefit of humans. This theme is found in the Genesis account of creation. Animals are used for sacrifices in Islam during festival time. Thousands of years ago they were used in the Jewish sacrificial system. Many people now feel unhappy with any religious practice that encourages people to think of animals as tools.

4. 'Christians do not agree with each other about animal rights.' Is this comment accurate? Show, in your answer, that you have considered more than one point of view.

4. There are many points about the animal world on which Christians agree. They believe that animals and humans are essentially different – human beings have a spiritual awareness and animals do not – expressed in the statement that human beings are 'made in the image of God'.

- Many Christians do not agree with the Roman Catholic belief that because animals do not have a soul they do not any rights. However, it does not follow from this that Roman Catholics feel animals should not be treated with love and respect. The belief that animals do not have any rights means that many Christians do not have a problem with vivisection.

- To give animals rights means that the value of animal life is the same as that of human life. Most Christians would not agree with this. The Christian Churches agree that experiments on animals are acceptable if they are to further medical research – because human life is much more important than animal life. Christians, though, do not all agree over such controversial issues as factory farming and hunting.

5. Describe the attitude of ONE religion, other than Christianity, towards animal rights.

5. The chosen religion is Judaism.

- The Jewish scriptures gave human beings permission to eat meat. At the same time, it must be meat killed in a certain way (kosher) with the blood totally drained out of the carcase.

- The laws in the Jewish scriptures underline that animals must always be treated properly. They are to be rested from their work for one day each week – this follows from the fact that human beings give up one day to rest as well.

- Animals are here to serve man. To make this possible they must be treated with care – never cruelly. Part of the service of animals to human life is their use in medical research. Jews find this acceptable. Another part of their service is the use of organs taken from animals to save human life; again, Jews find this acceptable.

CHAPTER 8: CONFLICT AND CRIME

8:1　War – the facts

What is the cost of war?

> I pursued my enemies and overtook them; I did not turn back till I destroyed them. I struck them down, and they could rise no more; they lay fallen at my feet.
>
> ... THE TANAKH (PSALM 18.38–39)

War has always been a fact of life. There is certainly no reason to think that human beings are finding new and peaceful ways of solving their conflicts and disagreements. The period since the end of the Second World War, in 1945, has seen more conflicts than any other similar period in history.

Wars of different kinds

During the twentieth century more that 100 million people died throughout the world as a direct result of war. The nature of war has changed during the last 100 years. During the First World War (1914–18) 95 per cent of casualties were soldiers, but in recent years up to 90 per cent of those killed in conflict have been civilians. In the First World War, 9 million people died and there were over 21 million who were seriously injured. In the Second World War (1939–45) there were 55 million deaths of which 16 million were soldiers and 39 million civilians. With modern weapons, and the way that wars are now fought, civilians will always pay a much higher price than professional soldiers.

A war is any armed conflict that lasts for longer than 60 minutes and in which regular armed forces from at least one side are involved. These conflicts fall into three groups.

1. **Conflicts between nations.** Since 1945 there have been more than 270 armed conflicts.

2. **Civil wars and wars of 'liberation'.** When the two main tribes in Rwanda were involved in a civil war in the 1990s it is thought that more than 1 million people from one tribe alone were slaughtered.

3. **War against terrorism.** The conflict in Afghanistan fits into this category. The war in Afghanistan began after the events of 11 September 2001. The war against terrorism is unlike other war.

The cost of war

The cost of war must be measured in terms of:

- **Destruction.** The number of people killed and injured; the destruction of towns, villages and countryside and the number of families whose lives have been shattered all need to be taken into account when considering the cost of war. When the Allied Forces led by the USA and Britain undertook the Gulf War in 1991 against Iraq the cost is believed to have been $71 billion but this did not take into account the cost of rebuilding a devastated land.

- **Refugees.** War forces thousands of people to leave their homes and, often, their countries as well. This turns them into refugees, people without a home. This is a lasting effect of war.

- **Economic cost.** War inevitably destroys homes, crops, water, power supplies, industry, hospitals and schools. All of these vital services have to be replaced once the war is over. This uses up vast amounts of money – money and resources that poor countries cannot afford. Angola, one of the poorest of countries, suffered a civil war throughout the 1980s and 1990s. The developing countries of the world spend 22 times as much money on buying military weapons as they do on feeding their poorest citizens and improving the facilities in the country.

IT'S A FACT

In 2001 there were estimated to be 12 million refugees in the world. Some Palestinian Arabs, dispossessed when the State of Israel was formed in 1948, have been refugees since that date: they do not have a country of their own.

✓ Exam tip
Although you should never become bogged down with facts and figures a few of them, carefully used, can give your answer greater substance.

> The arms race is one of the greatest curses on the human race and the harm it inflicts on the poor is more than can be endured.
>
> ... CATECHISM OF THE CATHOLIC CHURCH

▲ In 1991, Kurdish refugees from Iraq crossed into Turkey and made camps in the mountains.

Tasks

1.a. What is a war?

b. Into which **THREE** groups can wars be divided? Write a sentence about each of them.

2. Describe **ONE** change that took place in the way that war was conducted in the twentieth century.

3.a. What is a refugee?

b. Why are there refugees?

c. Why do you think that the refugee problem has been described as one of the greatest challenges facing the modern world?

4. What is the cost that has to be paid because of war?

SUMMARY

1 Modern warfare is very different from that in previous centuries. The civilian casualty rate is much higher.

2 There are different kinds of war – wars between nations, civil wars and wars against terrorism.

3 The cost of war can be measured in terms of the destruction, the number of refugees created and the economic cost to the countries involved.

8:2 Two modern conflicts

What created conflict in the Middle East?

The United Nations was set up in New York after the end of the Second World War. It was established to promote international peace and security and 'to save succeeding generations from the scourge of war'. The United Nations also encourages nations to work together to solve their economic, social and humanitarian problems, as well as promoting human rights throughout the world.

Most people agree that the original intention of the United Nations – to prevent war and promote peace – was unrealistic. It could never hope to secure world peace and this mission has clearly failed. Occasionally nations debate problems rather than use force to solve them but, far too often, they resort to force before they seek reconciliation. On occasions a United Nations force is sent in to keep the peace in a troubled area.

The Middle East

> We are destined to live together in the same land. We say to you today in a loud and clear voice, 'Enough of blood and tears. Enough. We have no desire for revenge, we harbour no hatred towards you ... . We are today giving peace a chance.'
>
> **... YITZHAK RABIN, ISRAEL'S PRIME MINISTER, SPEAKING TO PALESTINIANS, 1993**

Since the 1990s one of the most troublesome conflicts in the world has been that between the Israelis and the Palestinians.

- Jews believe that they were given the land of Israel, called 'the Promised Land', by God in the distant past. King David conquered the city of Jerusalem around 1000BCE and this became the capital of Israel. The Romans expelled the Jews from Judea in 132CE and the territory was renamed Palestine. For very different reasons this city is sacred to Jews, Muslims and Christians. Jerusalem is important to the Jews because the Temple, the focus of their religion, was situated there. Jerusalem is important to Muslims as the third most important site in Islam.

- Centuries later the ancient land that had been called Israel became an Arab state (a Muslim country). During

the First World War, the British captured the land and, in the famous 1917 Balfour Declaration, offered to establish a Jewish homeland there. At the same time the Palestinians were promised an independent State.

- After the First World War Jewish migration to the area from Eastern Europe continued. It was still ruled at the time by the British. When the Second World War ended the Jews in the country revolted and set up the State of Israel in 1948. The British were forced to leave. Many Palestinians went to what is now Jordan, whilst others became permanent refugees.

- In 1967 the Six Day War saw a victory for Israel over her Arab neighbours. Israel took the land to the west of the River Jordan – known as the West Bank. It is this land that it is envisaged will form the basis of a Palestinian state.

- In 1987 a Palestinian uprising (Intifada) in the West Bank saw the beginning of extensive terrorist activity in the area. These actions died down for several years but re-ignited in 2001 with many suicide bombings that have resulted in hundreds of Palestinians and Israelis being killed. The Israeli army went into the West Bank towns in search of terrorists. Hundreds were killed, including many civilians.

The Israelis say they will end the conflict if the Palestinians recognise their borders and guarantee their security. The Palestinians want an independent state. There is much dispute over Jerusalem as it contains many different holy sites. Palestinians believe that the building of Jewish settlements in the occupied territories means the Israelis do not intend to leave the land. In 2002, the stalemate remained.

Afghanistan

- In 1978 a Communist government took over in Kabul, the capital of Afghanistan. It retained power because the USSR sent supplies and soldiers. In 1979 the USSR sent in its army to fight against the rebels in the country. The Russian army could not defeat the rebels and it left in 1989. In 1994 a group of Muslim extremists, the Taliban, took control of the country and imposed a very strict form of Islam on the population. They also gave refuge to a wealthy terrorist, Osama bin Laden, and allowed him to use the country to plan his worldwide terrorist activities. On 11 September 2001, bin Laden organised attacks on the World Trade Center twin towers in New York in which over 3000 people were killed. An American-led invasion of Afghanistan overthrew the Taliban three months later, but by June 2002 bin Laden had still not been found.

▲ Israeli tanks entered the West Bank town of Jenin, 5 June 2002. A Palestinian suicide attacker exploded a powerful car bomb next to an Israeli bus killing at least 17 people in a major setback to international peace efforts. Hours later, Israeli tanks rolled into the bomber's home town.

 Think about ...

There is a very important religious component in both the Middle East and the Afghanistan conflicts. Why do you think that religion has sometimes led to fanaticism?

Tasks

1.a. Who conquered Jerusalem around 1000BCE?

 b. Why is Jerusalem such an important city in the world today?

2. What are the Israeli and the Palestinian demands in the Middle East?

3.a. Who are the Taliban?

 b. What happened in Afghanistan in 2002 and how was this connected with what happened in New York in 2001?

4. Choose **ONE** conflict in the modern world and explain why it is being fought.

SUMMARY

1 Some Israelis believe that God has given them the land of Israel. The State of Israel came into existence in 1948. The Israelis have taken land and forced many Palestinians to become refugees. The Palestinians want a land of their own. The Israelis want peace and security for their country.

2 Since 1993 the Taliban controlled Afghanistan. They harboured Osama bin Laden who was behind the destruction of the World Trade Center in September 2001. The US retaliated by attacking the Taliban in Afghanistan but could not find bin Laden.

8:3 Nuclear war

Why have nuclear weapons opened up new issues in the debate about war in the modern world?

> " *The monstrous power of nuclear weapons will have fatal consequences for life on earth. Justice, right reason and humanity therefore urgently demand that the arms race should cease … . Nuclear weapons must be banned.* "
>
> **… ROMAN CATHOLIC DOCUMENT, PACEM IN TERRIS, 1963**

The first atomic bombs were developed by the USA during the Second World War and dropped for the first, and only, time on the Japanese cities of Hiroshima and Nagazaki in 1945.

The nuclear club

When the first atomic bombs were dropped, only the USA had the capacity to manufacture such weapons. It was not long, however, before other countries developed the raw materials and the necessary technology to join the 'nuclear club'. The basic ingredient needed to make a nuclear bomb is plutonium and this is produced by nuclear reactors.

Soon the 'nuclear club' expanded. In 1949 the USSR developed, and tested, its own nuclear weapons. A nuclear arms race soon began between the USA and the USSR as they competed against each other to produce bigger, better and more powerful nuclear weapons. Within a few years this club had five members, with France, the UK and China joining the USA and the USSR. The modern nuclear club is much larger and is thought to include Israel, Pakistan, India, South Africa, Iran and North Korea. Many other countries are also thought to have the ability to make nuclear weapons and may already have done so.

The balance of terror

Although there have been over 270 armed conflicts since 1945, none of them developed into a worldwide conflict. Some people argue that this was because of the 'balance of terror' which exists in the world. This stops one country using nuclear weapons because of the fear of what other countries will do in retaliation. Others do not find this argument convincing. They point out that the world almost suffered a nuclear catastrophe on at least one occasion, such as during the Cuban Missile Crisis in 1962.

The 'balance of terror' seems a flimsy foundation on which to build world peace.

The deterrent argument

The debate about nuclear weapons revolves around whether or not such weapons act as a deterrent.

Nuclear weapons – a deterrent

Some people believe that when a particular country has nuclear weapons this will stop other countries using theirs.

- It seems to work as there has not been a world war since 1945.
- The possession of nuclear weapons is bound to deter others because of the immense consequences of using such weapons against a country that also has them.
- Nuclear weapons give a country a bargaining chip – they can give up such weapons if other countries agree to do so.

Nuclear weapons – not a deterrent

Some people believe countries that develop nuclear weapons are playing a dangerous game.

- The growth of nuclear weapons – and the number of countries now having them – make their use more, not less, likely.
- The use of such weapons could not be justified under any circumstances; other countries know this and so the deterrent argument does not work.
- The vast amounts of money spent on nuclear weapons could be far better used in solving the problems of poverty, hunger and bad housing.
- Although some steps have been taken towards disarmament, these steps are very small and the world remains a very dangerous place.

Disarmament

It is clear that the countries of the world do not need their vast arsenals of nuclear weapons. Everyone agrees that disarmament is essential for future peace. There are two possible approaches to this:

1. **Unilateral disarmament.** This calls for one country to give up its arms in the hope that others will be encouraged to follow. Both the Roman Catholic and Anglican Churches have encouraged this approach in the past but it is unlikely to happen.
2. **Multilateral disarmament.** This involves every country with nuclear weapons disarming at the same time. A few steps have been taken along this path but the journey is going to be long – if it ever happens!

▲ The mushroom-shaped cloud of a nuclear explosion.

 Before the bomb, man had to live with the idea of his death as an individual; from now onwards, mankind has to live with the idea of death as a species.

... ARTHUR KOESTLER, AUTHOR

IMPORTANT WORDS

Nuclear weapon; a bomb or a weapon that takes its destructive force from the energy released by a nuclear reaction

Tasks

1. What is the 'nuclear club'?

2.a. What is the 'balance of terror'?

   b. Why do some people argue that the 'balance of terror' has kept peace in the world since 1945?

   c. Do you feel comfortable living in a world where peace is only kept by the balance of weapons held by different countries? Explain the reasons for your answer.

3. What are the arguments for and against the belief that nuclear weapons act as a deterrent in the modern world?

Think about ...

In the 1960s and 1970s people were terrified at the thought of nuclear weapons being used. Now many hardly seem to give it a thought. The threat, though, is no less. Why do you think people are not still worried?

SUMMARY

1 Many countries now have nuclear weapons and the number is growing. The first and only use of atomic weapons in war was against Japan in 1945. The countries that have nuclear weapons make up the so-called 'nuclear club'.

2 Since 1945 some argue that relative peace has been maintained through the balance of terror in the world – opposing sides having equally destructive weapons.

3 There are strong arguments for and against many countries having nuclear weapons.

4 Two kinds of disarmament are discussed – unilateral disarmament (one country disarming first) and multilateral disarmament (many countries disarming at the same time).

8:4 Holy wars, just wars and pacifism

What is the difference between a holy and a just war and can either be justified today?

>
> *Prepare for war; call your warriors.*
>
> **... THE BIBLE (JOEL 3.9)**
>

Christians believe that war is wrong. Most Christians, though, also believe that war is sometimes an unfortunate necessity to overcome evil. The Bible contains opposing viewpoints on war: there is mention of holy war as well as the opposing view from Jesus who told his followers to turn the other cheek when someone hits them (Matthew 5.39).

Holy war

The idea of a 'holy war', carried out on the authority of God, is prominent in the Old Testament. The Israelites had to fight their way into the Promised Land, the country that they believed God had given them to be their home. This is the country now known as Israel. Many battles were fought in the name of God to conquer the land but the final victory was always assured. In the eleventh century later during a series of bloody battles known as the Crusades, Christian armies, about to wage war against the Muslim army, were told by Pope Urban II:

- they were fighting for a holy and noble cause
- they were being led into battle by God
- since God was with them, those who opposed them were the enemies of God.

Holy wars are essentially wars of aggression launched against those thought to be the enemies of a particular faith. In past centuries Christians have fought holy wars. Today, a similar claim is sometimes made by Muslim fanatics who claim to be fighting a jihad, but the majority of Muslims believe that this is a misinterpretation of the teaching of the Qur'an.

Just war

> It is lawful to Christian men, at the commandment of the magistrate [government] to wear weapons and serve in wars.
>
> **... ARTICLE 37 OF THE CHURCH OF ENGLAND**

Christians have always realised that war is not compatible with the teaching of Jesus in the Gospels. To justify it, though, St Augustine put forward ideas to support a 'just' war and laid down some ground rules by which such a war should be fought. These were later developed by St Thomas Aquinas (1225–74), a Dominican friar. He taught that to be just a war must:

- be declared by the government of a country
- have a just cause, such as self-defence or the reclaiming of lost territory
- be for good, or against evil – law and order must always be restored.

The Catholic Church later added two more rules:

- war must be a last resort
- use only necessary and not excessive force.

Most Christians feel unhappy about claiming any conflict to be 'just' even though there seems to be evidence for this approach in the Bible. They point out that warfare in the thirteenth century, when the 'rules' were drawn up by Aquinas, was very different from warfare today. Even then, it was felt necessary to restrict conflict within certain limits and that could be done. Such a hope is unrealistic today. Modern warfare kills many more civilians than military personnel. Of the conflicts fought since the beginning of the twentieth century it would be impossible to claim that many of them were 'just'.

Pacifism

A pacifist is someone who is against all war and the use of violence in every possible situation. Not all pacifists are Christians, but many Christians are pacifists. They believe that there is a solid foundation in the life and teaching of Jesus to support a pacifist approach to life. Only one branch of the Christian Church, however, has officially adopted pacifism and that is the Quakers. They believe that the only way to achieve peace in the world today is to appeal to that part of God that is in every human being. In times of war most pacifists now register as 'conscientious objectors' carrying out war duties that do not involve the carrying and using of arms.

>
> *It is impossible to conceive of a just war in a nuclear age.*
>
> **... POPE JOHN XXIII**
>

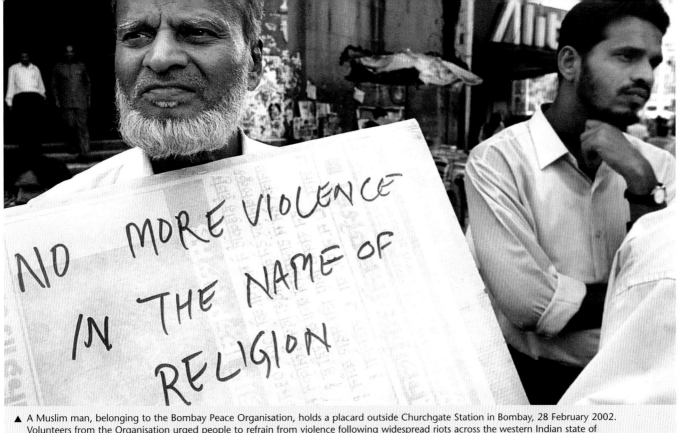

▲ A Muslim man, belonging to the Bombay Peace Organisation, holds a placard outside Churchgate Station in Bombay, 28 February 2002. Volunteers from the Organisation urged people to refrain from violence following widespread riots across the western Indian state of Gujarat in revenge for the 27 February train attack that left 58 Hindus dead.

IT'S A FACT

Mahatma Gandhi was a Hindu who believed in non-violence. He encouraged his followers in India to achieve their aims, the expulsion of the British from their country, by peaceful, non-violent means. He sometimes went on hunger strike to achieve his goals.

IMPORTANT WORDS

Holy war; a war fought in the belief that the will of God is being carried out and so final success is guaranteed

Just war; a war that is fought in the belief that the cause is just and that it should be fought according to certain 'just' principles

Pacifism; the belief that war and the use of violence are unacceptable in any situation; during a war pacifists are known as 'conscientious objectors'

Tasks

1. Write **TWO** sentences about each of the following:
   a. just war
   b. holy war
   c. pacifism.

2. What were the Christian soldiers, fighting against the Muslims in the Crusades, told by Pope Urban II?

3.a. With which **TWO** Christian thinkers is the idea of a 'just' war associated?
   b. What are the conditions laid down for a 'just' war?

4. Considering the weapons that are in the world do you think a 'just war' is possible today? Give **TWO** reasons for your answer.

SUMMARY

1 A holy war is a battle fought in the name of God: the final victory being justified for this reason.

2 A just war is one carried out for a just cause; conducted on certain just principles and one that safeguards the safety of civilians.

3 Pacifism is against the use of violence in any situation. The teaching of Jesus suggested that the pacifist approach was the only one in keeping with his principles.

8:5 Christianity and war

What is the Christian teaching about war?

> *Happy are those who work for peace; God will call them his children!*

... THE BIBLE (MATTHEW 5.9)

War and peace

Although the ideas of both holy and just wars have been associated with the Christian religion over the centuries, there is nothing in the teaching of Jesus to support either. Although there is evidence that Jesus supported a pacifist approach to life, not all Christians are pacifists. However, all Christians want peace. The Bible calls God 'the God of Peace' and Jesus 'the Prince of Peace'. The Old Testament looked forward to the time when the Messiah would arrive: the prophet Micah said that this would usher in a time of peace. Paul said that people who have been put right with God through faith 'have peace with God through our Lord Jesus Christ' (Romans 5.1). The biblical pattern is that peace with God will lead to peace with other human beings.

Peace means much more than simply not being at war. At the heart of the Christian message is the belief that the life and death of Jesus gives people peace with God and peace within themselves. It was in these terms that Jesus spoke of the peacemakers *(see quotation)* who would themselves be called 'the children of God'. They were called this because peace between God and human beings was the very heart of the message that Jesus came to bring.

Those who work for peace with God and peace between human beings are those who are continuing the very work that Jesus died to secure. Peace in society does not happen by accident. It needs to be worked for. It will involve the removal of injustice, poverty and hunger. Peace is only possible in a just and humane society in which all human beings feel valued and needed.

Violence is unacceptable

Taking its lead from the teaching of Jesus, it seems that the early Christian Church was almost totally pacifist. Very few Christians joined any army until the Emperor Constantine became a Christian at the start of the fourth century. Then Christianity became the religion of the Roman Empire and Christians felt able to join the armed forces.

Christians today would maintain that this was a departure from the ideals that Jesus came to teach. They would point to the commandment, 'Thou shalt not kill' in the Torah and maintain that killing, in any circumstances, is against the Christian ideal of love. They would point, in particular, to two passages in the Gospels to support their case:

- **Matthew 5.38–46.** Jewish justice was based on the principle that punishment should return like for like – 'an eye for an eye, a tooth for a tooth'. Jesus replaced this with another principle – violence should never be returned. Indeed, his followers should go a step further and meet an act of violence with one of love.

- **Luke 22.35–43.** At the Last Supper Jesus told his disciples that matters had come to a head. Jesus used the symbol of buying a sword but his disciples misunderstood what he was saying – they believed that he wanted them to fight to defend him. Later, in the Garden of Gethsemane, he ordered his disciples not to fight when he was arrested. One of them, Peter, cut off the ear of the High Priest's servant with his sword. Jesus told Peter that this, the way of violence, was not his way and he healed the man. As Jesus himself said, those who live by the sword will also die by the sword.

▼ In the First World War pacifists refused combat duties and instead worked for the Red Cross.

It is very difficult to escape the conclusion that Jesus himself was a pacifist and that he wanted his followers to act in this way as well. A famous 'declaration' to this effect was presented by Quakers to King Charles II in 1660 and this summarises perfectly the pacifist position.

 We utterly deny all outward wars and strife; and fightings with outward weapons, for any end or under any pretence whatsoever. And this is our testimony to the whole world. The Spirit of Christ, by which we are guided, is not changeable, so as to command us from a thing as evil and again to move unto it, and we do certainly know, and so testify to the world, that the Spirit of Christ, which leads us into all Truth, will never move us to fight and war against any man with outward weapons, neither for the kingdoms of this world.

... QUAKER DECLARATION, 1660

! Think about ...

Some people think that pacifism is an unrealistic approach to war and violence. Do you think that it is unrealistic or is it a bold attitude to adopt?

Tasks

1. If peace is not just an absence of war, then what is it?

2. Describe **THREE** examples that show peace is a very important part of the Bible's teaching.

3. Is violence always seen as unacceptable by Christians?

4. Describe what we learn from the following two biblical references about war, violence and peace:
   a. Matthew 5.38–46
   b. Luke 22.35–43

5. Write down **THREE** things you would advise a world leader to do to create a peaceful world for future generations.

▲ A reminder to Christians to pray for those who suffer injustice and brutality throughout the world.

SUMMARY

1 Although ideas of holy war and just war have been associated with Christianity, pacifism is much closer to the teaching of Jesus.

2 True peace is a state of being at peace with God and with one's fellow human beings. Jesus called the 'peacemakers' of the world 'the children of God'.

3 Some teachings of Jesus state that acts of violence and war have no place amongst his followers. Turning the other cheek was the way of Jesus.

8:6 Judaism, Islam and Hinduism, and war

How do Judaism, Islam and Hinduism differ in their teachings about war?

▐ JUDAISM

> ❝ If a person intends to kill you, be the first to kill him. ❞
>
> **... THE TALMUD, A JEWISH HOLY BOOK**

In the Jewish Scriptures there are several examples of holy wars. These took place when the early Jews were trying to conquer the Promised Land of Israel and make it their homeland. The teaching of the Scriptures showed that war should only be used as a last resort when everything else had failed and that any damage caused by violence must be carefully limited. Occasionally a pre-emptive strike is permitted if another country is waiting to launch an attack on Israel. This happened in 1967; Israel attacked Egypt and Syria discovering that these two countries were intending to launch an attack of their own. This is known as the 'Six Day War'.

There is no tradition of pacifism in the Jewish religion. However, peace is always held out as the most desirable state. The Jewish prophets looked forward to the everlasting kingdom of peace that would be established by the Messiah, God's chosen leader, who would come at the end of time. Jews believe that forgiveness should always be offered but that no one can forgive on behalf of someone else. Some crimes, like the Holocaust, are so horrific that God alone can forgive them.

▐ ISLAM

There is a concept in Islam called the 'jihad' or holy war. Most Muslims understand this to refer to the struggle, called by God, to fight against all forms of evil. Some fanatical Muslim extremists have adopted this sacred term and claim it should be understand in the more literal sense of a war which can legitimately be waged against the 'enemies' of Islam. The teaching is that such a war can only be waged against an aggressor who threatens the very existence of Islam. Anyone who dies in a holy war is promised immediate entrance to heaven.

Although the word Islam means 'submission' it can also mean 'peace'. Such peace does not necessarily mean the absence of war. Sometimes war is necessary to bring about peace if the enemies of Islam need to be resisted. The society that is truly peaceful is one in which everyone is equal and free to live without being threatened. In this new state all people will live in peaceful harmony under the authority of Allah.

▐ HINDUISM

Many Hindus are opposed to war in any form. The majority, though, believe that war can be justified in certain situations, especially if it is fought in self-defence.

The doctrine of ahimsa (non-violence) is one of the most important in Hinduism. It includes the need to fight against injustice and overcome evil by peaceful means. Many Hindus believe that violence in all senses is wrong, as a violent act will lead to bad karma. This means that the person who shows violence in this life will themself, suffer from violence either in their present life or in a future reincarnation.

This does not mean, though, that war is forbidden in Hinduism. The oldest Hindu holy texts, the Vedas, describe how the gods are sometimes asked for success in battle. One of the four castes into which Hindu society is divided, is the kshatriya – a warrior caste – and it has the responsibility of defending Hindu society if this is necessary. As the quotation shows, fighting in such a righteous war is a sacred duty since to do so opens the gates of heaven, so making future reincarnation unnecessary.

> ❝ Think thou also of thy duty and do not waver. There is no greater good for a warrior than to fight in a righteous war. There is war that opens up the gates of heaven, Arjuna! Happy the warrior whose fate is to fight such a war. ❞
>
> **... GOD KRISHNA SPEAKING TO HINDU WARRIOR ARJUNA, BHAGAVAD GITA (2.31–2)**

> ✓ **Exam tip**
> You will need to be very careful to distinguish between the teachings of these three religions on war and conflict, because they have similarities, including the concept of the 'holy war'.

SUMMARY

1 There is a 'holy war' tradition in Judaism. There is no pacifist tradition. Jews look forward to the Messiah's future reign of peace.

2 In Islam jihad is 'striving in the way of Allah'. Sometimes this involves going to war, to fight against enemies of Islam.

3 The important Hindu teaching of ahimsa rules out the use of violence for many Hindus. However, there is a warrior caste in Hindu society.

▼ Israelis (Jewish majority) and Palestinians (Muslim majority) demonstrate together for peace.

8:7 The law and justice

Why are laws so important in our society?

> *... pay the Emperor what belongs to the Emperor and pay God what belongs to God.*
>
> **... THE BIBLE (MARK 12.17)**

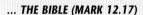

Criminal activity, the breaking of the law, both fascinates and disturbs us. It fascinates us, as numerous television programmes demonstrate, because criminal activity can be made to appear exciting. We find the constant battle between the forces of good and evil in society compelling. If we think seriously about it, it also frightens us because it threatens the very fabric of the society in which we live. It occasionally involves ourselves or people we know as victims. The increasingly violent form that criminal activity is taking is one of the greatest problems facing society in the UK.

The importance of laws

There are two kinds of law in England.

1. **Bye-laws.** These are laws that relate to our local area and are made by the council that we elect. These laws have the power to determine, for instance, where people can park their car or which roads they can, and cannot, use. If we break a bye-law we do not have a criminal record and it does not usually involve the law-breaker in a court appearance.

2. **Parliamentary laws.** Bye-laws only apply locally whereas laws passed by Parliament apply nationally. New laws are coming into place all the time whilst existing laws are frequently changed or up-dated. These laws have created two kinds of offence:

   - **Non-indictable offences.** These cover minor offences, such as petty theft, and less serious motoring offences. They are dealt with in a magistrates' court and usually involve a fine for the guilty person.

   - **Indictable offences.** These are much more serious crimes such as manslaughter, murder, armed robbery and rape. These matters are dealt with in a Crown Court by a judge and jury. The penalties that can be imposed include substantial fines or periods in prison.

Why have laws?

Laws are established by a society in order to control the behaviour of its citizens. Laws tell people what behaviour is socially acceptable and what is unacceptable. They also lay down the forms of punishment that will be applied if the laws are broken. The laws reflect the kind of government that is in place and the religious background of the country. In the UK, where we have a democratic form of government in a traditionally Christian country, this is reflected in our laws. Some countries, though, have a totalitarian dictatorship and this is reflected in the laws imposed on the country. Countries with a Muslim government may put in place laws and forms of punishment that reflect the Shariah laws of the Qur'an. Many Muslim countries have a mixture of civil laws and those taken from the Qur'an.

The law in most countries sets out to protect its most vulnerable members. All law-abiding citizens are vulnerable in some areas of life and so the law is very important for the protection that it gives to everyone. Everyone would be vulnerable when faced with an armed robber, murderer or potential rapist. At the same time the young, the elderly and those in the front line of the battle against crime need special protection. The law exists to make living in society as safe as it possibly can be. A sin is an offence against the laws of God.

The UK has had a democracy and a Parliament to pass laws longer than any other country. This means that there are a large number of laws included in the statute book. New laws continue to be made. In the last half-century, for instance, the laws regarding abortion and homosexual activity have been drastically altered in most of the UK. In these two instances, changes in the law have brought about changes in moral and religious attitudes as well. Once a law is passed by Parliament it has to be enforced. The police exist to make sure that laws are obeyed and that people who break them are arrested. At this stage the judiciary (the court system and the judges) take over, apply the law, determine guilt and apply the punishment, which is laid down by Parliament.

> *Rulers are not to be feared by those who do good, but by those who do evil. Would you like to be unafraid of those in authority? Then do what is good and they will praise you, because they are God's servants working for your own good. But if you do evil, then be afraid of them, because their power to punish is real. They are God's servants and carry out God's punishment on those who do evil. For this reason you must obey the authorities.*
>
> **... THE BIBLE (ROMANS 13.3–5)**

IMPORTANT WORDS

Crime; an offence against the laws of a country
Justice; the administration of the law and its punishments
Law; the rules of a community or state
Sin; an offence against God and His laws

Think about …

Can you imagine what it would be like to live in a society where the law was very weak or non-existent? In such a situation, what would frighten you most?

Tasks

1. What are the main differences between bye-laws and those passed by parliament?

2.a. Why do countries have their own laws?

b. How do the laws reflect the type of government in a country?

c. What does law set out to do?

d. Why do laws matter?

3. If you had the opportunity, which **THREE** laws do you think you would pass to make life safer and more pleasant for everyone?

4. Discuss the difference between a sin and a crime. Think of **TWO** examples of each.

SUMMARY

1 Laws are very important in each society. In this country local laws are called bye-laws. The most important laws are those passed by Parliament.

2 Offences can be divided into non-indictable (less serious) and indictable (those responsible are liable to be charged with a crime). Only the most serious are tried in front of a judge and jury.

3 The UK is a democracy with a Christian background. Most of its laws reflect this. The laws exist to protect the most vulnerable members of society.

▼ Supreme court in Islamabad, Pakistan.

8:8 Why punish?

What does punishment set out to achieve?

> *Do not judge others, so that God will not judge you, for God will judge you in the same way as you judge others.*
>
> ... THE BIBLE (MATTHEW 7.1)

Punishment is the way in which society makes people pay for a crime they have committed. This payment may involve the loss of personal freedom (prison); the inconvenience of having one's freedom restricted (probation, community service or tagging) or the payment of a sum of money (a fine). Tagging is a new method of punishment that involves fitting an electronic device to someone released from prison so that the authorities know where they are and what they are doing. This leads us to ask a very basic question – what does any punishment, whatever it is, set out to achieve?

Five answers are usually given to this question.

1. **Retribution.** This means making a person pay for the crime they have committed. The criminal owes society a debt – the more serious the crime the greater the debt. The problem lies in deciding which punishment is appropriate for the crime. This becomes particularly difficult when we consider capital punishment. Whatever the punishment, the criminal is paying the debt that society considers to be appropriate.

2. **Deterrence.** Each punishment is intended to deter someone who has committed a crime from doing the same thing again. It is also intended to remind other people what they can expect to receive if they commit the same, or a similar, crime. Opinion is divided as to how effective punishment is as a deterrent. Over 80 per cent of UK criminals are 'recidivists', that is they offend more than once. Many criminals return to prison time and time again. The death penalty should be the ultimate deterrent yet, since it was re-introduced in the USA in 1976, there has been a large number of murders. As a simple deterrent it is a failure.

3. **Protection.** Criminals threaten the stability of society and they are a threat to the most vulnerable members of the community. Everyone agrees that society needs to be protected from hardened criminals. Locking people away guarantees that society is safe from them whilst they are in prison. Most people see this as the main reason for passing a prison sentence.

However, it has been argued that during a prison sentence, prisoners are mixing with other criminals and this could reinforce tendencies to break the law; prison has often been called 'a university of crime'.

4. **Reformation.** Whilst a person is locked away it is very important to make an attempt to reform him or her. Over 200 000 young people pass through the juvenile courts each year and it is crucial that an attempt is made to reform them before they become hardened criminals. In some prisons, attempts are made to educate prisoners, teach them a trade, find them somewhere to live when they are released and arrange a job for them. At the same time, sessions are held to help them see the effect their crime has had on their victims. Prisons, though, are severely overcrowded and this makes it very difficult, and often impossible, to carry out effective reformative work.

5. **Vindication.** Few of us would enjoy living in a lawless society in which chaos reigned. If people break the law they must understand what they are doing and the punishments that are used to uphold (vindicate) the law.

> *You have heard that it was said, 'An eye for an eye and a tooth for a tooth'. But now I tell you: do not take revenge on someone who wrongs you. If anyone slaps you on the right cheek, let him slap your left cheek too,*
>
> ... THE BIBLE (MATTHEW 5.38–39)

▼ The number of inmates in most UK prisons has exploded in recent years.

▲ Tagging is a modern way of keeping track of criminals without keeping them in prison.

Tasks

1. What is meant by describing punishment as:
    a. retribution
    b. a deterrent
    c. vindication?

2. What do you think is the most important objective of punishment?

3.a. Write down **TWO** ways in which the prison system attempt to reform inmates.

   b. Write down **TWO** reasons why it is important that an attempt should be made to reform as well as to punish prisoners.

4. Imagine that you are the Home Secretary. You have been asked by the Prime Minister to reduce overall levels of crime in the country. Which **TWO** measures would you introduce and why?

5. Place the five purposes of punishment in what you consider to be their order of importance. Give **TWO** reasons for the order that you have chosen.

 Think about ...

Do you think that criminals should be made to help or compensate their victims? How do you think this could be put into practice?

SUMMARY

1 Punishment is the way in which society makes a criminal pay for his or her actions.

2 Punishment has five purposes: to exact a penalty; to deter; to protect society; to reform the prisoner and to uphold the law.

8:9 Capital punishment

What are the arguments for and against the death penalty?

Capital punishment – the facts

The practice of putting someone to death for killing someone else or committing a very serious crime is not new. The Romans, for example, crucified murderers and those found guilty of treason if they were not Roman citizens and beheaded those who were.

In eighteenth-century England, over 200 crimes were punishable by death. In 1957 Parliament restricted the death penalty to those found guilty of killing a policeman; killing during an armed robbery; killing by causing an explosion and killing more than one person. The last two people were executed in the UK in 1964. A year later the death penalty was abolished for a trial period of five years and in 1969 it was abolished altogether. We now know that several people were unjustly executed.

Capital punishment has been abolished throughout Europe. It is still used in countries, including the USA, China and in Muslim countries which are ruled by Shariah law. In 2001, over 3048 executions were carried out in 31 different countries. Over 2400 were executed in China alone. Hundreds were also killed in Iran, the Congo and Afghanistan.

IT'S A FACT

By 2002:
- 74 countries had abolished the death penalty altogether.
- 15 countries had retained the death penalty only for exceptional crimes such as wartime offences and treason.
- 22 countries had the death penalty but had not executed anyone for at least 10 years.
- 84 countries retained and used the death penalty.

Arguments for the death penalty

- The death penalty is the most appropriate punishment for someone who has taken the life of someone else.
- Some people are so violent that they only understand the language of violence. It is the only effective deterrent for violent people.
- Putting a murderer to death is the only really effective way of protecting society – they cannot kill again.
- Society must protect its most vulnerable members. Society must also protect those at the forefront of the fight against crime, especially police officers.
- A 'life' sentence does not really mean life. Most murderers are freed before they complete their sentence and this places society at risk.

Arguments against the death penalty

- The justice system is not infallible and we know that many innocent people were executed in the past.
- Only God can ultimately judge – He gave life and He alone can take it away.
- There is no evidence that the death penalty acts as a deterrent. 80 per cent of all murderers are known to their victims and are often family members. Domestic murderers are very unlikely to murder again.
- Executing people who kill for political reasons would turn them into martyrs and this could lead to more deaths.
- Execution is barbaric. Life is sacred and it should not be taken in this way in a civilised society. Society is little more than a murderer itself if it executes criminals.

The death penalty is a very emotive subject. It is very difficult to feel any sympathy for the person who kills a defenceless victim. However, many people feel that the death penalty is not appropriate in a civilised society.

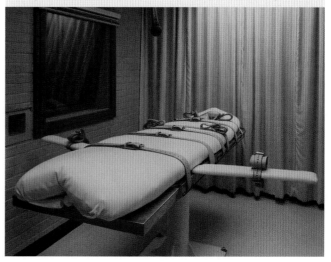

▼ In the USA, there is still a majority of people in favour of capital punishment. One form of execution involves the convicted person being strapped to a 'bed' and a fatal mix of chemicals being injected into their arm.

▲ Amnesty International is at the forefront of those campaigning for abolition of the death penalty.

Tasks

1.a. What is capital punishment?

b. 'The death penalty has no place in a civilised society.' Do you agree with this opinion? Give **TWO** reasons for your answer.

c. What arguments can be put forward for retaining the death penalty?

d. What arguments can be put forward for abolishing the death penalty?

2. Write a paragraph making out your own case for either abolishing or retaining the death penalty.

3. 'Execution is less degrading than keeping someone locked up for life.' Produce **TWO** arguments either supporting or opposing this argument.

Think about ...

Some murderers have been told that they will never be released from prison. Do you think this is a good or a bad thing from the point of view of the murderer, the victim's relatives and society?

SUMMARY

1 The death penalty was abolished in the UK in 1969. It is still retained in countries including the USA, China and several Muslim countries.

2 Arguments in favour of the death penalty stress its deterrent and protective value in a society which has vulnerable people.

3 Arguments against the death penalty stress its barbarism, the possibility of making a mistake and the dangers of killing people who commit political crimes.

8:10 A prisoner of conscience – Georgi Vins

Who was Georgi Vins and how did he suffer for his religious faith?

During the 1960s and 1970s many people in the Soviet Union suffered for their religious faith. Because their 'crime' was nothing more than a refusal to give up their religious faith these people became known as 'prisoners of conscience'. One such prisoner was Georgi Vins (1928–98) who was a Baptist minister.

The prisoner of conscience

Georgi Vins was a Russian Baptist minister who suffered a great deal at the hands of the authorities in his country during the 1960s and 1970s. For almost the whole of this time, he was either in prison or on the run from the authorities before, having served half of a ten-year prison sentence, he was released to live in the USA in exchange for two Soviet spies. Following the collapse of the Soviet Union in the late 1980s he was able to return home and follow a full ministry as a Baptist minister preaching, writing and taking church services.

New laws in 1960 in the Soviet Union required children to be excluded from public worship, discouraged the adult baptism of people between the ages of 18 and 30 and curtailed preaching activities. This was against everything that many Baptists believed about religious freedom. Vins rebelled against these new laws and by 1962 over 100 of his followers were also in prison. This figure soon rose to 170 and even as late as 1981 95 were still in prison.

Vins was the son of an American Baptist missionary who was executed in 1936. Georgi was brought up by his Christian mother and he withstood the many attempts during his time at school to make him give up his faith. He soon became a Baptist minister but the law required him to continue working as an electrical engineer. He met secretly with other Baptists for worship and Bible study – sometimes in different homes and sometimes in the forest. This was a very risky thing for them to do.

When his request to be able to give up his job was refused he went underground to continue to serve his fellow Baptists. He was first arrested in 1966 after organising a mass demonstration that demanded freedom of worship for all Christians in the Soviet Union. Vins was invited to discuss the issue with the authorities, arrested and released three years later, with poor health after having suffered torture for more than a year, followed by two years in a labour camp.

A committee was formed to keep people in the West informed about Georgi Vins and other 'prisoners of conscience'. Vins was soon arrested again and sent to prison for 12 months for 'parasitism'. He went on the run for five years until he was captured and sentenced to five years in a Siberian labour camp, to be followed by five years internal exile in the Soviet Union.

International Representation

It was at the end of the first five years of this sentence, in 1979, that Georgi Vins was released to go to the USA, after first being stripped of his Soviet citizenship. In the USA, Vins set up the organisation 'International Representation', which set out to raise funds and other forms of help for the Baptists in Russia who were being persecuted. Somehow he also managed to continue to lead the persecuted Baptists in Russia. Sadly, Vins did not find it easy to adapt to life in the West and he made few friends. He only trusted a few close associates.

This was the time when great changes were taking place in the Soviet Union. The old laws of oppression were replaced by new laws that guaranteed religious and cultural freedom. The Christian Church was able to engage freely in worship, teaching and social activity. Churches and monastic buildings were handed back to the Church in large numbers after they had been closed or turned into museums for a long time. Vins was able to return home. For the next seven years, before his death, he was able to play a full part in the life of the Baptist Church in Russia. He was to be found preaching in churches, schools and in the open air.

> **IT'S A FACT**
>
> The strongest anti-religious campaign in the USSR at this time took place between 1959 and 1964. During this time 14 000 churches were closed and turned into museums. 7000 churches remained unchanged until the late 1980s when the Churches in Russia were free to open more churches if they wished.

 Think about ...

Throughout history there have been many attempts to wipe out religious movements by suppressing them. Few have been totally successful. Why do you think that oppression and suppression have this effect on those who hold strong religious beliefs and motivations?

1. What is a prisoner of conscience?

2. What made Georgi Vins decide to become an underground leader of the Baptist Church in the Soviet Union?

3.a. Describe what happened to Georgi Vins between 1966 and 1979.

 b. What was the organisation 'International Representation' and what did it try to achieve?

4. What did Georgi Vins do in 1990 and how did he end his days?

SUMMARY

1 Georgi Vins was a Baptist minister who became a prisoner of conscience. He suffered several spells in prison. Whilst he was on the run he led some members of the Baptist Church in their opposition to the government of the Soviet Union.

2 Vins was released from prison and allowed to go to the US. He was not happy there, but did form the organisation 'International Representation'.

3 When the Soviet Union fell in 1990 Vins returned to Russia. New laws allowed him, and others, to worship, teach and meet together freely.

▼ Georgi Vins at a press conference in New York in 1979.

8:11 Christianity: justice and forgiveness

What is the Christian approach to justice and forgiveness?

> Then Peter came to Jesus and asked, 'Lord, if my brother keeps on sinning against me, how many times do I have to forgive him? Seven times?' 'No, not seven times,' answered Jesus, 'but seventy times seven.'
>
> **... THE BIBLE (MATTHEW 18.21–22)**

> If someone has done you wrong, do not repay him with a wrong. Try to do what everyone considers to be good. Do everything possible on your part to live in peace with everybody. Never take revenge, my friends, but instead let God's anger do it. For the scripture says, 'I will take revenge, I will pay back, says the Lord.'
>
> **... THE BIBLE (ROMANS 12.17–21)**

In approaching the issue of punishment, Christians try to find a middle way between the demands of justice and the need for mercy and forgiveness. Christians would not agree with an approach to punishment that says 'lock the door and throw away the key'. They believe that it should be possible for everyone to find forgiveness from God and from society – whatever they have done.

Christians and justice

Christians believe in justice because they believe in a God who deals with everyone fairly. Throughout the Old Testament people were told that they must be absolutely fair in their business dealings with others. They must not cheat and, if they do, they can only expect to experience the justice of God. The same message is carried on in both the words of Jesus and those of Paul in the New Testament. Jesus emphasised that this sense of justice must always be tempered with mercy. In the Beatitudes – eight sayings which sum up his whole teaching – Jesus said, "Happy are those who are merciful to others; God will be merciful to them!" (Matthew 5.7) The need to show mercy to others was highlighted in the parable that Jesus told about the unmerciful servant (Matthew 18.21–35). A servant who owed his master a large sum of money is called to account but, after begging for mercy, has his debt cancelled. The servant then goes out and finds someone who owes him much less money. Rather than cancel the debt, he has the man thrown into prison. When he hears this, the master reinstates the servant's debt and has him thrown into prison to be tortured. Jesus used the parable to remind his followers of the debt they owed God. If God could forgive their debts then they could certainly forgive the debts owed to them by others.

Forgiveness

Jesus had more to say about forgiveness than about anything else. He reminded his listeners that God was ready to forgive anyone who repented of their sins and sought His forgiveness. Here are some examples:

- The three parables in Luke 15 – the lost sheep, the lost coin and the lost son – all have the same theme. There is great joy when the sheep and coin are found and when the son returns to his father. In the parable of the lost son, his father is overjoyed when his son returns home and seeks his father's forgiveness.

- Forgiveness is a two-way business. In the Lord's Prayer Jesus included the phrase – "Forgive us our debts as we have forgiven our debtors." He adds: "If you forgive others the wrongs they have done to you, your Father in heaven will also forgive you. But if you do not forgive others, then your Father will not forgive the wrongs you have done." (Matthew 6.14) These words of Jesus would seem to apply, amongst other situations, to the relationship between criminal and victim. It seems almost impossible to forgive a serious crime, such as rape or grievous bodily harm, but Jesus implies that we all need God's forgiveness and this depends on our ability to forgive others.

Paul underlined that revenge is not a Christian emotion although it might be a natural response. He attacked the idea that Christians should ever return evil for evil. Revenge belongs to God. Christians should respond by feeding and giving water to their enemies. As Jesus told Peter, there should be no limit to the forgiveness they are prepared to show others. This forgiveness should bring about the reconciliation of the criminal with society. Punishment should always be designed to rehabilitate the criminal into the community.

Think about ...

Can you think of a practical way in which the teaching of Jesus about forgiveness could become a part of our approach to dealing with law-breaking – to the benefit of the victim, the criminal and society generally?

Tasks

1. What do Christians mean when they say that they try to find a middle way between the demands of justice and the need for mercy?

2. How does the Christian belief in God make demands on the way that people treat one another?

3. What did Jesus say about:

   a. forgiveness   **b.** mercy?

4. 'Some crimes are so bad they should never be forgiven.' Do you agree? Give reasons to support your opinion and refer to different points of view, including Christianity.

SUMMARY

1 Christians believe that both justice and mercy should be reflected in any dealings with criminals. God deals with everyone fairly and so should we.

2 Christians believe that justice must always be tempered with mercy. Forgiveness was an important theme in the teaching of Jesus. Forgiveness is a two-way thing. To be forgiven one must forgive others. God's forgiveness depends on a person's willingness to forgive others.

▼ A prison chaplain and his wife help a prisoner to seek God's forgiveness.

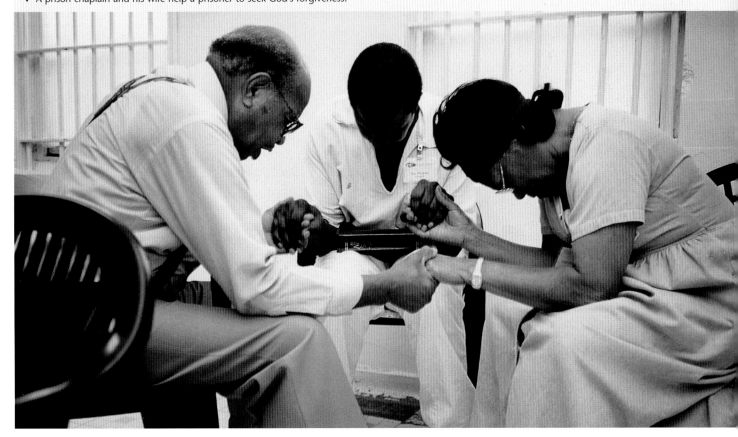

8:12 Judaism, Islam and Hinduism: justice and forgiveness

How do Jews, Muslims and Hindus differ in their approaches to justice and forgiveness?

 ## JUDAISM

> *Repentance, charity and devotion can change a grim fate.*
>
> ... **YOM KIPPUR ORDER OF SERVICE**

Traditional Jewish punishments were intended to be harsh but fair. The scriptures insisted that anyone suspected of a crime be given a fair trial. The most serious of crimes, including idolatry and witchcraft as well as murder, were punished by execution ranging from stoning to burning to death. In practice, though, the laws of trial were so strong that it was almost impossible for the death penalty to be passed. Witnesses had to be found who saw the accused committing the crime and their testimonies had to be in complete agreement. A number of other crimes were punished with 39 lashes with a whip. The punishments carried out in Israel today are not those laid down in the Torah and Talmud.

Rabbis are sure that a person who repents of their sins will be forgiven. To show that the repentance is genuine, three courses of action are open to the person:

1. **Prayer.** If the person showed their sincerity by praying for forgiveness then they could be sure that they would be forgiven both by God and the people.

2. **Charity giving.** Giving to those in need is a spiritual obligation on all Jews. This action can show genuine repentance.

3. **Fasting.** This is a traditional religious way of showing that one is genuinely sorry.

IT'S A FACT

In the Talmud, Rabbi Eliezer recommended that everyone should repent on the day before they died. When questioned as to how someone would know the day on which they were going to die he replied: "Exactly. One should repent every day."

ISLAM

Islam teaches that everyone is equal in the eyes of the law and must be dealt with in the knowledge that on the Day of Judgement each human being will stand before Allah – the all-knowing One – to account for the way they have lived. There are four crimes which are particularly condemned in the Qur'an:

• murder

• adultery

• the making or drinking of alcohol

• theft.

These crimes are seen as being particularly dangerous within society since they lead to many other undesirable things. Punishments are designed to stop people stepping over the boundaries that Allah has laid down.

Forgiveness plays an important part in dealing with the law-breaker. Only Allah is able to forgive. The teaching of Islam is that Allah will always do this if the person is genuinely sorry for what they have done. Those who show that they are sorry by forgiving others will be rewarded on the Day of Judgement.

> *If a person forgives and makes reconciliation, his reward is due from Allah.*
>
> ...**THE QUR'AN (42.40)**

 ## HINDUISM

In most of the Hindu holy texts the right to punish is only given to rulers. In India in the past, most punishments were carried out by the elders or headsmen of a village or clan. The king had to maintain a balance between all the different interests. Murder was identified as the most serious offence. Sometimes, though, it was legitimate to kill, such as when a potential assassin was prevented from carrying out his evil will. The Laws of Manu, an important Hindu text, makes it clear that murdering a Brahmin, a member of the highest caste, is particularly serious and was punishable with death. It is also believed that the people who are never caught and punished for their crime will suffer because of the law of karma. Punishment is inevitable: they will be punished in this life or the next.

According to Hindu teaching there are three reasons for punishment.

1. **To restrain.** The criminal is prevented from committing further crimes.

2. **Retribution.** Society takes its revenge on the criminal who has broken its laws.

3. **Reformation.** To make the criminal realise that they have done wrong and so change their ways.

Tasks

1. The harsh punishments laid down in the Torah and the Talmud have not been applied within the Jewish community for centuries. Why do you think that things have changed over time?

2. How could a Jewish person show that they are genuinely sorry for what they have done?

3. What does the Qur'an teach about forgiveness and the way in which it can be obtained?

4. How was law and order maintained in early Hindu societies?

5. What are the three things that Hindu punishments set out to achieve?

✓ Exam tip
The holy books are extremely important. Try to learn one piece of text from each to illustrate an important point.

SUMMARY

1 Early Jewish punishments were harsh but the door to repentance and forgiveness was always open.

2 Everyone is equal before Allah, who alone is able to grant true forgiveness. To receive this, a person must be genuinely sorry for what they have done.

3 The oldest Hindu texts gave the king, or ruler, the sole right to punish. The purpose of punishment is to restrain, to take retribution and to reform.

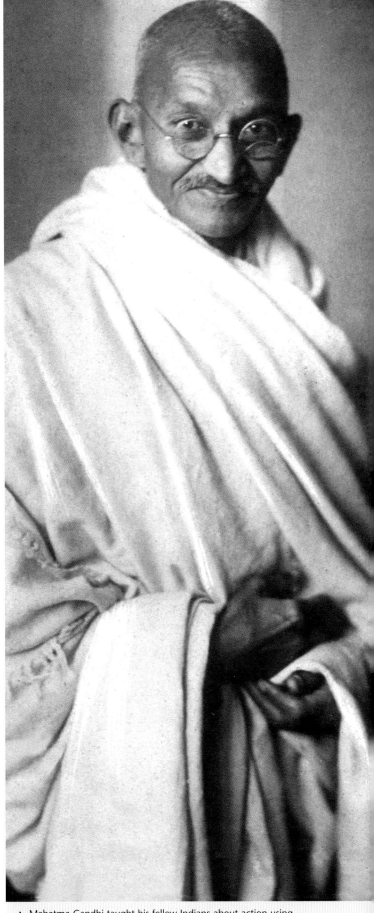

▲ Mahatma Gandhi taught his fellew Indians about action using non-violence.

✓ Exam help ...

This section brings together the moral and religious issues that surround war and crime. You should be able to indicate clearly the different attitudes of the various religions towards war and conflict. It is important to remember the difference that nuclear weapons have made to any debate about whether war can be justified or not. The attitude of society towards criminal behaviour and the punishment of the offender is very important today, particularly as the crime rate for particular crimes is rising. Ensure you know what punishment is and what it is intended to achieve.

1.   Why do some Christians believe that it might be necessary and right for them to fight in a war?

1.   Christians believe that they should be working for peace in today's world. In the Beatitudes, Jesus picked out the peacemakers as those who would enjoy a great spiritual blessing. Jesus himself said he came to bring peace into the world. Yet Christians do not always agree about war. Some wars are more serious than others because more is at stake. Most Christians would think that war can be justified in some circumstances.

   • The idea of the just war was first set forward by St Augustine at the start of the fifth century. It was amplified by St Thomas Aquinas in the thirteenth century. A war may be just if the cause is just; it is declared by the government of a country and the purpose is to promote good and therefore is fighting evil. It must not target civilians.

   • Although Jesus seemed to be a pacifist he did not condemn soldiers. Paul taught that the civil powers must be obeyed – this might involve war. Jesus said that his followers should give to Caesar what belongs to Caesar – this might justify war.

2.   Why are some Christians pacifists?

2.   A pacifist is someone who believes that violence cannot be justified in any situation. Not all Christians are pacifists and the Quakers are the only Christian Church that supports pacifism. During a time of war Christian pacifists try to register as 'conscientious objectors'.

   • The teaching of Jesus was strongly pacifist. In the Sermon on the Mount, Jesus taught his followers that they should meet acts of violence with acts of love. At the Last Supper he told his followers that they must not fight to defend him. He healed the ear of the High Priest's servant after Peter had struck him with a sword. The death of Jesus was to secure peace – between God and human beings and between human beings.

   • For centuries the early Christians did not join the Roman army. The early Church appears to have been pacifist. Christians only began to join the army when the Roman Emperor became a Christian.

3.   'It is unthinkable that a Christian should support the gathering or using of nuclear weapons.' Do you agree? Show that you have considered more than ONE point of view.

3.   Nuclear weapons and other weapons of mass destruction (cruise missiles, inter-continental ballistic missiles etc.) raise enormous issues for Christians.

   • Christians believe that this is God's world. Human beings are intended to be stewards of God's creation. That means that they are entrusted with its care. They must pass it on to the new generation in a perfect state. Clearly that would be impossible if a nuclear war were to take place. The world itself might be destroyed. The number of people killed would be incalculable and the suffering indescribable. The risk of accidentally exploding a nuclear device is very high.

continued ...

- Many people say that the 'balance of terror' is the only thing that keeps the world safe. This can only give a very fragile peace.

- The just war theory provides the only possible Christian justification for war. The just war theory cannot apply to a nuclear world. This was emphasised by Pope Paul VI. It would be impossible to keep any war between nuclear powers within limits, which is the basis of the just war theory.

- **Conclusion.** We live in a nuclear age. Nuclear weapons will not go away. Christians and non-Christians are very worried about the future. Most Christians feel that multilateral disarmament is the best hope for the future of the world. Christian organisations like Pax Christi work to this end.

4. Outline the teaching of ONE religion, other than Christianity, on war and conflict between nations.

4. The chosen religion is Islam.

- The word Islam means submission and derives from a word meaning 'peace'. Islam accepts that war is sometimes necessary. If Islam as a religion is under threat then it is right to resist the aggressor.

- Islam has its own understanding of a holy war – called a 'jihad'. Most Muslims understand this to be a war against evil in the world: to extremist fanatical Muslims, it is a military battle against those opposed to Islam. An extreme Muslim group, the Taliban, tried to argue that their actions that led to the events of 11 September 2001 were a holy war. However, Muslims across the world were appalled by their actions. Those who die in a jihad are promised immediate entry into heaven – hence its appeal to some.

- For some Muslims the ideal society is one in which the laws of the Qur'an are applied, called Shariah law, and everyone lives under the rule of Allah.

5. What is the Christian teaching on forgiveness?

5. Christian teaching is that the way to forgiveness should always be left open – no matter what a person has done.

- The way to forgiveness is through the confession of sins. In the Roman Catholic Church such forgiveness is through Confession (the Sacrament of Penance). The person seeking forgiveness must show contrition (heartfelt repentance) and carry out acts of penance.

- Christians should forgive others because God has forgiven them – compare the parable of the 'Ungrateful Steward'. No one can be forgiven their sins unless they have first forgiven others – 'Forgive us our sins ask we forgive others' in the Lord's Prayer.

- St Peter asked Jesus how often his followers should forgive others. The normal Jewish teaching was that a person should be prepared to forgive someone else seven times. Jesus, though, said that they should be prepared to forgive others seventy times seven times!

6. Outline the teaching of ONE religion, other than Christianity, on justice and punishment.

6. The chosen religion is Hinduism.

- Although the right to punish is only given in the holy books to rulers, most punishments in India were traditionally carried out by the tribal elders. Crimes against Brahmins, the highest of the castes, were punished most severely.

- Even if a person is never caught and punished for a crime it is believed that they will be punished in the next life by the law of karma. Punishment is intended to restrain the behaviour of people, to bring retribution on the criminal and to help the criminal realise the error of their ways.

What can be done today to help couples who are unable to conceive a baby?

Infertility is when a man or a woman is unable to conceive a baby. Difficulties in conceiving a baby affect far more couples than is generally known. Over 10 per cent of couples have problems starting a family; 1 in every 10 of these is described as 'inexplicably infertile'. Infertile couples, left to their own efforts, would not become parents.

Some couples do not want to have a family. Some couples, finding that they cannot conceive, accept their infertility and still enjoy a happy and fulfilling relationship. Although most couples want to have their own family it is not essential for a happy marriage. Other couples, finding that they are infertile, turn to medical science for help. Such help is not usually available on the NHS and costs over £3000 for a course of treatment.

Ways of assisting conception

In vitro fertilisation (IVF). 'In vitro' means 'in glass' and people often refer to this method of conceiving as 'test-tube babies'. This procedure was first used in 1978 and is now quite common: 12 out of every 1000 babies are now conceived in this way. This technique was developed to help women with blocked fallopian tubes to conceive, since their eggs could not reach their uterus to be available for fertilisation by their partner's sperm. To solve the problem, a woman is given drugs to help her to produce eggs, which are then fertilised by her partner's sperm outside her body. If successful, the resulting embryos are placed inside the uterus where they can develop normally. Usually two or three fertilised eggs are placed in the uterus to increase the chances of one growing through to full term, so multiple births can result.

Artificial insemination by donor (AID). AID has been used in the UK since the 1950s. If the male partner is infertile, sperm from an anonymous donor are placed in the neck of the womb from where they can travel to fertilise an egg. This technique is used frequently with animals, but is still very controversial with humans. One reason is that the child may not know who their father is. The Roman Catholic Church is strongly opposed to AID, considering it to be little different from adultery. Similar objections are raised by other religions.

Artificial insemination by husband (AIH). This can take place when a man and woman cannot conceive and there is nothing wrong with their eggs or sperm. Most religious people find this more acceptable than AID.

Egg or sperm storing. It is now possible to store a woman's eggs or a man's sperm in case they are needed at a future date. If a man dies it must be clear that he would have consented to his sperm being used. In 2002, Diane Blood announced that she was expecting her second baby using the sperm of her dead husband. Before her first child was conceived she had to go to court to prove that her dead husband would have consented to his sperm being used.

Fertility drugs. There are now many fertility drugs available. One problem is that the number of babies conceived after treatment cannot be controlled, often leading to multiple births.

The Human Fertilisation and Embryology Act 1990

This important Act states that:

- a man who donates sperm and a woman who donates eggs must remain anonymous

- a donor, male or female, has no rights over any baby that may result

- frozen embryos may be stored for up to ten years, but must then be destroyed

- scientific experiments may be carried out on an embryo for up to 14 days. After this time it must not be kept alive.

Surrogacy

Surrogacy takes place when a woman becomes pregnant for someone else, who is infertile. This can be done by using the sperm of the infertile woman's partner or using a donor's sperm. For some couples this is the only alternative to childlessness. The Surrogacy Arrangements Act 1985 made it illegal for anyone to advertise surrogacy or for anyone to pay an agency to make a surrogacy arrangement. It later became illegal for any money, apart from expenses, to be paid for such an arrangement.

! Think about …

In the past, childlessness was looked on as the will or punishment of God. Do you think that anyone might think like this today?

Tasks

1. What is infertility?

2. Write **TWO** sentences about each of the following:

   a. IVF   **b.** AID   **c.** AIH
   d. egg or sperm storage.

3.**a.** If you needed to, would you be prepared to use any of the methods mentioned in this unit?

   b. Are there any methods you might feel unhappy about? Give **TWO** reasons for your answer.

4. 'Couples who cannot conceive should simply accept this and get on with their lives.' Do you agree with this comment? Write down **TWO** reasons to support or oppose it.

IMPORTANT WORDS

AID;	a donor's sperm is used to fertilise a woman's egg
AIH;	when a woman's partner's sperm is placed in her uterus to fertilise an egg
IVF;	when an egg is taken from the mother's womb, fertilised in a test-tube and then placed in the womb to grow normally
Surrogacy;	a surrogate mother is one who agrees to carry and give birth to a baby for someone else

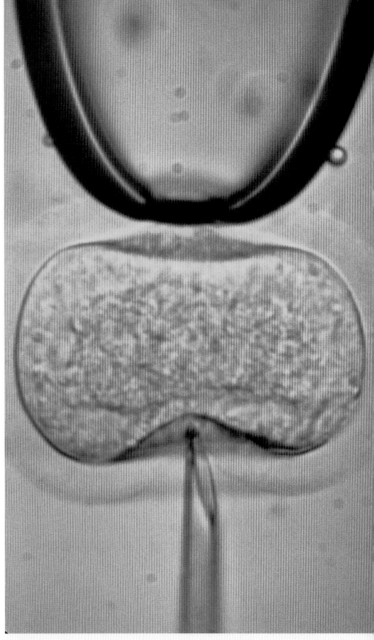

▲ IVF research, showing a needle injecting a sperm cell into an egg.

SUMMARY

1 A large number of couples are unable to have children – or find it difficult to do so.

2 There are several ways in which infertile couples can be helped to conceive, including IVF, AIH, AID and other fertility treatments. Many people have reservations about AID and it is discouraged by most religions.

3 Surrogacy is occasionally used; it involves a woman carrying a baby and after birth giving the baby to someone else.

9:2 Christianity and infertility

What does Christianity teach about infertility?

> Techniques that entail the dissociation of husband and wife, by the intrusion of a person other than the couple ... are gravely immoral.

... CATECHISM OF THE CATHOLIC CHURCH, 1994

Like other religions, Christianity teaches that life is sacred and human beings are created to enjoy a unique spiritual relationship with God. It is within this understanding that Christians look at the question of infertility.

Infertility

There is no specific teaching in the Bible about infertility treatments because at the time the Bible was written medical science did not exist. If people were childless then this was because God intended it to be that way. There was nothing that could be done about it and it had to be accepted – although childlessness was looked upon with disfavour in Jewish society. Abraham asked of God, "What good will your reward do me, since I have no children?" (Genesis 15.2) Rachel cried to her husband Jacob, "Give me children, or I will die." (Genesis 30.1) The following quotation demonstrates how the Old Testament described the childlessness of one woman.

> Hannah had no children ... because the Lord had kept her from having children.

... THE BIBLE (1 SAMUEL 1.2,5)

Infertility today

Today, the medical situation is very different and so is our understanding of the causes of infertility. Few people seriously put forward the view that infertility is the will of God and so must be accepted. Within the Christian community there exist two different viewpoints on this subject.

All of the Christian Churches, except the Roman Catholic Church, accept that infertility treatment is acceptable as long as it is the wife's egg and the husband's sperm which is being used – AIH and IVF. This, it is argued, is a proper use of science that, to many Christians, is a way of discovering God's intricate secrets of life and the universe as He chooses to reveal them. In the case of AIH and IVF, science is making use of its understanding of life and using that knowledge to increase human happiness. The embryos that are discarded because they are not needed to bring about conception are not foetuses and so are not yet human beings.

The Catholic view on infertility

The attitude of the Roman Catholic Church is different. It bans any form of embryo technology. It is also strongly opposed to IVF, AIH and AID. IVF involves the fertilisation of some eggs that are not used in the treatment. These eggs are either destroyed at the end of the treatment or are used for scientific experimentation – in both cases the same objection applies as to abortion. AID, AIH, IVF and surrogacy are ruled out because they involve male masturbation and this has always been regarded by the Catholic Church as a grave moral sin.

> Masturbation is an intrinsically and gravely disordered action.

... CATECHISM OF THE CATHOLIC CHURCH, 1994

The Catholic Church believes that it is very important that each child should have the right to know the identity of its parents and to be brought up by them. Although this is not a problem with AIH and IVF, it is not possible under AID and surrogacy – at least as present UK law stands. This, in itself, is sufficient to rule out both procedures.

Any scientific procedure that involves conception taking place without sexual intercourse is condemned. The Catholic attitude towards contraception makes clear every sexual act must be open to the possibility of the creation of new life. Likewise, the creation of new life can only stem from the act of sexual intercourse and in no other way. This is the way God designed and planned it.

Infertility is a cross that many couples are called by God to bear. Although it is natural for every couple to want to have children they do not have an absolute right to do so. The ends do not always justify the means. A couple without children can adopt a child or perform services for others instead.

Think about ...

Do you think that every couple has the 'right' to become parents? Explain your answer.

Tasks

1. How is childlessness explained in the Bible?

2. Which infertility treatments are acceptable to all Christians, except Roman Catholics, and why are they accepted?

3. Give **THREE** reasons why the Roman Catholic Church is opposed to all forms of infertility treatment.

4. 'People who cannot have children should accept this and not try to interfere with nature.' Do you agree? Give reasons to support your opinion and explain what a Christian viewpoint might be.

SUMMARY

1 Childlessness in Biblical times was looked upon as the will of God and so had to be accepted.

2 Most Churches today accept IVF and AIH as being acceptable, because childlessness is no longer viewed as being God's will.

3 The Roman Catholic Church is opposed to all infertility treatment as it often involves the destruction of some embryos; it involves the sinful activity of masturbation and denies the right of every child to know the identity of both parents.

▲ The gift of new life is treated within the Christian community with great excitement.

9:3 Judaism, Islam and Hinduism, and infertility

How do Jews, Muslims and Hindus differ in their approaches to infertility?

▋ JUDAISM

> 66 *Whoever adds even one Jewish soul is considered as having created an [entire] world.* 99
>
> ... **MOSES MAIMONIDES, TWELFTH-CENTURY JEWISH THINKER**

IVF and AIH treatments for infertility do not cause any problems for Jews and some are prepared to accept AID treatment as well, although the majority do not. Many rabbis have taught that if procreation cannot be achieved through normal sexual intercourse then other means are acceptable. Family life is extremely important within the Jewish community and infertility is a source of great sadness. Most Jews are unhappy about AID because, technically, it seems to be a form of adultery and that is strictly against the teaching of the Ten Commandments. Surrogacy is forbidden by most rabbinic authorities. One reason is that a child's religious identity comes through its Jewish mother. Jews believe that whoever gives birth is the child's actual mother.

▋ ISLAM

> 66 *To Allah belongs the dominion of the heavens and the earth. He creates what He wills (and plans). He bestows (children) male and female according to His Will (and plan). Or He bestows both males and females, and He leaves barren whom He will: for He is full of knowledge and power.* 99
>
> ... **THE QUR'AN (42.49–50)**

The creation of children is a very important part of a Muslim marriage and life can be difficult for a couple who have not been blessed by Allah with the gift of children. Muslims accept that if a couple have difficulty conceiving they may need medical help. There is no objection to IVF or AIH, but Muslims see little difference between AID and adultery, which is strictly forbidden in the Qur'an. Surrogacy is also forbidden because, as the Qur'an teaches, no one can be a child's mother, except the woman who carried it. Muslim men are allowed by the Qur'an to have up to four wives and this may happen if a wife is unable to give her husband any children – so making surrogacy unnecessary.

▋ HINDUISM

> 66 *I look upon all creatures equally, none are less dear to me and none more dear.* 99
>
> ... **THE BHAGAVAD GITA (9.29)**

Family life is extremely important within the Hindu community. Couples are anxious, in particular, to have at least one son, since it is the eldest son who carries out the most important religious rites at the death of a parent. He lights the funeral pyre and carries out other rituals within days of death to guarantee that the soul finds a new home. If this does not happen, the soul can return to trouble the dead relative's family.

If a couple do not manage to conceive a baby then, under Hindu laws, they can divorce. A barren woman is pitied in Hindu society. It is part of the natural order of things that a Hindu man should be the father of sons before he reaches old age. Traditionally, he is only free to seek God in old age when his children are grown up and have left home.

Hindu men and women are happy to use medical science to help them conceive and they have no problems with IVF or AIH. AID, however, does present a problem because a child conceived in this way would not know what caste they belonged to. It would be difficult to guarantee that the father belonged to the same caste as the mother. Although the caste system has been outlawed in India for more than 50 years, it still exercises influence, especially over the choice of a marriage partner.

Tasks

Tasks

1. How do the three religions agree in their approach to the problem of infertility?

2. How do the three religions disagree in their approach to the problem of infertility?

3. Why is surrogacy forbidden for members of the Jewish community?

4. Both Judaism and Islam are strongly opposed to adultery. How does this affect their attitudes towards infertility treatment?

5. Explain why it is very important for every Hindu married couple to have at least one son.

 Think about ...

Do you think that receiving AID is the same as committing adultery, as most religions believe, or not?

 Exam tip
You will find that the different religions often have similar attitudes to the same social issues – although for very different reasons. You must make sure that you know what these different reasons are.

SUMMARY

1 Jews are willing to use IVF and AIH but, for many, AID has similarities with adultery. Surrogacy causes problems about the child's Jewish identity and so is not supported.

2 Children are very important in a Muslim marriage. Couples who cannot conceive are encouraged to seek help. IVF and AIH do not cause any problem, but AID is equated with adultery, which is strictly forbidden in Islam. Surrogacy is also forbidden.

3 Each Hindu couple hopes to have one son to perform their funeral rites. A woman with no children is pitied in Hindu society. AID causes a problem because of the caste system.

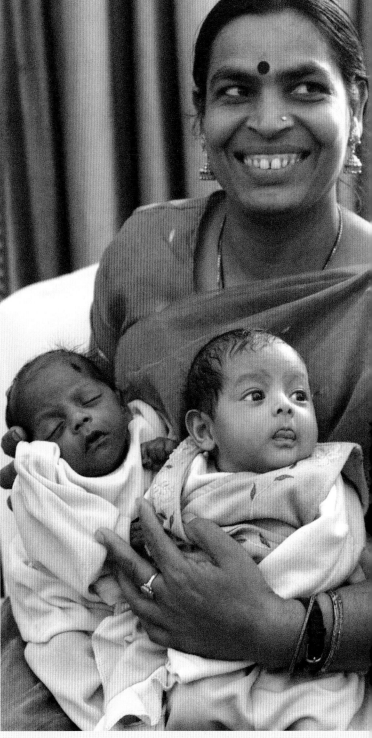

▲ Malti Devi holds her test-tube twins in New Delhi, India, in 2002.

9:4 Genetic engineering and transplant surgery

What is genetic engineering?

In 1953, one of the greatest scientific discoveries of the twentieth century was made by James Watson and Francis Crick. They unravelled DNA – a complex molecule found in all cells – which holds the blueprint for everything that happens in the human body. It has been called 'the building-block of life'. The Human Genome Project, which began in 1990, is an attempt to map out the DNA structure of human beings. This will make it possible to see how individual genes work – and ultimately could lead to the development of drugs to deal with many human diseases.

Manipulating the genes

Within a decade or so it will be possible to manipulate most of the genes in the human body. There are three possible uses of this.

1. **Genetic engineering.** This is the process of manipulating DNA directly, so allowing a particular characteristic to be deleted, altered or replaced. By changing the genetic code the new characteristic will be passed on to the next generation.

2. **Gene therapy.** This involves replacing a defective gene with a new one. This could be done to help people with cystic fibrosis and other conditions. Cloning processes can now be used to grow healthy cells to replace the malfunctioning ones in the body. This involves creating stem cells from embryos, which are produced for IVF treatment and not used, or by developing them from bone marrow or blood.

3. **Xenotransplantation.** This is a method of transplanting organs between one species and another. Pig organs, for instance, have been used as short-term replacements for human organs in the last few years.

Moral and religious issues

Genetic engineering raises immense moral and religious issues.

- Should insurance companies be allowed to ask for genetic tests before providing life insurance? The results of these tests would tell them a lot about the future life of each person.

- Should unborn foetuses be tested for conditions that lead to an early death? This would give parents the opportunity to seek an abortion if they wish. It would be possible to tell if a foetus had cystic fibrosis, for example, or might have a tendency to contract a condition such as breast cancer later in life.

The questions raised by genetic engineering are far-reaching. On the positive side, some 'killer' diseases could become things of the past by around 2020. On the negative side it could mean the whole map of a person's life being laid bare. It will mean that human beings will be given the power to 'play God' more and more in the future. This is bound to have a great effect on the faith that many people have in God.

Organ transplantation

In the last 20 years it has become possible to transplant many different human organs and tissues. This is offering thousands of people the opportunity to have an improved lifestyle. At the same time, these techniques have introduced a series of hotly debated issues ranging from our attitudes to the dead body, the scarcity of available organs and the use of animal organs and tissues in the future. Two kinds of human organ transplantation can take place: bone marrow and kidney transplants.

1. **Transplants in which the donor is living.** To be successful there must be a perfect match between recipient and donor. People can live a normal life with only one kidney. In the UK it is illegal for someone to be paid to donate a kidney, although this sometimes happens in many Third World countries.

2. **Transplants in which the donor has died.** This may take place after someone dies in a car accident. Many people carry donor cards giving permission for their organs to be used in the case of a sudden and unexpected death. The organ must be removed very soon after death and presents close relatives with a difficult emotional decision.

IT'S A FACT

It is now possible to transplant at least 25 different organs and tissues – including bone and cartilage tissue, kidney, pancreas, heart, lung, cornea and liver – from one person to another. These operations were revolutionary when first introduced, but most are now routine.

▲ A horse's body has a pig's head superimposed on it. Could this become a possibility with genetic engineering?

Exam tip

Topics such as genetic engineering and organ transplantation are immensely important areas of debate in the modern world. You will not be expected to have a detailed knowledge of them. You will be expected, however, to have a basic understanding and an awareness of the difficult issues that each topic raises.

SUMMARY

1 Genetic engineering involves the manipulation of genes, allowing particular characteristics to be changed. This could lead to cures for many fatal diseases. Gene therapy involves replacing a defective gene with a new one.

2 Genetic engineering raises many moral and religious issues. It could give people a map of their entire life.

3 Organs for transplantion can be taken from living and dead people.

Tasks

1.a. What is genetic engineering?

  b. Write about DNA and the Human Genome Project.

2. Describe **TWO** possible reasons scientists might have for manipulating the genes in a human being.

3. 'Insurance companies should not be allowed to ask for genetic tests. People should be allowed to keep this information private.' Present **TWO** reasons for this argument and **TWO** against.

4. What are the **TWO** different kinds of organ transplantation?

9:5 Christianity and genetic engineering

How do Protestants and Roman Catholics differ in their attitudes towards genetic engineering?

> Since it must be treated from conception as a person, the embryo must be defended in its integrity, cared for, and healed, as far as possible, like any other human being.
>
> ... **THE CATECHISM OF THE CATHOLIC CHURCH, 1994**

Genetic engineering is one of the most controversial issues in modern society. Christians reflect the general confusion on the matter and these different opinions are widely reflected in the Christian Church. These opinions can generally be divided into two.

The Protestant viewpoint

Protestants, such as the Church of England and the Methodist Church, do not object to research being carried out on human embryos – as long as it is properly controlled and is only performed on embryos less than 14 days old (that is within the present UK law). Protestants are happy to support this research because they do not believe that human life begins at conception. Some believe human life starts when the body is fully formed in the womb at about 12 weeks; some believe that it starts at the time of 'viability' when the baby could exist on its own and others believe it is at the time of birth. The work of the Human Fertilisation and Embryology Authority is very important. It is sometimes asked to adjudicate on scientific matters that have important moral and ethical, as well as religious, implications.

Protestants believe that human beings have a God-given responsibility to look after the whole of creation. They are sometimes worried that scientists may, through genetic engineering, overstep the authority that God has given them. It is thought that generally the scientific community does act responsibly in this and other matters. An essential part of the ministry of Jesus was to heal the sick: the deaf, the blind, the physically and mentally incapacitated. The Christian Church should support this work today and if genetic engineering is the most effective way of doing this then the Church should give its support. However, people do have reservations, for example Christians feel uncomfortable with the idea of human cloning. The creation of human life must remain with God and the means that He has provided to bring this about – sexual intercourse. Nothing must be allowed to interfere with this.

The Roman Catholic viewpoint

Some Roman Catholics are totally opposed to genetic engineering. They believe that it is the genetic makeup of a person that gives them their unique identity – an identity that is God-given. Any interference with this amounts to interference with God's plan. In attempting to interfere with this genetic makeup humans are exceeding the authority that God has given them – even if they are trying to better people's lives. Suffering is a necessary, and valuable, part of life's journey through which people learn spiritual lessons which they cannot learn in any other way.

Other Roman Catholics accept that the possible benefits of genetic engineering are considerable, but cannot accept the desirability of carrying out research on human embryos. They oppose this even if human embryos can be used to create replacement cells to help people suffering from such diseases as Parkinson's and diabetes. This is because of the Roman Catholic understanding of when human life begins. This is a hotly disputed scientific question, but Roman Catholics, for various reasons, believe that life begins at conception. Just as abortion at any time is an inhumane act so is the using of embryos for research purposes (see quotation). The killing of human life is strictly forbidden both by the Bible and also by the Christian Church.

Few Christian Churches have a problem with organ donation and transplantation, whether the donor is dead or alive. They see it as the gift of life from one person to another. If the death of one person can lead to new life for another then that is good.

> We support the recommendation that research, under licence, be permitted on embryos up to 14 days old, and agree that embryos should not be created just for scientific research.
>
> ... **CHURCH OF ENGLAND REPORT, 1994**

Donor Card

I would like to help someone to live after my death.

Let your relatives know your wishes, and keep this card with you at all times.

▲ Christians support the giving of organs to people who might otherwise die.

Think about ...

'Christians should support research into genetic engineering because this could result in millions of people being helped and cured.' Do you agree with this comment? Do you support such research?

Tasks

1.a. What is the Protestant view on embryo research?

  b. What is the Protestant attitude towards genetic engineering?

2. What is the main difference between the two attitudes in the Catholic Church to genetic engineering?

3. What is the reason why Roman Catholics are opposed to research being carried out on human embryos?

SUMMARY

1 Most Protestants support human embryo research as long as strict safeguards operate. They believe that the prize of being able to cure many serious illnesses is very important.

2 Most Roman Catholics are against all human embryo research – stemming from the Catholic belief about when human life begins. Some Catholics, though, support genetic engineering if human embryos are not used.

9:6 Judaism, Islam and Hinduism, and genetic engineering

What are the similarities and differences in the approaches adopted by Jews, Muslims and Hindus towards genetic engineering?

◼ JUDAISM

> *Whoever destroys a single life is considered as if he had destroyed the whole world and whoever saves a single life as if he had saved the whole world.*
>
> **... THE MISHNAH, A JEWISH HOLY BOOK**

Genetic research is supported by most Jews, because the Tanakh clearly teaches that everything should be done to eliminate disease. Some, however, disagree with research on human embryos because the embryo is a human life and killing is forbidden in the Ten Commandments. Many Jews applaud the way in which science is able to improve the quality of human life since this is what God has always wanted human beings to do in their role as God's stewards on earth. A steward not only passes on God's gift to the future generations but also tries, where possible, to improve that gift. Clearly it would greatly improve the standard of life for many people if some diseases were eliminated.

Most Jews are happy to allow transplant surgery as long as the organ is taken from a living person, but many are unhappy with the idea of an organ being taken from a person who has just died. This is because of the enormous care that Jews take of a dead body in the few hours between death and burial.

◼ ISLAM

The Qur'an teaches that all human life is sacred. Embryos left over from IVF treatment may be used for medical research, but they cannot be created specifically for this purpose. Concerning genetic engineering, some Muslims believe that Allah alone can determine the genetic make-up of a person and any attempt to alter this is forbidden. Many believe, however, that the Qur'an clearly teaches that everything possible should be done to cure disease and help those who are suffering. If this involves genetic engineering then it should be supported. Muslims, though, are totally against the cloning of human beings.

> *If anyone has saved a life, it would be as if he had saved the life of the whole people.*
>
> **... THE QUR'AN (5.32)**

Muslims have strict rules about the treatment of the human body after death and this leaves the majority of them opposed to organ transplantation. Allah ordains when each person will die and so to take an organ from a dead person and use it to sustain life in someone else is against the will of Allah. There is, however, some disagreement amongst Muslims if the donor is living and donating their kidney to keep someone, usually a relative, alive. Many Muslims believe that this does not break any of the Muslim laws or traditions about death.

◼ HINDUISM

Hindus believe that everything should be done to cure human beings from disease. Doctors and scientists should work together to make this increasingly possible. Some Hindus accept that human embryos are used in genetic research, as long as no attempt is made to clone human beings. They believe that embryos do not become human beings until well after conception. Other Hindus, though, are strongly opposed to all genetic research and, especially, to the use of human embryos in research. They argue that the law of karma, which covers the whole of life, determines that if a person is suffering now that is because of something they have done in a past life. It is not possible to escape the consequences of karma and if they are evaded in this life they will have to be faced up to in the next.

Organ transplantation does not cause any problems to Hindus. When a Hindu dies the body is burned whilst the soul seeks out another body to inhabit. What happens to the body is not important. If an organ is taken from a dead body and given to another that does not create any problems.

▲ Religious teaching is strongly against the creation of 'designer' babies.

 Think about ...

The attitude of most religions to the use of human embryos in genetic engineering depends on when an embryo or foetus becomes a human being. Why do you think this is a particularly difficult question to answer?

Tasks

1.a. What **TWO** attitudes are there within the Jewish community towards genetic engineering?

b. Give **ONE** reason for each of these attitudes.

2.a. Which **TWO** attitudes are found in the Muslim community towards genetic engineering?

b. Give **ONE** reason for each of these attitudes.

3.a. Which **TWO** attitudes are found in the Hindu community towards genetic research?

b. Give **ONE** reason for each of these attitudes.

4. Write down **TWO** ways in which you agree or disagree with the religion you have studied about genetic engineering.

SUMMARY

1 Jews believe that everything should be done to eliminate disease but many are unhappy about using human embryos in genetic research.

2 Muslims believe that all life is sacred. Muslims disagree over whether human beings have the authority to tamper with the human genetic make-up. Organ transplantation interferes with the very strict Muslim laws about how a dead body should be treated.

3 Some Hindus believe that human embryos can be used in research but the belief in karma stops many Hindus supporting genetic research.

9:7 The Jewish and Christian cosmologies

What do Jews and Christians believe about the creation of the universe?

Christianity and Judaism share the same myth about the creation of the universe, the creation of the world and the creation of all forms of life. This story is found in the first three chapters of the book of Genesis. In fact, not one but two stories are told there and one, it seems, is much older than the other.

1. Genesis 1.1–2.4. The first story moves in sequence through the six days of creation, beginning with creation of the physical habitat, the universe (days 1–4), birds and aquatic animals (day 5) and ending with the creation of land animals and human beings (day 6). On the seventh day the Creator, God, rested after announcing that He was highly satisfied with His work. Each day's creative activity ends with the comment: "Evening passed and morning came … ." After each day of creative activity we are told that "God was pleased with what He saw." The whole story ends with the comment: "That was how the world was created."

This account reflects the importance that religious festivals (1.14) and the sabbath day (2.3) had in the life of the Jews at a much later date. In particular, the sabbath day is linked with the story of creation to show the importance of the holy day – a day of rest and a day in which to worship God.

2. Genesis 2.5–25. The second story concentrates on the creation of the first man, Adam, and the first woman, Eve. In this account the first man is created before the first animals. The man is given the task by God of naming the animals but, after he has done so, he doesn't find that he can make friends with any of them. It is then that God creates woman to be man's companion. The main purpose of this account is to establish God's will for humankind in terms of family life. We discover that God has created the man and the woman so that the earth can be peopled. This account is full of colourful details about what God said and did.

Behind the stories

By calling these stories 'myths', we are indicating that they are not literal descriptions of fact. They are myths or poems; stories intended to convey some important ideas about God and His activity in the world. Some Christians, called 'creationists', disagree with this view but they are in the minority. They wish to maintain that the world is

much younger than the scientists tell us, a matter of a few thousand years old at the most, but this idea wins little scientific support.

Most Jews and Christians feel that a scientific and a biblical account of creation need to be set side by side to provide two pictures of the single story of creation. From one we learn how the world came into being (the scientific account) whilst from the other (the biblical story) we discover how God was involved. The biblical story does not give us any factual information about how the world was created but sheds light on God's activity and the dependence of human beings on Him.

Creation out of nothing

Jews and Christians, therefore, both teach that God created the world. There is no official teaching, however, as to how this creation took place. It is often assumed that both believe that God created the world 'out of nothing' (*creatio ex nihilo*). This is not necessarily the case. The rabbis point out that the scriptures suggest that the man and the woman were made 'out of the dust of the ground'. This, though, is not a scientific statement. Both Jews and Christians accept the scientific explanation of how the world began without too much trouble.

There are many 'creation myths' but the Jewish and Christian story is special. The first chapter of the Bible introduces God – who later shows Himself to be the ruler of the universe, lawgiver, judge, loving father, lord of history and Creator. The universe and human beings are not divine, like God is – they are created. God is uncreated. That is the real message behind the two creation stories in Genesis.

▼ The book of Genesis states that God created light 'to show the time when religious festivals begin'. Passover is an important Jewish festival.

! Think about ...

Every ancient culture has its own creation story. Why do you think it is important to have an explanation of how the universe, the world and human life began?

IMPORTANT WORD

Cosmology;   the study of the universe as a whole; the structure and parts of the system of creation

Tasks

1.a. Outline the story told in the first account of creation found in the book of Genesis.

b. Why do you think that this account stresses that God was pleased with His handiwork after each stage of creation?

c. Which parts of Jewish religious life are linked with creation in this account?

2.a. Outline the story told in the second account of creation in the book of Genesis.

b. Why is the sabbath day linked with God and creation in this second account?

3. According to the second account of creation:

a. What did man give to the animals?

b. Why was woman created?

c. Why were marriage and family life created?

SUMMARY

1 Jews and Christians share the same cosmology and the same creation stories. They are found in the book of Genesis and there are two stories that are very different. The first concentrates on the creation of the physical world at the command of God. The second revolves around the creation of the first man and woman.

2 The stories are myths – they teach religious and moral but not scientific truth.

3 In Judaism and Christianity, God the Creator is also the law-giver and the lord of history. God is divine – human beings are not.

▲ Both Judaism and Christianity depend upon the same creation story.

9:8 The Muslim and Hindu cosmologies

What cosmologies are found in Islam and Hinduism?

> *And We send down from the sky rain charged with blessing, and We produce therewith gardens and grain for harvests; And tall (and stately) palm-trees, with shoots of fruit-stalks, plied one over another – As sustenance for (Allah's) Servants – and We give (new) life therewith to land that is dead: Thus will be the Resurrection.*
>
> **... THE QUR'AN (50.9–11)**

ISLAM

The Qur'an leaves the reader in no doubt – Allah is the creator of all that exists. By a simple word of command Allah speaks and all that is exists. Everything in the world is a 'sign' so that everyone can see Allah. This work of creation continues beyond the world to the after-life, as Allah brings everyone from the grave to the place of judgement *(see quotation)*.

The ummah

Muslims believe that all things come from Allah. Everyone who belongs to the faith of Islam forms a single community (the ummah) and this gives people real safety in Allah. This is the way that Allah created all things. The Qur'an tells us how this happened.

- Allah created the sun, moon, stars and planets before separating the night from the day.

- After water was sent by Allah to the earth, vegetation began to grow up and sprout. He then created the birds, fish and animals.

- The first human being, Adam, was created out of the clay into which Allah breathed life *(see quotation)*.

> *Man we did create from a quintessence (of clay). Then we placed him as (a drop of) sperm in a place of rest, firmly fixed; Then We made the sperm into a clot of congealed blood; then of that clot We made a (foetus) lump; Then We made out of that lump bones and clothed the bones with flesh; then we developed it into another creature.*
>
> **... THE QUR'AN (23.12–14)**

Adam was made the khalifah (ruler) of the earth and God told all the angels to bow down in front of him. Adam and Eve, his wife, were then thrown out of paradise because they listened to the temptations of Iblis (Satan) and disobeyed God. There is a very close similarity between this picture of creation and that in the Jewish scriptures.

HINDUISM

Just as Hinduism can take many forms, so there are many creation stories. They fall into two clear groups.

1. Stories that suggest the world began at a definite time at some point in the distant past. In the Rig Vedas, for example, there is a cosmic egg from which all creatures come forth. Brahma, the creator god, is often pictured as the first to come out of Brahman, who is the architect of the gods.

2. Stories that suggest that the world did not have a definite starting point. It was an 'emanation' from Brahman: it came out of Brahman. Some people thought of creation as a wave. The water rises to form a crest before falling into a trough. The process goes on and on. Creation is seen to be the same as it is always in the process of being created. It is always slipping into disorder and chaos.

As the quotation shows, Hindus do not claim to know how creation came into being. The 'Hymn of Creation' in the Rig Vedas shows that many more questions can be asked about creation than answers found. Hindus today are perfectly happy to leave scientists to provide the information as long as room is left for the universal force behind the universe, Brahman, who is eternal and never-ending whilst the universe is born, dies and is reborn again. It is not difficult to see how this way of understanding creation could provide a simple link with the theory of evolution.

▲ Historical engraving of an early Hindu idea of the Earth and the Universe. The Earth was thought to be a hemisphere supported by four elephants. The elephants are standing on a giant tortoise floating on the universal ocean.

> *Neither being nor non-being was as yet. There was no air, no sky that lies beyond it. What was concealed? And where? And in whose protection? Who really knows? Who can declare it? Whence was it born and whence came this creation? The gods were born later than the world's creation, so who knows from where it came into existence? None can know from where creation has arisen.*

... ADAPTED FROM THE RIG VEDA (10:124.2—7)

SUMMARY

1 The Qur'an emphasises that Allah is the creator of everything – the physical world being a 'sign' to those with faith in Allah. The creative process continues with the resurrection of everyone from the grave to the place of judgement.

2 Hindu creation stories, of which there are many, divide between those which look back to the time of creation and those which see creation as an ongoing process. The second type suggest a link with the process of evolution.

Tasks

1. 'Everything in the world is a sign so that we can see Allah clearly.' What does this statement mean?

2.a. Write down **THREE** stages in the creation process that are found in the Qur'an.

   b. Write down **TWO** similarities that you can find between the Jewish and the Muslim creation stories.

3. Into which **TWO** groups do the Hindu creation stories fall?

4. Why does **ONE** creation story in Hinduism liken the act of creation to the rise and fall of a wave?

✓ **Exam tip**
On many issues there are different viewpoints within the same religion. Hindu cosmology is a good example of this. Make sure that you realise that are two broad points of view. A good exam answer will need to show this.

9:9 The scientific cosmology

What are the key elements in the scientific understanding of the universe, the world and life?

> *There is grandeur in this view of life, with its several powers, having been originally breathed by the Creator into a few forms or into one; and that, whilst this planet has gone cycling on according to the fixed laws of gravity, from so simple a beginning endless forms most beautiful and most wonderful have been and are being evolved.*
>
> **... CHARLES DARWIN, ON THE ORIGIN OF SPECIES**

Since the holy texts of the world's religions were completed scientists have told us a great deal about the origins of the universe and life on earth. In many ways this information has revolutionised the way in which we look at life – and our place, as human beings, in the vast universe.

The Copernican revolution

A great change took place in the sixteenth century and is associated with the name of Nicholas Copernicus (1473–1543). Copernicus, a Christian priest, was also an astronomer. Until his time, people thought that the earth was at the centre of the universe with the sun, moon and the stars being no more that lights in the heavens to light up earth. The whole world was thought to revolve around the earth. Copernicus declared that Earth is just one of billions of planets in the solar system. The solar system, one of millions in the universe, travels around the sun and not vice versa.

The origins of the universe

The study of the origin of the universe is called 'cosmology'. There has been a lively debate in the last century over the age of the universe. Most scientists now think that it is between 18 and 20 billion years old. Some scientists, though, dispute whether the universe ever came into existence at a definite time.

Most scientists believe that the universe started with a Big Bang. For reasons that are not fully understood, this explosion led to plasma being sent flying throughout the universe at a great speed. This eventually led to the formation of galaxies and these are still moving away at great speed. As the galaxies travel through the universe they cool and slow down. The universe is still expanding but at a much slower rate than at first. The cooling of the gases led to the formation of stars and planets, including the Earth.

The origin of life

The theory of evolution was the most important scientific theory to emerge in the nineteenth century. It is associated with the name of Charles Darwin, who spent some years on the Galapagos Islands studying plant and animal life. His work convinced him that all forms of life developed (evolved) over a long period of time. As they grew so they adapted to meet the changing conditions around them. If they did not, they died out. As the different species adapt so they change; this is called 'natural selection'. The best adapted survive whilst the weakest die; this is called 'the survival of the fittest'. Darwin realised that what he had found out about animals and plants was also true of human beings. It was this that religious people found so difficult to accept. Human beings share some of their physical characteristics with apes and so the two must be related. You can imagine why the people, who had always thought that human beings were special and unique, were so upset.

Science and religion

Religion is much older than science. Many holy books put forward myths to explain how the universe and human life began. It is natural that many people conclude that religion and science would always be on a collision course. Yet there are some interesting thoughts that might lead us to challenge this conclusion.

- Science deals with facts and how they should be understood. Many of these facts have to be discovered and investigated. To investigate them we need to use our senses. Religion claims to deal with 'facts' but they are discovered spiritually. To understand life fully, perhaps we need both a scientific and a religious understanding.

- Most world religions claim that the world was created by God and based on laws that He put in place. Science believes that its task is to discover these laws and understand them. Science and religion could be two sides of one coin. Many scientists are religious believers.

▲ Scientists believe the universe began with a 'big bang'.

IT'S A FACT

In 1999 the morning news programme on BBC Radio 4 invited listeners to name 'the most significant British figure of the second millennium'. Almost everyone mentioned Shakespeare or Churchill. There was barely a mention, though, of any scientist!

Tasks

1.a. What was the Copernican revolution?

   b. Why did this revolution upset so many people in the sixteenth century?

2. What do scientists mean when they talk of the Big Bang?

3.a. What is 'the theory of evolution'?

   b. What does 'natural selection' mean?

   c. What is meant by 'the survival of the fittest'?

4. Outline **TWO** reasons for thinking that the gap between science and religion may not be as wide as some people think.

SUMMARY

1 The great scientific revolution associated with Copernicus was the realisation that the Sun, and not the Earth, was the centre of the solar system.

2 Cosmology is the study of the origins of the universe. Modern science dates the age of the universe at between 18 and 20 billion years. Scientists think the universe was formed through a Big Bang; the planets and stars were formed as gases cooled. The universe is still expanding.

3 Evolution is the generally accepted explanation for the beginning of human life. Species that survive are those that adapt to their surroundings – natural selection. The best adapted survive whilst others die out – the survival of the fittest.

 **Exam help ...**

This chapter raises some of the most controversial, and difficult, issues confronting society today. Religious people are finding their faith under challenge from infertility and genetic engineering. Another kind of challenge comes from scientific explanations about the beginning of the universe and human life. You must be aware of the kind of challenge that this new scientific knowledge presents to religious faith. Christians, in particular, have tried to respond to it in different ways.

1.a. Outline the different treatments available to a couple suffering from infertility.

b. Explain why there are different reactions within the Christian Church to these treatments.

1.a. There are four main treatments open to an infertile couple.

- **In vitro fertilisation (IVF).** 'In vitro' means 'in glass'. Often referred to as 'test-tube' babies. Now a common technique. Fertilisation takes place outside a woman's body, in a laboratory. Fertilised eggs are placed back in her body.

- **Artificial insemination by donor (AID).** Sperm from a donor is placed in a woman's body. Commonplace in animals, but controversial in humans.

- **Artificial insemination by husband (AIH).** A woman's egg is fertilised by husband's sperm and replaced in her body. Less controversial method.

- **Surrogacy.** Where a women carries a fertilised egg, gives birth and then hands the baby over to somebody else who will become the child's parent. Strict laws surround surrogacy; it cannot be advertised and it is illegal to pay an agency to make any arrangement.

continued ...

b. Within Christianity there are mixed feelings about infertility treatments.

- The Roman Catholic Church objects to all forms of infertility treatment. Along with other Churches, it maintains that AID is wrong because this is the same as adultery. Other forms of infertility treatment are objected to because they involve masturbation, which is a grave sin according to the Roman Catholic Church. It is felt that procreation should only take place as a result of sexual intercourse; objections to surrogacy are raised for the same reason.

- Other Christian Churches also object to AID and some have great reservations about surrogacy. Churches do not object to AIH or IVF.

2. What is the attitude of Christianity towards genetic engineering?

2. Genetic engineering involves manipulating genes in the human body to make it possible for a gene to be altered or replaced. This would make it possible for medical conditions to be 'phased out' – dependent on scientists knowing the structure of each gene in the body. The Human Genome Project is hoping to make this possible within a short time.

- Christians believe that each individual is created by God. Altering the genetic make-up has serious implications for people who believe in God. Are we 'playing God'? If so, does this alter the faith that people have in God? Would it lay the 'map' of each person's life bare? Do we want this? Can we cope with the knowledge? Each person's medical history will be known before it happens. What are the implications of having this knowledge? Many Christians feel only God is entitled to have such knowledge.

continued ...

- On the positive side, it opens up the possibility of being able to cure many diseases and eradicate some completely.
- The Roman Catholic Church is opposed to embryo research. It believes such embryos to be human beings. The Church also believes that it is God who gives each person their individual identity and are opposed to anything that changes this. Protestants do not believe that the embryo is a human being and they are not opposed to embryo research. Protestants support anything that offers long-term benefits to the human race.

3. Choose ONE religion and explain the attitude of that religion to genetic engineering and organ transplantation.

3. The chosen religion is Judaism.

- Jews believe that everything should be done to improve life and eliminate disease. Jews, though, are opposed to genetic engineering. Like Roman Catholics, they believe that the embryo is a human life and so any research on embryos is unacceptable.
- Some Jews believe that the situation is not so clear-cut. As God's stewards on earth, Jews want to hand His gifts on to the next generation – in a better state. Clearly eliminating serious illnesses would be a major step forward.
- Jews accept organ transplantation as long as the organ is taken from a living person, such as with some kidney transplants. Many, though, are very unhappy about the idea of taking an organ from a dead person for transplantation; this is because of the great care that Jews take of a dead body.

4. Describe the Biblical cosmology that Jews and Christians share.

4. Jews and Christians share the cosmology that is found in the first two chapters of Genesis. There are two stories of creation there.

- The first story moves swiftly through the six days of creation – the creation of the physical order; the creation of the universe; the creation of birds and aquatic animals; the creation of land animals and, finally, the creation of human beings. This story reflects the importance of religious festivals and the sabbath day.
- The second story concentrates on the creation of the first man and woman. After being created, man names the animals but cannot find a close companion among them, so God creates woman. This places importance on family life so explaining how the world came to be peopled.
- Much debate has centred on whether God created the world 'out of nothing'. God is before everything else – uncreated. Human beings are created; they are not divine.

5. What are the different attitudes that Christians adopt to the Biblical cosmology?

5. There are three different attitudes that Christians adopt to the Biblical cosmology.

- The creationist viewpoint. This accepts that the Genesis account is giving us literal, scientific truth. This means that the world and the human race are much younger than science tells us – only a matter of a few thousand years.
- The conservative viewpoint. Takes both the biblical and the scientific accounts seriously. The 'days' in the Genesis account could be long periods of time. The suddenness of the Genesis account of the creation of light could refer to the Big Bang.
- The liberal viewpoint. This is the viewpoint of those who believe that science tells us how the world was created. The biblical account tells us the role that God played in creation.

Additional Quotations

Suffering

CHRISTIANITY

I was born with nothing, and I will die with nothing. The LORD gave, and now he has taken away. May his name be praised!

... THE BIBLE (JOB 1.21)

Every illness can make us glimpse death. ... Very often illness provokes a search for God and a return to him.

... CATECHISM OF THE CATHOLIC CHURCH

JUDAISM

Bear in mind that the LORD your God disciplines you just as a man disciplines his son.

... THE TORAH (DEUTERONOMY 8.5)

When God brings suffering upon people, he is educating us – making us realise our mistakes, just like a loving father sometimes has to smack his child.

... RABBI MEIR SIMCHA HACOHEN OF DVINSK (1843–1926)

The potter does not test cracked vessels, because if he taps them even once they break. He only tests good vessels, because no matter how many times he taps them they do not break. So God does not test the wicked but only the righteous.

... THE TALMUD

HINDUISM

Great souls who have become one with Me have reached the highest goal. They do not undergo rebirth, a condition which is impermanent and full of pain and suffering.

... BHAGAVAD GITA (8.15)

The result of a virtuous action is pure joy; actions done out of passion bring pain and suffering; ignorance arises from actions motivated by 'dark' intentions.

... BHAGAVAD GITA (14.16)

Sanctity of life

CHRISTIANITY

We need to affirm the sacredness of all human life. Every person is somebody because he is a child of God.

... MARTIN LUTHER KING JR, AMERICAN CHRISTIAN LEADER, (1929–68)

Do you not know that your body is the temple of the Holy Spirit, who lives in you and who was given to you by God? You do not belong to yourselves but to God.

... THE BIBLE (1 CORINTHIANS 6.19)

JUDAISM

And God created man in His image, in the image of God He created him, male and female He created them.

... THE TORAH (GENESIS 1.27)

You shall not murder.

... THE TORAH (EXODUS 20.13)

ISLAM

That it is He who granteth laughter and tears; That it is He who granteth death and life.

... THE QUR'AN (53.43–44)

[Do not] take life ... except for just cause. And if anyone is slain wrongfully, We have given his heir authority to demand retribution or to forgive.

... THE QUR'AN (17.33)

Life after death

CHRISTIANITY

Then I saw a great white throne and the one who sits on it. Earth and heaven fled from his presence and were seen no more. And I saw the dead, great and small alike, standing before the throne. Books were opened, and then another book was opened, the book of the living. The dead were judged according to what they had done, as recorded in the books. ... Then I saw a new heaven and a new earth. The first heaven and the first earth disappeared, and the sea vanished. And I saw the Holy City, the new Jerusalem, coming down out of heaven from God, prepared and ready, like a bride dressed to meet her husband.

... THE BIBLE (REVELATION 20.11–12; 21.1–2)

And he [one of the criminals executed with Jesus] said to Jesus, 'Remember me, Jesus, when you come as King!' Jesus said to him, 'I promise you that today you will be in Paradise with me.'

... THE BIBLE (LUKE 23.42–43)

This is how it will be when the dead are raised to life. When the body is buried, it is mortal; when raised, it will be immortal. When buried, it is ugly and weak; when raised, it will be beautiful and strong. When buried, it is a physical body; when raised, it will be a spiritual body. There is, of course, a physical body, so there has to be a spiritual body.

... THE BIBLE (1 CORINTHIANS 15.42–44)

I believe in ... the forgiveness of sins, the resurrection of the body and the life everlasting.

... APOSTLES' CREED

JUDAISM

A visitor to paradise was amazed to find it filled up with old men taken up with studying the Torah. Astonished, he turned to his heavenly guide who told him: 'You are mistaken if you think these men are in heaven. Heaven is in these men.'

... JEWISH FABLE

When a man leaves this world [no riches] accompany him, but only the Torah he has learnt and the good works he has carried out.

... ETHICS OF THE FATHERS

I believe with perfect faith that there will be a resurrection of the dead at a time when it will please the Creator, blessed be His name, and exalted be the remembrance of Him for ever and ever.

... THIRTEEN PRINCIPLES OF FAITH, NUMBER 13

Hear, O Israel: You shall love the Lord your God with all your heart, with all your soul and with all your strength. Let these matters, which I command you today, be upon your heart. Teach them thoroughly to your children and speak of them while you sit in the home, while you walk on the way. When you retire and when you arise. Bind them as a sign upon your arm and let them be tefillin between your eyes. And write them on the doorposts of your house and upon your gates.

... THE SHEMA, OFTEN SAID BY DYING JEWS

ISLAM

Muslims believe that each dead person is visited by two angels who put certain questions to them. To help them with the answers, these words are said over the grave after burial: *O [fe]male servant of God, remember the covenant made while leaving the world, that is, the statement that there is no God but God himself, and that Muhammad is the Messenger of God, and the belief that paradise is a truth, that the Doomsday shall come, there being no doubt about it; that God will bring back to life those who are in the graves, that thou hast accepted God as thy Lord; Islam as thy religion; Muhammad as thy Prophet, the Qur'an as thy guide, the Ka'bah as the direction to turn for the service of worship and that all believers are thy brethren. May God keep thee firm in this trial.*

On the Day of Judgement the whole of the earth will be but His handful, and the heavens will be rolled up in his right hand ... The trumpet will be sounded, when all that are in the heavens and on earth will swoon, except such as it will please Allah (to exempt). Then will a second one be sounded, when, behold, they will be standing and looking on! And the earth will shine with the glory of its Lord.

... THE QUR'AN (39.67–69)

... that Day shall (all men) be sorted out. Then those who have believed and worked righteous deeds, shall be made happy in a Mead of Delight. And those who have rejected faith and falsely denied Our signs and the meeting of the Hereafter – such shall be brought forth to punishment.

... THE QUR'AN (30.14–16)

Those who believe (in the Qur'an), those who follow the Jewish (scriptures) and the Sabians and the Christians – any who believe in Allah and the Last Day, and work righteousness – on them shall be no fear, nor shall they grieve.

... THE QUR'AN (5.69)

From the (earth) did We create you, and into it shall We return you, and from it shall We bring you out once again.

... THE QUR'AN (20.55)

HINDUISM

Whoever, at the hour of death, abandoning his mortal frame, bears me in mind, he accedes to my divinity, have no doubt of that.

... BHAGAVAD GITA (8.5)

Lead me from the unreal to the real, from darkness to light, from death to immortality.

... BRIHADARANYAKA UPANISHAD (1.28)

Euthanasia

Anything that says to the very ill that they are a burden to their family and that they would be better off dead is unacceptable. What sort of society could let its old folk die because they are 'in the way'?

... DR CICELY SAUNDERS, FOUNDER OF ST CHRISTOPHER'S HOSPICE

I will use treatment to help the sick according to my ability and judgement, but never with a view to injury and wrongdoing. Neither will I administer a poison to anybody when asked to do so, nor will I suggest such a course ... . I will keep pure and holy both my life and my art.

... HIPPOCRATIC OATH

CHRISTIANITY

By giving terminally ill children permission to be who they are and ensuring that they are kept in a loving, supportive environment, it is possible to help them to meet death with a dignity and with a nobility which in no way denies grief.

... MOTHER FRANCES DOMINICA, FOUNDER OF HOSPICE FOR CHILDREN IN OXFORD

I sincerely believe that those who come after us will wonder why on earth we kept a human being alive against his own will, when all dignity, beauty and meaning of life had vanished ... and when we would have been punished by the State if we had kept an animal alive in similar circumstances.

... DR LESLIE WEATHERHEAD, METHODIST MINISTER

ISLAM

There was a man ... who had an affliction that taxed his patience, so he took a knife, cut his wrist and bled to death. Upon this God said, 'My subject hastened his death. I deny him paradise.'

... THE PROPHET MUHAMMAD, HADITH

HINDUISM

As a goldsmith, taking a piece of gold, reduces it to another newer and more beautiful form, just so this soul, striking down this body and dispelling its ignorance, makes for itself another newer and more beautiful form.

... BRIHADARANYAKA UPANISHAD (4.4.4)

The one who tries to escape from the trials of life by committing suicide will suffer even more in the next life.

... YAJUR VEDA (40–43)

Marriage and divorce

CHRISTIANITY

Now, to the unmarried and to the widows I say that it would be better for you to continue to live alone ... . But if you cannot restrain your desires, go ahead and marry – it is better to marry than to burn with passion.

... THE BIBLE (1 CORINTHIANS 7.8–9)

Fornication is carnal union between an unmarried man and an unmarried woman. It is gravely contrary to the dignity of persons and of human sexuality which is naturally ordered to the good of spouses ...

... CATECHISM OF THE CATHOLIC CHURCH

You have heard that it was said, 'Do not commit adultery'. But now I tell you: anyone who looks on a woman and wants to possess her is guilty of committing adultery with her in his heart.

... THE BIBLE (MATTHEW 5.27–28)

Despite the many pressures modern society brings to bear, traditional Christian teaching – for good reason – continues to say that sex should be kept for marriage and that outside marriage it is a sin.

... SIMON AND CHRISTOPHER DANES, TODAY'S ISSUES AND CHRISTIAN BELIEFS

At the beginning of creation God made them male and female. For this reason a man will leave his father and mother and be united to his wife and the two will become one flesh. So they are no longer two but one. Therefore what God has joined together, let man not separate ... Anyone who divorces his wife and marries another commits adultery.

... THE BIBLE (MARK 10.6–9,11)

Judaism
The LORD God said, 'It is not good for man to be alone; I will make a fitting helper for him. And the LORD God formed out of the earth all the wild beasts and all the birds of the sky, and brought them to the man to see what he would call them; ... but for Adam no fitting helper was found. So the LORD God cast a deep sleep upon the man; and, while he slept, He took one of his ribs and closed up the flesh at that spot. And the LORD God fashioned the rib that He had taken from the man into a woman; and He brought her to man. Then the man said, 'This one at last is bone of my bones and flesh of my flesh. This one shall be called Woman, for from man was she taken. Hence a man leaves his father and mother and clings to his wife, so that they become one flesh.'

... THE TORAH (GENESIS 2.18–24)

Accordingly they both entered this covenant of love and companionship of peace and friendship to create a Jewish home to the glory of the Holy One, blessed be He, who makes His people Israel holy through the covenant of marriage.

... MARRIAGE CONTRACT, REFORM GROUP OF SYNAGOGUES

Every man needs a woman and every woman a man and both of them need the divine presence.

... RABBINIC SAYING

Over him who divorces the wife of his youth even the altar of God sheds tears.

... RABBINIC SAYING

A man takes a wife and possesses her. She fails to please him because he finds something obnoxious about her, and he writes her a bill of divorcement, hands it to her, and sends her away from his house ...

... THE TORAH (DEUTERONOMY 24.1)

Islam
A woman is taken in marriage for three reasons: for her beauty, for family connections or for lure of wealth. Choose the one with faith and you will have success.

... THE PROPHET MUHAMMAD, HADITH

If a wife fears cruelty or desertion on her husband's part, there is no blame on them if they arrange an amicable settlement between themselves; and such settlement is best ... If ye come to a friendly understanding, and practise self-restraint, Allah is Oft-Forgiving.

... THE QUR'AN (4.128–30)

It is He who has created man from water, then has He established relationships of lineage and marriage.

... THE QUR'AN (25.54)

Family life

Christianity
In creating man and woman, God instituted the human family ... Its members are persons equal in dignity. For the common good of its members and of society, the family necessarily has manifold responsibilities, rights and duties.

... CATECHISM OF THE CATHOLIC CHURCH

Respect your father and your mother, so that you may live a long time in the land that I am giving you.

... THE BIBLE (EXODUS 20.12)

Judaism
Listen to your father who begot you; do not disdain your mother when she is old.

... KETHUVIM (PROVERBS 23.22)

Blessed are You, our God, King of the universe, Who has created everything for His glory ... Who fashioned the Man in His image, in the image of His likeness. And prepared for him – from himself – a building for eternity ... Bring intense joy – and exultation to the barren one – through the gathering of her children amidst her gladness ... Blessed are You ... who created joy and gladness, groom and bride, mirth, glad song, pleasure, delight, love, brotherhood, peace and companionship.

... EXTRACT FROM SEVEN WEDDING BLESSINGS

May the All-Merciful bless the father and mother of this child; may they be worthy to rear him, to initiate him in the precepts of the Law and to train him in wisdom; from this eighth day and henceforth may his blood be accepted and may the Lord his God be with him.

... PRAYER AT CIRCUMCISION OF JEWISH BOY

Hinduism
The husband who wedded her ... always gives happiness to his wife. If a wife obeys her husband she will for that (reason alone) be exalted in heaven.

... THE LAWS OF MANU (5.153, 155)

Contraception

Christianity
All the Christian Churches at one time taught that contraception was sinful. It was held that God intended sex for the creation of new life and people should not interfere with this. ... Protestant Christians today see no moral problem in using contraceptives to help them limit the size of their families or delay starting a family for financial or other practical reasons.

... SIMON AND CHRISTOPHER DANES, TODAY'S ISSUES AND CHRISTIAN BELIEFS

Every action which … proposes, whether as an end or as a means, to render procreation impossible is intrinsically evil.

… CATECHISM OF THE CATHOLIC CHURCH

The purpose of human sexual activity is to express love and create new life within the context of marriage. Any sexual activity or expression that is not consistent with, or violates, this purpose is considered to be morally wrong because it opposes the divine plan. That is why artificial means of birth control, masturbation, fornication and pre-marital sex are always immoral.

… THE HARPERCOLLINS ENCYCLOPAEDIA OF CATHOLICISM, RICHARD P. MCBRIEN (ED), 1995

JUDAISM

For thus said the LORD, The Creator of heaven who alone is God, Who formed the earth and made it, Who alone established it - He did not create it a waste, but formed it for habitation.

… NEVI'IM (ISAIAH 45.18)

ISLAM

If Allah wishes to create a child you cannot prevent it.

… THE PROPHET MUHAMMAD, HADITH

Homosexuality

CHRISTIANITY

If a man has sexual relations with another man, they have done a disgusting thing, and both shall be put to death.

… THE BIBLE (LEVITICUS 20.13)

For homosexual men and women permanent relationships characterised by love can be appropriate and the Christian way of expressing their homosexuality.

… METHODIST CHURCH REPORT 1979

The number of men and women who have deep-seated homosexual tendencies is not negligible. They do not choose their homosexual condition: for most of them it is a trial. They must be accepted with respect, compassion and sensitivity.

… CATECHISM OF THE CATHOLIC CHURCH

We do not reject those who believe that they have more hope in growing in love for God and neighbour with the help of a loving and faithful homophile relationship.

… CHURCH OF ENGLAND REPORT ON HOMOSEXUALITY

ISLAM

If two men among you are guilty of lewdness, punish them both. If they repent and amend, leave them alone; for Allah is Oft-Returning, Most Merciful.

… THE QUR'AN (4.16)

HINDUISM

If sex itself is a somewhat difficult topic for a Hindu, homosexuality is virtually swept under the carpet.

… WERNER MENSKI IN ETHICAL ISSUES IN SIX RELIGIOUS TRADITIONS, PEGGY MORGAN, CLIVE LAWTON (EDS.), (EDINBURGH UNIVERSITY PRESS, 1996)

Social harmony

CHRISTIANITY

The LORD God said, 'It is not good for the man to live alone. I will make a suitable companion to help him.'

… THE BIBLE (GENESIS 2.18)

JUDAISM

If your wife is short, bend down to listen to her advice.

… THE TALMUD, A JEWISH HOLY BOOK

And to the woman He said, 'I will make most severe your pangs in childbearing; in pain shall you bear children. Yet your urge shall be for your husband, and shall rule over you.'

… THE TORAH (GENESIS 3.16)

ISLAM

Men are the protectors and maintainers of women, because Allah has given the one more (strength) than the other, and because they support them from their means.

… THE QUR'AN (4.34)

And say to the believing women that they should lower their gaze and guard their modesty, that they should not display their beauty and ornaments except what (must ordinarily) appear thereof.

… THE QUR'AN (24.31)

And stay quietly in your houses, and make not a dazzling display, like that of the former Times of Ignorance.

… THE QUR'AN (33.33)

… women shall have rights similar to the rights against them, according to what is equitable; but men have a degree (of advantage) over them.

… THE QUR'AN (2.228)

Modesty and faith are joined closely together; if either of them is lost, the other goes also.

… THE PROPHET MUHAMMAD, HADITH

The Believers, men and women, are protectors one of another: they enjoin what is just, and forbid what is evil: they observe regular prayers, practise regular charity, and obey Allah and His Messenger. On them will Allah pour His mercy.

… THE QUR'AN (9.71)

Other religions

CHRISTIANITY

The shift in the attitudes of many Christians that has taken place in the twentieth century owes a great deal to the increased knowledge and understanding that Christians now have of faiths other than their own and many Christians are involved in interfaith dialogue.

… TREVOR SHANNON IN ETHICAL ISSUES IN SIX RELIGIOUS TRADITIONS, PEGGY MORGAN, CLIVE LAWTON (EDS.), (EDINBURGH UNIVERSITY PRESS, 1996)

JUDAISM

When a stranger resides with you in your land, you shall not wrong him. The stranger who resides with you shall be to you as one of your citizens; you shall love him as yourself, for you were strangers in the land of Egypt.

… THE TORAH (LEVITICUS 19.33–34)

Let there be no compulsion in religion: Truth stands out clear from error.

... THE QUR'AN (2.256)

Muslims are required to deal with non-Muslims kindly and justly. Jews and Christians and all those who believe in one God have been given a special position in the Qur'an since their religions were originally based on revelation.

... MASHUQ IBN ALLY IN ETHICAL ISSUES IN SIX RELIGIOUS TRADITIONS, PEGGY MORGAN, CLIVE LAWTON (EDS.), (EDINBURGH UNIVERSITY PRESS, 1996)

Racism

CHRISTIANITY

We affirm that racism is a direct contradiction of the gospel of Jesus. We welcome the multi-racial nature of society in Britain and assert our unqualified commitment to it.

... METHODIST CONFERENCE 1987

ISLAM

And among His signs is the creation of the heaven and the earth, and the variations in your languages and your colours; verily, in that there are signs for those who know.

... THE QUR'AN (30.22)

All mankind is from Adam and Eve, an Arab has no superiority over a non-Arab nor a non-Arab has any superiority over an Arab; also a white has no superiority over a black nor a black has any superiority over a white except by piety [holiness] and good action. Learn that every Muslim is a brother to every Muslim and that the Muslims constitute the one brotherhood.

... THE PROPHET MUHAMMAD IN LAST SERMON AT MAKKAH 632

Wealth and poverty

Freedom from fear and want has been proclaimed as the highest aspiration of the common people ... to promote social progress and better standards of life in larger freedom. All human beings are born free and equal in dignity and rights.

... UNIVERSAL DECLARATION OF HUMAN RIGHTS

CHRISTIANITY

What God the Father considers to be pure and genuine religion is this: to take care of orphans and widows in their suffering and to keep oneself from being corrupted by the world.

... THE BIBLE (JAMES 1.27)

For the love of money is a source of all kinds of evil.

... THE BIBLE (1 TIMOTHY 6.10)

There is surely a moral imperative to bring sanity to this crazy deadly situation [about food wastage], to restore human dignity, to promote development and the possibility of peace. We must look at ourselves and our lifestyle. We must examine and change the processes and structures of the world, which at the moment promote division and ultimately bring death.

... CARDINAL BASIL HUME

The church should concern itself first, and indeed second, with the poor and needy, whether in spirit or in body.

... ARCHBISHOP'S COMMISSION ON CHURCH AND STATE, CHURCH OF ENGLAND

JUDAISM

If, however, there is a needy person among you, ... do not harden your heart and shut your hand against your needy kinsmen. Rather, you must open your hand and lend him sufficient for whatever he needs.

... THE TORAH (DEUTERONOMY 15.7–8)

Do not toil to gain wealth; have the sense to desist.

... KETHUVIM (PROVERBS 23.4)

... whenever a man does eat and drink and get enjoyment out of all his wealth, it is a gift of God.

... KETHUVIM (ECCLESIASTES 3.13)

ISLAM

Riches are sweet and a source of blessing to those who acquire them by the way; but those who seek them out of greed are like people who eat but are never full.

... THE PROPHET MUHAMMAD, HADITH

HINDUISM

Recall the face of the poorest and the most helpless man you have seen, and ask yourself if the step you contemplate is going to be of any use to him.

... MAHATMA GANDHI

He who seeks happiness must strive for contentment and self-control; happiness arises from contentment, uncontrolled pursuit of wealth will result in unhappiness.

... THE LAWS OF MANU (4.12)

Social responsibility

Since 1945 the UK has developed a Welfare State in which people are able to claim benefits, medical treatment and other services as a right. Before that time, many of these were seen as charity and were organized by individuals – they decided who should and should not receive help and on what terms.

... ACTIVATE 2 ENQUIRIES INTO NATIONAL CITIZENSHIP, PAULINE HUDSON AND ANNE KNAPP, (NELSON THORNES, 2002)

CHRISTIANITY

Everyone must obey the state authorities, because no authority exists without God's permission, and the existing authorities have been put there by God.

... THE BIBLE (ROMANS 13.1)

Remind your people to submit to rulers and authorities, to obey them, and to be ready to do good in every way. Tell them not to speak evil of anyone, but to be peaceful and friendly, and always to show a gentle attitude towards everyone.

... THE BIBLE (TITUS 3.1–2)

The Church, in her doctrine, life and worship, perpetuates and transmits to every generation all that she herself is, all that she believes.

... CATECHISM OF THE CATHOLIC CHURCH

A human being must always obey the certain judgement of his conscience. If he were deliberately to act against it, he would condemn himself ... A good and pure conscience is enlightened by true faith, for charity proceeds at the same time from a pure heart and a good conscience and sincere faith.

... CATECHISM OF THE CATHOLIC CHURCH

The books of scripture must be acknowledged as teaching solidly, faithfully and without error that truth which God wanted put into sacred writings for the sake of salvation.

... SECOND VATICAN COUNCIL OF THE CATHOLIC CHURCH, 1962–5

SUMMARY OF THE TEN COMMANDMENTS
1.   You shall have no other gods before me.
2.   You shall not make for yourself an idol.
3.   You shall not misuse the name of the Lord your God.
4.   Remember the Sabbath Day by keeping it holy.
5.   Honour your father and mother.
6.   You shall not murder.
7.   You shall not commit adultery.
8.   You shall not steal.
9.   You shall not give false testimony against your neighbour.
10. You shall not covet your neighbour's house. You shall not covet your neighbour's wife.

... THE BIBLE (EXODUS 20.3–17)

The environment

We, members of the major world religions and traditions, and men and women of good will, are gathered here, in this marvellous Church of St Francis, to awaken all people to their historical responsibility for the welfare of Planet Earth, our Sister and Mother, who in her generous sovereignty feeds us and all her creatures.

... FATHER LANFRANCO SERRINI, OPENING OF WORLD FAITH GATHERING, ASSISI, 29 SEPTEMBER 1986

Scientists predict the rate of sea level rise in 2100 will be 10 times that recorded in 1860 and global temperatures have risen fastest in the last 100 years compared to general decreases in the previous millennium.

... STATEMENT BY THE METEOROLOGICAL OFFICE

CHRISTIANITY
Christ is the visible likeness of the invisible God. He is the firstborn Son, superior to all created things. For through him God created everything in heaven and on earth, the seen and the unseen things, including spiritual powers, lords, rulers and authorities. God created the whole universe through him and for him.

... THE BIBLE (COLOSSIANS 1.15–17)

The world and all that is in it belong to the LORD; the earth and all who live on it are his.

... THE BIBLE (PSALMS 24.1)

The universe as a whole is a product of God's creative and imaginative will. Men and women are to be stewards and curators not exploiters of its resources, material, animal and spiritual.

... METHODIST CHURCH

Use of the mineral, vegetable and animal resources of the universe cannot be divorced from respect for moral imperatives. Man's dominion over inanimate and other living beings granted by the Creator is not absolute; it is limited by concern for the quality of life of his neighbour ...

... CATECHISM OF THE CATHOLIC CHURCH

JUDAISM
Six years you shall sow your land and gather in its yield; but in the seventh you shall let it rest and lie fallow. Let the needy among your people eat of it, and what they leave let the wild beast eat. You shall do the same with your vineyards and your olive groves.

... THE TORAH (EXODUS 23.10–11)

Some twenty centuries ago they told the story of two men who were out on the water in a rowboat. Suddenly, one of them started to saw under his feet. He maintained that it was his right to do whatever he wished with the place that belonged to him. The other answered him that they were in the rowboat together: the hole that he was making would sink both of them. We have a responsibility to life, to defend it everywhere, not only against our own sins but also against those of others. We are all passengers together in this same fragile and glorious world. Let us safeguard our rowboat – and let us row together.

... JEWISH DECLARATION ON NATURE, ASSISI, 29 SEPTEMBER 1986

ISLAM
For the Muslim, mankind's role on earth is that of a 'khalifa', vice-regent or trustee of God. We are God's stewards and agents on earth. We are not masters of the earth; it does not belong to us to do as we wish. It belongs to God and he has entrusted us with its safekeeping. His trustees are responsible for maintaining the unity of His creation, the integrity of the earth, its flora and fauna, its wildlife and its natural environment.

... MUSLIM DECLARATION ON NATURE, ASSISI, 29 SEPTEMBER 1986

HINDUISM
Modern India does have severe environmental problems both as a result of industrial expansion and disasters such as the Bhopal gas leak, but also because of increased pressure on the environment of a growing population. Development of environmental consciousness seems to be more advanced among certain groups of western people than among Hindus.

... WERNER MENSKI IN ETHICAL ISSUES IN SIX RELIGIOUS TRADITIONS, PEGGY MORGAN, CLIVE LAWTON (EDS.), (EDINBURGH UNIVERSITY PRESS, 1996)

In the ancient spiritual traditions, Man was looked upon as part of nature ... This is very much marked in the Hindu tradition, probably the oldest religious tradition in the world ... Let us declare our determination to halt the present slide towards destruction, to rediscover the ancient tradition of reverence for all life and, even at this late hour, to reverse the suicidal course upon which we have embarked. Let us recall the ancient Hindu dictum: 'The earth is our mother and we are all her children.'

... HINDU DECLARATION ON NATURE, ASSISI, 29 SEPTEMBER 1986

This whole universe must be pervaded by a lord, whatever moves in this moving world ... loves not the goods of anyone at all.

... ISA UPANISHAD 1

Animal rights

CHRISTIANITY
In the end, a lack of regard for the life and well-being of an animal must bring with it a lowering of man's self-respect, and it is important to our Christian faith that this world is God's world and that man is a trustee and steward of God's creation.

... DR ROBERT RUNCIE, FORMER ARCHBISHOP OF CANTERBURY

The Church recognises the need for animals to be used in certain research to improve medical understanding, veterinary or behavioural knowledge, and to test for the safety of chemicals, and to understand that such testing is a requirement of law. It also, however, affirms that responsible stewardship of the natural world requires all animals to receive careful and sympathetic treatment, both during their lives and in the manner of their dying.

... WHAT THE CHURCHES SAY, CEM, 1993

We believe that the air, sea, earth, forests, animals and ourselves are all intimately connected, and the way in which we treat all of those things reflects on ourselves and consequently on God.

... RELIGIOUS SOCIETY OF FRIENDS [QUAKERS]

JUDAISM

All of them look to You, to give them food when it is due. Give it to them, they gather it up; open Your hand, they are well satisfied.

... KETHUVIM (PSALMS 104.27–8)

A righteous man knows the needs of his beast, But the compassion of the wicked is cruelty.

... KETHUVIM (PROVERBS 12.10)

When the whole world is at peril, when the environment is in danger of being poisoned and various species, both plant and animal are becoming extinct it is our Jewish responsibility to put the defence of the whole of nature at the very centre of our concern.

... JEWISH DECLARATION ON NATURE, ASSISI, 29 SEPTEMBER 1986

ISLAM

The Holy Prophet Muhammad was asked by his companions if kindness to animals was rewarded in the life hereafter. He replied, 'Yes, there is a meritorious reward for kindness for every living creature.'

... THE PROPHET MUHAMMAD, HADITH

Those who are kind and considerate to Allah's creatures. Allah bestows his kindness and attention on them.

... THE PROPHET MUHAMMAD, HADITH

There is not an animal (that lives) on the earth, nor a being that flies on its wings, but (forms part of) communities like you. Nothing have We omitted from the Book, and they (all) shall be gathered to their Lord in the end.

... THE QUR'AN (6.38)

One day the Prophet passed by a camel which was so thin that its back had shrunk to its belly. He said, 'Fear Allah in these beasts – ride them in good health and free them from work while they are still in good health.' The Prophet said, 'It is a great sin for man to imprison these animals who are in his power.'

... THE MUSLIM EDUCATIONAL TRUST

HINDUISM

He who hates no creature, who is friendly and compassionate to all ... he My devotee is dear to Me.

... BHAGAVAD GITA (12.3–4)

All creatures born from you, move round about you. You carry all that has two legs, three or four.

... HYMN TO THE EARTH, ATHARVA VEDA

Turning to the animal world, we find that animals have always received special care and consideration. Numerous Hindu texts remind us that all species should be treated as children.

... HINDU DECLARATION ON NATURE, ASSISI, 29 SEPTEMBER 1986

War and peace

CHRISTIANITY

If I saw a drunken driver racing down the street, I would not consider it my duty to bury the victims. It would be more important to wrench the wheel out of his hands.

... DR DIETRICH BONHOEFFER, CHRISTIAN ANTI-NAZI CRUSADER, (1906-45)

You are going to hear the noises of battles close by and the news of battles far away; but do not be troubled. Such things must happen, but they do not mean that the end has come.

... THE BIBLE (MATTHEW 24.6)

Respect for and development of human life require peace. Peace is not merely the absence of war and is not limited to maintaining a balance of powers between adversaries. Peace cannot be attained on earth without safeguarding the goods of persons, free communication between men, respect for the dignity of persons ...

... CATECHISM OF THE CATHOLIC CHURCH

Peace is what I leave with you; it is my own peace that I give you. I do not give it as the world does.

... THE BIBLE (JOHN 14.27)

For we no longer take sword against nation, nor do we learn any more to make war, having become sons of peace for the sake of Jesus who is our leader.

... ORIGEN, THIRD-CENTURY CHRISTIAN LEADER

JUDAISM

Proclaim this among the nations: prepare for war! Arouse the warriors, let all the fighters come and draw near! Beat your ploughshares into swords and your pruning hooks into spears.

... NEVI'IM (JOEL 3.9)

When siege is laid to a city for the purpose of capture, it may not be surrounded on all four sides but only on three in order to give an opportunity for escape to those who would flee to save their lives.

... MOSES MAIMONIDES, TWELFTH-CENTURY JEWISH THINKER

Thus He will judge among the nations and arbitrate for the many peoples, and they shall beat their swords into ploughshares, and their spears into pruning hooks: nation shall not take up sword against nation; they shall never again know war.

... NEVI'IM (ISAIAH 2.4)

ISLAM

Fight in the cause of Allah those who fight you, but do not transgress limits; for Allah loveth not transgressors.

... THE QUR'AN (2.190)

But if the enemy incline towards peace, do thou (also) incline towards peace, and trust in Allah: for He is the One that heareth and knoweth (all things).

... THE QUR'AN (8.61)

But those who are slain in the Way of Allah – He will never let their deeds be lost. Soon will He guide them and improve their condition and admit them to the Garden [paradise] which He has announced for them.

... THE QUR'AN (47.4–6)

But when the forbidden months are past, then fight and slay the Pagans wherever ye find them, and seize them, beleaguer them, and lie in wait for them in every stratagem (of war). But if they repent and establish regular prayers and practise regular charity, then open the way for them: for Allah is Oft-forgiving.

... THE QUR'AN (9.5)

Hate your enemy mildly; he may become your friend one day.

... THE PROPHET MUHAMMAD, HADITH

The most excellent jihad is to speak the truth in the face of a tyrannical ruler.

... THE PROPHET MUHAMMAD, HADITH

The Prophet was asked about people fighting because they are brave, or in honour of a certain loyalty, or to show off. Which of them fights for the cause of Allah? 'The person who struggles so that Allah's word is supreme is the one serving Allah's cause.'

... THE PROPHET MUHAMMAD, HADITH

HINDUISM

I have already slain these men, you are only an instrument.

... BHAGAVAD GITA (11.33)

Do works for Me, make Me thy highest goal. Be loyal in love to Me. Cast off all other attachments, Have no hatred for any being at all; For all who do thus shall come to Me.

... BHAGAVAD GITA (11.55)

If you are killed, you win heaven; if you triumph, you enjoy the earth; therefore, Arjuna, stand up and resolve to fight the battle!

... BHAGAVAD GITA (2.37)

Non-violence is more powerful that all the armaments in the world. It is mightier than the mightiest weapon of destruction devised by the ingenuity of man. In non-violence the masses have a weapon which enables a child, a woman, or even a decrepit old man to resist the mightiest government successfully.

... MAHATMA GANDHI

Capital punishment

The death penalty is irrevocable – it sends innocent people to their deaths. It is a particularly cruel, calculated and cold-blooded form of killing. It does nothing to prevent violent crime. It is a violation of the right to live.

... AMNESTY INTERNATIONAL

Innocent people have been hanged in the past and will be hanged in the future, unless the death penalty is abolished worldwide or the fallibility of human judgement is abolished and judges become superhuman.

... ARTHUR KOESTLER, AUTHOR

CHRISTIANITY

The Laws of the Realm may punish Christian men with death for heinous and grievous offences.

... ARTICLE 37 OF THE THIRTY NINE ARTICLES OF THE CHURCH OF ENGLAND

Preserving the common good of society requires rendering the unjust aggressor unable to inflict harm. The traditional teaching of the Church has acknowledged the right and duty of legitimate public authority to punish criminals by means of penalties in keeping with the gravity of the crime, not excluding in cases of extreme gravity, the death penalty.

... CATECHISM OF THE CATHOLIC CHURCH

JUDAISM

He who fatally strikes a man shall be put to death.

... THE TORAH (EXODUS 21.12)

If a man commits adultery with a married woman ... both the adulterer and the adulteress shall be put to death.

... THE TORAH (LEVITICUS 20.10)

You shall not take vengeance or bear a grudge against your countrymen. Love your fellow as yourself.

... THE TORAH (LEVITICUS 19.18)

But if other damage ensues, the penalty shall be life for life, eye for eye, tooth for tooth, hand for hand, foot for foot, burn for burn, wound for wound, bruise for bruise.

... THE TORAH (EXODUS 21.23–24)

ISLAM

The law of equality is prescribed for you in cases of murder: the free for the free, the slave for the slave, the woman for the woman. But if any remission is made by the brother of the slain, then grant any reasonable demand, and compensate him with handsome gratitude; this is a concession and a Mercy from your Lord. After this whoever exceeds the limits shall be in grave penalty.

... THE QUR'AN (2.178)

The punishment of those who wage war against Allah and His Messenger, and strive with might and main for mischief through the land is: execution, or crucifixion, or the cutting off of hands and feet from opposite sides ...

... THE QUR'AN (5.33)

As to the thief, male or female, cut off his or her hands; a punishment by way of example, from Allah, for their crime: and Allah is Exalted in power.

... THE QUR'AN (5.38)

Those who are kind and considerate to Allah's creatures, Allah bestows his kindness and attention on them.

... THE PROPHET MUHAMMAD, HADITH

HINDUISM

If punishment is properly inflicted after due consideration, it makes all people happy. But inflicted without due consideration it destroys everything.

... THE LAWS OF MANU (7.19)

Justice and forgiveness

CHRISTIANITY

You give God a tenth of the seasoning herbs, such as mint and rue and all the other herbs, but you neglect justice and love for God.

... THE BIBLE (LUKE 11.42)

Happy are those who are merciful to others.

... THE BIBLE (MATTHEW 5.7)

The priest uses the ministry of forgiveness, a ministry which Jesus gave to his Church. It is not the priest who forgives the penitent but God. The priest merely offers a visible symbol that such forgiveness is given. This he does by placing his hands on the penitent.

... THE CATHOLIC EXPERIENCE, MICHAEL KEENE, (TRANS-ATLANTIC PUBLICATIONS, 1995)

I absolve you from your sins in the name of the Father, and of the Son and of the Holy Spirit.

... PRIEST IN SACRAMENT OF PENANCE AND RECONCILIATION

JUDAISM

You shall not judge unfairly: you shall show no partiality; you shall not take bribes, for bribes blind the eyes of the discerning and upset the plea of the just.

... THE TORAH (DEUTERONOMY 16.19)

When all Israel heard the decision that the king had rendered, they stood in awe of the king; for they saw that he possessed divine wisdom to execute justice.

... NEVI'IM (1 KINGS 3.28)

Would one who hates justice govern?

... KETHUVIM (JOB 34.17)

You shall not hate your kinsfolk in your heart. Reprove your kinsmen but incur no guilt because of him. You shall not take vengeance or bear a grudge against your countrymen. Love your fellow as yourself.

... THE TORAH (LEVITICUS 19.17–18)

ISLAM

And the firmament has He raised high, and He has set up the Balance (of Justice).

... THE QUR'AN (55.7)

Nor can Goodness and Evil be equal. Repel (Evil) with what is better: then will he between whom and thee was hatred become as it were thy friend and intimate!

... THE QUR'AN (41.34)

Hold to forgiveness; command what is right; but turn away from the ignorant.

... THE QUR'AN (7.199)

Stand out firmly for justice, as witnesses to Allah, even as against yourselves, or your parents, or your kin, and whether it be (against) rich or poor.

... THE QUR'AN (4.135)

HINDUISM

Punishment alone governs all created beings, punishment alone protects them, punishment watches over them while they sleep; the wise declare punishment to be identical with the law.

... THE LAWS OF MANU (7.18–19)

Though not all Hindus believe in rebirth, the threat of punishment in the next existence has, of course, a potentially powerful deterrent effect.

WERNER MENSKI IN ETHICAL ISSUES IN SIX RELIGIOUS TRADITIONS, PEGGY MORGAN, CLIVE LAWTON (EDS.), (EDINBURGH UNIVERSITY PRESS, 1996)

Who have all the powers of their soul in harmony and the same loving mind for all; who find joy in the good of all beings – they reach in truth my very self.

... BHAGAVAD GITA (12.4)

Fertility

CHRISTIANITY

Techniques of artificial conception are morally unacceptable, since they separate procreation from the fully human context of the sexual act ...

... POPE JOHN PAUL II

HINDUISM

The one who rules over both knowledge and ignorance ... alone presides over womb after womb and thus over all visible forms and all the sources of birth.

... SVETASVATARA UPANISHAD (5.2)

Genetic engineering, embryology and organ donation

Unless we ourselves have handicapped children we cannot really know what it means. Yes, of course, there is love. There is more love because the child is handicapped. But there is also great hardship, which none of us would want to take on ourselves.

... LORD ENNALS, HOUSE OF LORDS DEBATE 1990

I cannot accept that a man has a right to take life, bottle it, put it on a shelf, play with it and destroy it.

... LORD RAWLINSON, HOUSE OF LORDS DEBATE 1990

If one, or even a dozen animals have to suffer experiments in order to save thousands, I would think it right ... that they should do so.

... PRACTICAL ETHICS, PETER SINGER (CAMBRIDGE UNIVERSITY PRESS, 1993)

The suffering that can be relieved is staggering. This new technology heralds a new era of unparalleled advancement in medicine if people will release their fears and let the benefits begin. Why should another child die from leukaemia when, if the technology is allowed, we should be able to cure it in a few years time?

... HUMAN CLONING FOUNDATION

CHRISTIANITY

Jesus of Nazareth was a healer. He cured diseases and showed that God's purposes include overcoming 'those things in creation that spoil it and that diminish the life of his children'. Clearly where genetic manipulation is the means of healing diseases – in animals or humans – it is to be welcomed.

... WHAT THE CHURCHES SAY, METHODIST CHURCH

The end – research into new treatments for disease using stem cells – is good in itself but the means being proposed are quite immoral. To create and destroy human lives simply to extract cells for research is wrong. Such procedures use human lives as disposable objects.

... LETTER TO THE TIMES FROM ROMAN CATHOLIC ARCHBISHOPS OF WESTMINSTER AND GLASGOW, 14 DECEMBER 2000

JUDAISM

If one is in a position to donate an organ to save another person's life, it is obligatory to do so, even if the donor never knows who the beneficiary will be. The basic principle of Jewish ethics – 'the infinite worth of the human being' – also includes donation of corneas, since eyesight restoration is considered a life-saving operation.

... DR MOSES TENDLER, RABBI

Glossary

A

Abortion the surgical removal of an embryo or foetus from the womb so that it is destroyed

Abraham the father of the Jewish people who entered into an agreement with God and was given the Promised Land; also recognised as a prophet by Muslims

Absolutism the belief that there are absolute moral values in the bible which are always right whatever the situation – murder is always wrong

Adhan the prayer-call that is recited from the mosque five times a day to call Muslims to prayer

Agni the God of fire in Hinduism; the mediator between the gods and human beings

Agnostic a person who does not believe there is enough evidence to decide whether there is a God or not

Ahimsa the Hindu belief in non-violence

Allah the name for God in Islam

Ananda in Hinduism, the state of bliss, used to describe Brahman

Anglican Church worldwide Protestant Christian Church which is based on the teachings of the Church of England

Annulment a declaration issued by the Roman Catholic Church that declares that a marriage did not exist; the only form of 'divorce' recognised by the Catholic Church

Apartheid the policy of separate development of the races in South Africa between the 1950s and the early 1990s

Apostasy people who give up the faith to which they belong and become members of another religion

Apostles 'those who are sent'; word applies to missionaries in early Christian Church especially the 12 disciples of Jesus

Aqiqa Muslim birth ceremony, celebrated with prayers and fasting, carried out when a baby is seven days old

Archbishop of Canterbury the leader of the Anglican Church throughout the world

Ascetic a person who rigidly abstains from physical pleasure for a spiritual reason

Ashrama the four stages of life, including the student and householder stages, through which every Hindu passes

Atheist a person who believes that there is no God

Atman the soul, the real self, the principle of life in Hindu teaching

Authority in Christianity, the sources of authority include three which are recognised as being of prime importance by different parts of the Christian Church – the authority of the bible; the authority of the Church and the authority of the individual conscience

B

Baptist Church worldwide Protestant Church; teaching based on the baptism of adult believers by total immersion

Barmitzvah 'son of the commandment'; service that marks the coming of age of a Jewish boy carried out in the synagogue on the first Sabbath day after his thirteenth birthday

Batmitzvah 'daughter of the commandment'; service in some synagogues to mark coming of age of Jewish girl aged 12

Believer's baptism the act of baptising believing adults by full immersion in water; mainly carried out by the Baptist Church

Bet Din the traditional court of three rabbis that has the authority to pronounce on matters of Jewish law, this court hears applications for a divorce

Bhagavad Gita song of the blessed one; most popular of Hindu scriptures

Bible collection of scriptures sacred to the Jewish or Christian communities

Bishop a senior priest in the Anglican and Roman Catholic Churches

Brahman the power believed by Hindus to be present throughout creation; a God who is indescribable

Brahmin the highest of the four main Hindu varnas – the priestly caste

C

Caste division of classes within Hindu society (Brahmin – priest; Kshatriya – warrior; Vaishya – trader/farmer; Sudra – labourer)

Celibacy abstaining from sexual relations

Christmas the Christian festival that celebrates the birth of Jesus in Bethlehem

Chuppah the canopy that forms a holy space under which the bride and groom stand during a Jewish wedding

Church of England most important Church in England; part of the worldwide Anglican Church, led by the Archbishop of Canterbury

Circumcision practice performed on Jewish and Muslim boys; involves removing the foreskin of a boy's penis

Confession practice in the Roman Catholic Church of confessing one's sins to God through a priest, one of the seven sacraments recognised by the Church

Confirmation one of the seven sacraments in the Church of England and the Roman Catholic Church; the sacrament during which a person 'confirms' their faith in Christ

Contraception device used to prevent conception occurring after sexual intercourse

D

Dalit 'untouchables' in Hinduism; member of the lowest caste who carry out the lowest and most menial tasks in the community

Day of Judgement Christianity, Judaism and Islam believe that the human race will be judged by God at some future time, this day will mark the end of life as we have known it

Decalogue Ten Commandments given by God to Moses on Mount Sinai

Democracy system of government that guarantees people the right to vote for the parliamentary representatives of their choice

Deterrent a punishment which is intended to 'deter' [discourage] the criminal from offending again or someone else from committing the same offence

Dharma a series of obligations from the holy books that govern the life of a Hindu

Divali one of the major Hindu festivals; known as the festival of lights

E

Easter Christian festival at which believers celebrate the death and resurrection of Jesus

Ecosystem a unit which consists of a community of organisms and their environment

Education Act 1944 known as the Butler Education Act, set up universal education for all children aged 14 and under

Egg donation takes place when an unknown woman's egg is fertilised by a husband's sperm using IVF before being implanted in his partner's womb

Eid ul-Adha Muslim festival, marks the completion of the Ramadan month of fasting

Embryo donation takes place when both egg and sperm are given by unknown donors and then fertilised using IVF to be planted in a woman's womb

Encyclical a circular letter sent out by the pope to all Catholic churches to tell them of any changes in the church's beliefs

Environment the natural world, regarded by many as being at risk from the harmful influences of industrialised societies

Established Church the Church of England; the Church which is given privileges and responsibilities in England and Wales that are not given to any other Church

Euthanasia 'a good death', painless killing to relieve suffering, illegal in the UK

Extended family aunts, uncles, cousins and grandparents who live nearby; in some cultures it is common for members of the extended family to live in the same house

F

Faithfulness remaining loyal to a partner and never having a sexual relationship with anyone else

Fatwa a legal opinion or religious declaration made by a Muslim scholar declaring that some action is against the teaching of the Qur'an

Five Pillars the five beliefs at the heart of Islam – belief in Allah (Shahadah), prayer (Salah), giving to the poor (Zakat), fasting during Ramadan (Sawm) and pilgrimage to Makkah (Hajj)

Free Church Churches, such as the Baptist and Methodist Churches, which do not belong to the Anglican or Roman Catholic Churches; also called Nonconformist Churches

G

Ganesha the Hindu God of wisdom, prudence and salvation, one of the most widely worshipped of the Hindu gods, recognised by his elephant head

Genetic engineering manipulating DNA to delete, alter or replace a faulty gene

Get a Jewish bill of divorce, this alone can dissolve the marriage contract (the ketubah)

Global warming the slow increase in the earth's surface temperature caused by manufactured carbon dioxide in the atmosphere trapping excessive amounts of solar radiation, this radiation would otherwise be reflected back into space

Golden Rule the most important teaching of Jesus, the heart of the Christian message, states that the followers of Jesus must treat others as they themselves expect to be treated

Gospel one of four books in the New Testament (Matthew, Mark, Luke and John) which detail the life and teachings of Jesus

Guna one of three forces which make up all inner or outer nature in Hinduism; everything which is created is an interplay of these three gunas – harmony (satua), activity (rajas) and inertia (tamas)

Guru a teacher in an Eastern religion, especially Hinduism

H

Hadith a large collection of sayings thought to have come from Muhammad; not as important as the Qur'an but still has great authority

Hajj the obligation on each Muslim to undertake a pilgrimage to the holy city of Makkah, one of the Five Pillars of Islam

Halal term used to describe any action that is permitted or lawful for a Muslim, frequently used to describe the food that is lawful for Muslims to eat

Havan the offering of ghee and grains into the fire during many Hindu ceremonies

Heder the traditional Jewish preparatory school

Heterosexual a man or a woman who is sexually attracted to members of the opposite sex

Hijrah 'emigration', the migration of Muhammad and his followers from Makkah to Madinah in 622CE

Holocaust the slaughter of over six million Jews, and other groups, during the Second World War by the Nazis

Holy Spirit the third person of the Trinity, along with God the Father and God the Son; expresses the idea of God active in the world

Homophobia an extreme aversion to homosexuality and homosexual people

Homosexual a man or a woman who is sexually attracted to members of their own sex

Hospice a home, often Christian, that offers pain relief and care to the terminally ill

I

Iblis 'Satan'; the angel who disobeyed Allah by refusing to bow to Adam, the first man, after his creation; later became the tempter of mankind

Ihram state of sacredness in which a Muslim performs the Hajj

Incarnation the Christian belief that God took on human form when Jesus was born

Infertility the inability of a man or a woman to conceive

J

Jerusalem the ancient and modern capital of Israel, the city in which Jesus was crucified, the third most holy city of Islam after Makkah and Madinah

Jesus Christ Son of God; the second person of the trinity

Jihad the Muslim struggle on behalf of Islam; holy war against those opposed to Allah

K

Karma the law of cause and effect that governs the whole of life according to Hinduism, all good and bad actions produce their own effects in this life or the next

Kashrut the Jewish dietary laws

Ketubah the traditional Jewish wedding contract signed by the groom; sets out his financial responsibilities to his wife

Khalifah the successors to the prophet Muhammad who led the Muslim community but did not inherit the mantle of prophethood

Khutbah the sermon that is delivered in the mosque during the weekly gathering of Muslims for prayer

Kiddushin inital state of Jewish marriage

Kosher term applied to food that Jews are allowed to eat according to their dietary laws

Krishna the eighth avatar (coming in human form) of the God Vishnu, most popular of all Hindu Gods, with many followers

Kshatriya in Hinduism, the second of the four varnas – the warrior caste

L

Lakshmi Hindu goddess of prosperity, the consort of Vishnu

Last Day a Christian description of the Day of Judgement

Last Supper the last meal that Jesus ate with his disciples before he was crucified; re-created by Christians each time they celebrate Holy Communion

Law of double-effect drugs administered to a terminally ill patient that may also have the effect of hastening their death

Laws of Manu an important Hindu holy text written between 300BCE and 100CE

Lent 40 days in the Christian year leading up to the festival of Easter; traditionally a time of fasting and preparation for the most important of all Christian festivals

Lesbian a woman who is sexually attracted to members of her own sex rather than the opposite sex

Lord's Prayer the prayer that Jesus taught his disciples to use; used today in most Christian services

M

Madrasah a school for religious study of Arabic and the Qur'an

Magisterium the decision-making machinery of the Catholic Church including church councils, the pope and the bishops

Mahr the dowry traditionally paid to a Muslim bride by the groom and his family

Mandir a Hindu place of worship

Mantra a sacred formula or chant used in Hindu worship

Marriage a formal commitment recognised by the State that two people are legally bound to each other; divorce is a legal dissolution of the marriage

Mass the term used in the Roman Catholic Church for the service of Holy Communion

Meditation spiritual discipline used in several religions; quietening the soul by concentrating the mind

Messiah the promised leader expected by the Jews who will lead them into an era of peace; Christians believe that Jesus is the Messiah

Methodist Church a Protestant Christian denomination that came into being through the teachings of the Anglican priest John Wesley (1703–91)

Minister the leader of a Nonconformist Church

Minyan a group of ten men who must be present before a service can be held in an Orthodox synagogue

Miscarriage a spontaneous abortion, when the body expels the foetus, usually in the early weeks of pregnancy

Mitzvot individual instructions or obligations which are required by God of the Jews

Moksha release from cycle of rebirth in Hinduism

Monotheism any religion that believes that there is only one God

Moses the father of Judaism; received the Ten Commandments from God; led the Israelites to the Promised Land of Israel

Mosque the Muslim building used for public prayer

Muezzin the person who calls the faithful to prayer from a mosque

Muhammad the name of the last, and greatest, of the Muslim prophets; born around 570CE

N

Natural family planning family planning methods, favoured by the Roman Catholic Church, that do not make use of any 'unnatural' methods of preventing conception

New Testament the second part of the Christian Bible, which contains the four Gospels, the Acts of the Apostles and letters written by early Christians

Nirvana in Hinduism, the indescribable state of ultimate peace or bliss achieved by anyone who reaches enlightenment

Nonconformist Churches Protestant denominations other than the Church of England during the Reformation in the sixteenth and seventeenth centuries

Non-renewable those resources, such as coal and oil, which cannot be replaced once they have been used

Nuclear family parents and children living in one household

Nuptial Mass the special Mass that is celebrated by the bride and groom in a Roman Catholic Church during their wedding

O

Old Testament first part of the Christian Bible; contains the books that are sacred to Jews

Orthodox Church the Church that separated from the Catholic Church in the eleventh century

Orthodox Jews Jews who keep to the old traditions and beliefs of the faith

P

Pacifism the belief that war and violence are unjustifiable; a pacifist believes all disputes should be settled peacefully

Parable story told by Jesus and believed to have a moral or a spiritual message

Paul (St) originally a persecutor of Christians, converted after a vision of Christ; missionary who founded many churches; writer of many books in the New Testament

Peter (St) one of the disciples of Jesus; first leader of the Christian Church after death of Jesus

Pir a term in Islam for a Muslim saint

Pluralism a society in which many different cultures and beliefs are followed

Polygamy practice of a man marrying more than one woman, allowed by the Qur'an

Pontiff a highly ranked priest or bishop in the Catholic Church, most likely to be the pope

Pope 'Papa'; leader of the Roman Catholic Church; believed to be the successor of St Peter

Procreation to produce offspring by reproduction

Progeny a person's offspring or descendants

Prophet a man or woman who passes on the message of God to the people

Protestant a Christian who does not belong to either the Roman Catholic or Orthodox Churches

Puja a Hindu act of worship or ritual

Punishment a response by society to an individual's crime

Purgatory the place between earth and heaven; place where Roman Catholics believe that the human soul is cleansed of sin

Q

Quakers Christian group that began in the seventeenth century; largely silent form of worship; believes in pacifism

Qur'an believed by Muslims to be the final word or revelation of Allah to human beings

R

Rabbi 'my master'; a Jewish teacher

Rajas one of the three gunas in Hindu teaching – the active quality, the one which makes people go out and do things

Ramadan month of fasting for all Muslims

Reconstituted marriage this occurs when parents who have children from previous relationships live together

Reform one of the most important purposes of punishment is to reform the criminal and make them a law-abiding member of society

Reform Jews Jews who believe that some of the old laws need to be reinterpreted in the modern world

Reincarnation belief held by Hindus that the soul is reborn many times

Remarriage when a person who has been divorced or widowed gets married again

Renewable resources resources, such as trees, which are deliberately planted or grown to replace those resources which are used

Retribution when a crime is committed a person offends against society and its laws, society takes retribution for this by exacting a just punishment on the person

Roman Catholic Church oldest and largest Christian Church, led by the Pope in Rome

S

Sabbath Jewish day of rest (Friday evening to Saturday evening), in remembrance of God 'resting' on the seventh day after spending six days creating the world; the Christian sabbath day is Sunday

Sacraments seven special services celebrated by Roman Catholics and other Christians; times when God's blessing is specially given; the most important sacrament is Holy Communion

Sacred thread thread worn by many Hindu boys to show that they have been spiritually re-born

Sadaqah a good deed or a voluntary payment of charity by a Muslim, that is in addition to zakat

Salah the second Pillar of Islam – prayer five times a day

Salvation Army Protestant organisation formed in the nineteenth century, famous for its social work, bands and distinctive uniform

Samsara the material world; Hindu belief that each person is caught up in an endless cycle of birth, life, death and rebirth; cycle is only broken when the soul reaches liberation or moksha

Samskara the special rituals that are celebrated at different stages in a Hindu's life

Sannyasin the fourth stage of the Hindu understanding of the human life cycle

Satan also known as the Devil, leader of the evil spirits opposed to God

Satva one of the three gunas in Hindu teaching – the quality of harmony and balance that runs through the whole of creation

Satyagraha the philosophy of non-violent opposition which Gandhi used successfully against British control of India in the 1930s and 1940s

Sawm the fourth Pillar of Islam – fasting during Ramadan

Sermon on the Mount a collection of the teachings of Jesus found in Matthew 5–7

Shahadah the first Pillar of Islam – the basic belief in Allah and Muhammad

Shariah Muslim laws based on the teaching of the Qur'an

Shirk the Muslim sin of idolatry or regarding anything as equal or a partner to God

Situation ethics the teaching that a Christian should make a moral decision after summing up the right thing to do in a situation, there are no absolute moral values

Sterilisation the most permanent form of birth control, makes a man or a woman infertile

Sudra in Hinduism, the fourth, and lowest, of the varnas – the labouring class

Surrogacy woman having a baby for someone else

Synagogue 'gathering together'; the place where Jews meet for teaching, study and prayer

Synod the system of government followed by the Church of England made up of the house of bishops, the house of clergy and the house of laity

T

Tallit Jewish prayer shawl, mainly white with tassels; worn by men during prayers

Talmud the main source of Jewish law

Tamas one of the three gunas in Hindu teaching – dullness, inertia; the quality which tends to hold one back and which is averse to progress

Tanakh Jewish scriptures, contains Torah, Neviim (prophets) and Kethuvim (writings)

Tawhid important Muslim belief, a belief in the unity and oneness of Allah

Tefillin small leather boxes containing passages of scripture; worn around the arm and forehead by Jewish men during prayers

Ten Commandments in the Bible; most important of Jewish laws, recorded in the Torah and given by God to Moses for the Jewish people, part of a much larger law system of 613 commandments

Torah the first five books of the Jewish scriptures

Transmigration the belief that there is a continuity from one life to the next; same as rebirth

Tzedakah a term in Judaism to describe an act of charity, includes the tithing obligation on Jews to give away 10 per cent of wealth and income

U

Ummah the universal community of Muslims

Utilitarianism an approach to ethics which says that something is right if it is useful at the time

V

Vaishya the third of the four varnas in Hinduism, the merchant and farming caste

Varna a caste group in Hindu society

Vedas the earliest Hindu scriptures, written at some time between 1500 and 800BCE

Viability the stage reached by an unborn baby when it can survive outside the womb

Virgin Mary the mother of Jesus, an object of religious devotion in the Roman Catholic Church; prayers are addressed to the Virgin Mary by many Christians

Vishnu one of the most important Hindu gods

Vivisection the use of living animals for scientific research

W

Welfare state government provision for the health and welfare of people in the UK

Wudu the washing ritual followed by all Muslims before prayer

Z

Zakat third Pillar of Islam – requirement that all Muslims give 2.5 per cent of their income to help the poor

Religion in Life and Society

Index